'Humour informs Ayelet Waldman's lively diary of taking acid ... A smart writer with an easy tone' *Observer*

'It's a simple, delightful premise: a journal of microdosing. Then Waldman brings so much to the project that it turns into something else, something far more beguiling ... I don't know another writer like her'

William Finnegan, Pulitzer-prize winning author of *Barbarian Days*

'Raw, honest, and ultimately hopeful'

Dr David Eagleman, neuroscientist, author of *The Brain*

'Crisp, hilarious, and weirdly optimistic'

Jenni Konner, executive producer of Girls, co-founder of *Lenny Letter*

'Waldman proves a sharp debunker of the myths that have accrued around a potentially life-saving chemical' *Spectator*

'Ayelet Waldman is fearless, which is our good fortune and sometimes hers ... You could call this book her war on the war on drugs, but it's so much more, and so much more funny'

Rebecca Solnit, author of *Men Explain Things To Me*

Also by Ayelet Waldman

Fiction

Love and Treasure

Red Hook Road

Love and Other Impossible Pursuits

Daughter's Keeper

Nonfiction

*Bad Mother: A Chronicle of Maternal Crimes, Minor Calamities,
and Occasional Moments of Grace*

A Really Good Day

*How Microdosing Made a Mega Difference in
My Mood, My Marriage, and My Life*

....

Ayelet Waldman

corsair

CORSAIR

First published in the US in 2017 by Alfred A. Knopf
First published in Great Britain in 2017 by Corsair
This paperback edition published in 2019

1 3 5 7 9 10 8 6 4 2

Portions of this work originally appeared in different form in *T: The New York Times Style Magazine* (www.nytimes.com/section/t-magazine) as 'All the Rage' on February 15, 2012; in *Finesse* magazine (www.ThomasKeller.com/senses-issue) as 'Sensory Deprivation: An Insomniac's Lament' in September 2014; and on *This American Life* as 'Ellis Island' (m.thisamericanlife.org) on November 21, 2014.

Author's Note: This book relates the events surrounding the author's experiment in self-medication with microdoses of the drug lysergic acid diethylamide, or, as it is more commonly known, LSD. It is a criminal offense in the United States and in many other countries, punishable by imprisonment and/or fines, to manufacture, possess, or supply LSD. You should therefore understand that this book is intended for entertainment and not intended to encourage you to break the law. Notwithstanding the legality or illegality of the treatment in question, no attempt at self-diagnosis or self-treatment for serious or long-term mental or physical problems should be made without first consulting a qualified medical practitioner. The author and the publisher expressly disclaim any liability, loss, or risk, personal or otherwise, that is incurred as a consequence, directly or indirectly, of the use and application of any of the contents of this book. Everything in these pages did happen, though I have changed some names and identifying details, and taken liberties with dates and chronology in order to protect myself and others.

A CIP catalogue record for this book is available from the British Library.

ISBN: 978-1-4721-5289-3

Printed and bound in Great Britain by Clays Ltd, Elcograf S.p.A.

To Sophie

If the words "life, liberty, and the pursuit of happiness" don't include the right to experiment with your own consciousness, then the Declaration of Independence isn't worth the hemp it was written on.

—Terence McKenna

Prologue

....

This morning I took LSD.

The table I'm sitting at right now is not breathing. My keyboard is not exploding in psychedelic fireworks, lightning bolts shooting from the letters "R" and "P." I am not giddy and frantic, or zoned out with bliss. I feel no transcendent sense of oneness with the universe or with the divine. On the contrary. I feel normal.

Well, except for one thing: I'm content and relaxed. I'm busy, but not stressed. That might be normal for some people, but it isn't for me.

I did not drop a tab of acid. What I took is known as a "microdose," a subtherapeutic dose of a drug administered at a quantity low enough to elicit no adverse side effects yet high enough for a measurable cellular response. A microdose of a psychedelic drug is approximately one-tenth of a typical dose. A recreational user of LSD looking for a trip complete with visual hallucinations might ingest between one hundred and one hundred and fifty micrograms of the drug. I took ten micrograms.

Microdosing of psychedelics, so new and renegade a concept that I had to teach it to my computer's spellcheck, was popularized by a psychologist and former psychedelic researcher named James Fadiman in a series of lectures and podcast interviews and in a book published in 2011 called *The Psychedelic Explorer's Guide: Safe, Therapeutic, and Sacred Journeys*. Since 2010, Dr. Fadiman has been collecting reports from individuals who experimented with regular microdosing of LSD and psilocybin, a naturally occurring chemical found in a variety of different species of mushroom. Soon after his book's publication, in a lecture at a conference on the potential therapeutic value of psychedelic drugs, Fadiman presented what he had learned from reading the dozens of reports mailed and e-mailed to him, some though by no means all of them anonymously. He said about microdosing, "What many people are reporting is, at the end of the day, they say, 'That was a really good day.'"

A really good day. Predictably, regularly, unexceptionally. That is all I have ever wanted.

For as long as I can remember, I have been held hostage by the vagaries of mood. When my mood is good, I am cheerful, productive, and affectionate. I sparkle at parties, I write decent sentences, I have what the kids call swag. When my mood swings, however, I am beset by self-loathing and knotted with guilt and shame. I am overtaken by a pervasive sense of hopelessness, a grim pessimism about even the possibility of happiness. My symptoms have never been serious enough to require hospitalization, nor have they ever prevented me from functioning either personally or professionally, but they have made my life and the lives of the people whom I love much more difficult.

I have sought many treatments for these moods and miseries. Though I managed to be one of the only neurotic Jewish children growing up in the seventies and eighties in the New York area to stay out of a shrink's office, I did eventually dip my toe. Or, to be more accurate, I waded into therapy with the eagerness of a dehydrated camel sloshing into an oasis mud puddle. I wallowed in therapy of all kinds.

My first therapist was a psychiatric resident assigned to me by University Health Services when I was a third-year law student. I was looking for help dealing with a breakup that at the time felt tragic but that now seems like that moment when you look up from your phone just in time to avoid being plowed down by a city bus. I sat in my therapist's office and sobbed. Once I stopped crying (two or three sessions in), we talked about my boyfriend and my ambivalence about the breakup. We talked about the guy (and the other guys, and the one or two girls) I cheated on him with. We talked about my mother's anger and my father's emotional reserve, and about how hard it was to grow up in a home where two people spent so much time fighting.

Since that first series of appointments, I have spent hundreds of hours in the offices of psychiatrists and psychologists, social workers and licensed family therapists, wearing my unique assprint into so many leather couches. I've nattered on to Freudians and diligently filled out the workbooks assigned by cognitive behavioral therapists. I enjoy these sessions; I'm analytical and an extrovert, so I enjoy picking apart my life and my feelings, especially with people I'm paying for the privilege. I was a good student in elementary school, and I find workbooks soothing.

Even though I am a cynic about all things countercultural (nothing makes me roll my eyes faster than a yogini pressing her lily-white palms together in a Namaste), I have on occasion even abandoned mainstream therapy for the decidedly alternative. In my eighth month of pregnancy with my second child, desperate to avoid another Caesarean section, I engaged in a series of sessions of hypnotherapy, during which I "rebirthed" my oldest child. This would, the hypnotist promised, guarantee a vaginal birth this time. I lay on her couch, my knees bent up around my ears, as she guided me in excruciating detail through the vaginal birth I did not have. Together we imagined every twisting contraction, the burn of crowning, the exertion of pushing. I panted, I moaned, I gritted my teeth and bore down. It turns out that the only thing one is guaranteed to produce by such efforts is a massive and propulsive fart.

One month, two doulas, a midwife, and forty-four hours of nonimaginary contractions later, my son was delivered by an obstetrician who waited with surprising patience for me to finish futilely visualizing my cervix opening before he performed the second of what went on to be four C-sections.

I've done mindfulness-based therapy, which required me to spend torturous minutes meditating, and many more torturous hours discussing with my therapist why I hate meditating so much. I responded to a crisis in a friend's marriage by forcing my long-suffering husband into an infuriating kind of couples therapy that involved repeating back each other's words, theoretically in a tone not dripping with passive-aggressive fury. ("I hear that it upsets you when I criticize how you load the dishwasher, but I feel sad when you insist on putting the glasses on the bottom rack, and I feel rage because, despite your vaunted intelligence, you can't seem to learn that that's how they get broken." Oops.) We might still be frantically using "I" language with one another had my husband not pointed out that it was the therapy that was the most serious threat to our marriage. "I" had to agree.*

Despite all of these hundreds of hours of talk therapy, I can't say that I have ever experienced much in the way of a change of either outlook or behavior.

And then, one day, on my way home from giving a depressingly poorly attended reading in bucolic and beautiful Marin County,† I found myself considering the possibility of steering my wheel hard to the right and hurtling off the Richmond Bridge. The thought was more than idle, less than concrete, and though I managed to make it across safely, I was so shaken by the experience that I called a psychiatrist.

That psychiatrist diagnosed me with bipolar II disorder, a less

---

*Lately, we've started going to a more traditional kind of couples therapy, in which we each try to recruit the therapist to take our side against the other. She's annoyingly neutral—Switzerland in sensible shoes.

†The single audience member, a malodorous gentleman slumped in a rear seat, woke up halfway through the reading, gazed at me with pity, and trundled his shopping cart heaped with beer bottles out the door.

serious variant of bipolar I, which was once known as manic depression. Though this diagnosis was a shock, it wasn't a surprise. Bipolar disorder runs in families, and my father and other members of my family have it. I suppose in the back of my mind I always feared that my shifting moods might be an expression of the disease.

Bipolar disorder is characterized by changes in mood, energy, and activity levels. Most people experience these different emotional states, but in bipolar people they are intense, sometimes drastic and disturbing. Like "Maybe I'll spontaneously drive my car off this bridge!" disturbing. They can have a profound impact on daily functioning and relationships. Up to one in five people with bipolar disorder will commit suicide, and rates may even, paradoxically, be higher for those suffering from bipolar II. Psychiatrists posit that individuals with bipolar I, though their suffering is more intense, are less able either to formulate a desire to commit suicide, or to carry it out. People with bipolar II possess the competence necessary to end their suffering.

Though these statistics scared me, having a diagnosis was also in many ways a profound relief. It explained so much! Like my tendency to overshare at dinner parties and on the Internet. Or the day I stood, trembling with rage, as the dry cleaner shrugged his shoulders at the ruin he'd made of my expensive new shirt. The purchase itself was made in a period of overspending typical of bipolar disorder, and my reaction to the dry cleaner's perfunctory apology was a symptom of what's known as "irritability." Irritability, or "irritable mood," is a clinical term, a piece of jargon, defined in the fifth edition of the *Diagnostic and Statistical Manual of Mental Disorders* as "a mood state in which apparently minimal stimulus or irritant produces excessive reaction, usually characterized by anger, aggressiveness or belligerence." It seems kind of an anodyne way to describe shrieking at one's local dry cleaner.

My diagnosis gave me the language to understand the more

positive aspects of what was happening to me as well. It shed light on experiences like the time I wrote three novels in six months, with a clarity of focus and attention to detail that I had never before experienced. This type of sublime creative energy is characteristic of the elevated and productive mood state known as hypomania. So exhilarating and fruitful were these periods that I sometimes thought they were sufficient compensation for the other, dark side of the disease.

After my diagnosis, I embarked on seven years of psychotropic medications, suspended only for a brief period in the early stages of one of my pregnancies. The list of meds I've tried and rejected is so long that my friends use me as a kind of walking *Physicians' Desk Reference,* able to recite symptoms and side effects for anything their shrinks might prescribe, like the soothing voice-over at the end of a drug commercial: "Abilify is not for everyone. Call your doctor if you have high fever, stiff muscles, or confusion." Off the top of my head, I have over the long course of this journey in mental illness and mood alteration been prescribed the following medications: selective serotonin reuptake inhibitors (SSRIs) including: citalopram (Celexa), its nongeneric and thus more costly fraternal twin sister escitalopram (Lexapro), fluoxetine (Prozac), and sertraline (Zoloft); the serotonin-norepinephrine reuptake inhibitors duloxetine (Cymbalta), venlafaxine (Effexor), and venlafaxine XR (Effexor XR); the atypical antidepressant bupropion (Wellbutrin); the mood stabilizers lamotrigine (Lamictal) and topiramate (Topamax); amphetamine (Adderall, Adderall XR), methylphenidate (Ritalin and Concerta), and atomoxetine (Strattera); the benzodiazepines alprazolam (Xanax), diazepam (Valium), and lorazepam (Ativan); the atypical antipsychotic quetiapine (Seroquel) (a particularly bizarre prescription since I have never been remotely psychotic); the sleep aids zolpidem (Ambien) and eszopiclone (Lunesta). I'm sure I'm forgetting some. That can happen when you take a shit-ton of drugs.

Some of these medications worked for a little while—sometimes a few days, sometimes a few months. But with every new pill there were new side effects. Since SSRIs made me gain weight and deadened my libido, standard practice dictated that we add new meds to combat the weight gain and to pump up my sex drive. Those drugs made me irritable, so the doctor prescribed something else to calm me down; round and round in a seemingly futile cycle.

Unfortunately, this kind of trial-and-error experience is quite prevalent in mental health treatment. These drugs act on people in different and unexpected ways, and it is often difficult to concoct the precise cocktail to address an individual's array of issues. Furthermore, practitioners, even the best ones, still lack a complete understanding of the complexity and nuance both of the many psychological and mood disorders and of the many pharmaceuticals available to treat them. Were mental health research more adequately funded, perhaps there might be more clarity. Certainly, misdiagnosis might be less common.

Years after my initial diagnosis, while tumbling down an Internet rabbit hole the genesis of which I can't remember, I stumbled across an abstract of a clinical study on PMS that made me question whether my diagnosis of bipolar disorder was correct. My bipolar disorder did not comply with the requirements written in the *DSM-5*. My hypomania rarely lasted the requisite four days, and never toppled into mania, and, though I regularly fell into black moods, I had never had a major depressive episode. My moods were not as extreme as my father's, nor had I ever suffered any real professional or personal damage as a result of them.* Was I really bipolar?

When I got out the mood charts I'd been keeping since my

---

*Other than the time I was fired for cursing out a sexist boss. But I'd waited until my last week of work before taking on the guy. He was such a complete and utter shitheel that I consider that experience an example of forbearance rather than (or perhaps in addition to) loss of control.

diagnosis and compared them to my menstrual cycle, it became strikingly clear. My mood, my sleep patterns, my energy levels, all fluctuated in direct correspondence with my menstrual cycle. During the week before my period, my mood dropped. I became depressed, more prone to anger; my sleep was out of whack. I also noticed another dip in mood in the middle of my cycle, this one lasting only for a day or so. This dip happened immediately before ovulation, and was characterized not so much by depression as by fury. It was during these pre-period periods that I traumatized that poor dry cleaner and picked fights with my stoical husband over issues of global importance like the proper loading of the dishwasher.

I consulted a psychiatrist recommended by the Women's Mood and Hormone Clinic at the medical center of the University of California, San Francisco, a psychiatric clinic that treats women with mood disorders that can be attributed, in part, to hormonal influences on the brain. My new doctor immediately evaluated me for PMS.

PMS—defined as mood fluctuations and physical symptoms in the days preceding menstruation—is experienced in some form by as many as 80 percent of all ovulating women. Nineteen percent suffer symptoms serious enough to interfere with work, school, or relationships, and between 3 and 8 percent suffer from PMDD, or premenstrual dysphoric disorder, symptoms so severe that those who suffer from them can be, at times, effectively disabled.

Although it's long been known that 67 percent of women's admissions to psychiatric facilities occur during the week immediately prior to menstruation, only recently have researchers begun to consider the effect of PMS on women with mood disorders. Premenstrual exacerbation, or PME, is when an underlying condition is worsened during a phase of a woman's menstrual cycle. However, because I only ever experienced mood swings during two periods in my luteal phase (the days before ovulation and the week leading up to menstruation), my new psychiatrist concluded that I did not suffer from bipolar disorder at all, even bipolar disorder complicated by PME, but, rather, from mild PMDD, not so serious as to be disabling, but troubling nonetheless. Especially to my dry cleaner.

This change in diagnosis immediately felt right to me. Though there'd been comfort in having the bipolar diagnosis to explain my shifting moods, the fact that I never experienced serious mania or profound depression had always given me pause. Many a morning I would feel fine and stable, stare at the handful of pills in the palm of my hand, and wonder whether it really made sense to swallow something that I knew would soon make me irritable and/or sap my sex drive. And yet I also knew what happened to people with bipolar disorder who said, "I feel fine!" and stopped taking their meds, so I was a good soldier and took whatever my psychopharmacologist prescribed. Now, finally, I was on the right track.

Mood stabilizers don't work on PMDD. Instead, low doses of hormones, including birth-control pills, are often prescribed, as are SSRIs, the latter given only in the week or ten days preceding menstruation. Research has also shown a positive effect from calcium supplements, light therapy, and cognitive therapy.

Because evidence of the link between hormone replacement therapy and breast cancer made me skittish, I initially opted for the monthly short course of SSRIs. Though antidepressants normally take four to six weeks to become effective, in premenstrual women, as soon as SSRIs are absorbed, they inhibit the enzyme 3-ß-HSD from metabolizing progesterone. Because the drop in progesterone is the culprit in premenstrual blues, the change is immediate and profound. In my case, within twenty minutes of taking a pill, my mood lifted.*

---

*Incidentally, alcohol seems to act on the same receptors, so a glass of wine can have the same effect. As appealing as was the idea of spending a week of every month in a mild state of inebriation, I opted for the pills.

Unfortunately, SSRIs don't have the same magical effect prior to ovulation, when a woman's hormones shift rapidly, estrogen levels peaking and LH (luteinizing hormone produced by the pituitary gland) surging. As Dr. Louann Brizendine, the founder of the UCSF Women's Mood and Hormone Clinic, told me, "Abrupt changes in hormones are like the rug being pulled out from under the brain." Because SSRIs don't work during this period, I relied on techniques learned in cognitive behavioral therapy and, when I found myself flinging my children's toys across the room or starting a social-media flame war, the occasional anti-anxiety pill. A chill pill, if you will.

Once I understood the cyclical nature of my sleeplessness, I could wean myself off sleeping pills, and throw away most of my pharmacopeia. For a while, I was far better able to control my moods. I still cycled, but because I could anticipate my rages and my periods of sadness, I was able to plan for them and deal with them. I monitored my calendar the way a pilot monitors her cockpit controls, not only to determine when to start taking my medication, but also so that I could schedule important meetings and events to coincide with less volatile days of the month. Dr. Brizendine requires her patients' partners to take the initiative during the premenstrual period, urging them to stop all arguments, jot down the subject on a piece of paper, and reintroduce it later in the month, when it can be dismissed without rancor. My husband kept track of my cycle and developed a bland and pleasant tone in which to ask the question "Do you think you might need an SSRI today?" I did my part by neither defenestrating nor decapitating him, but instead taking my pill.

For five years, things were predictable and peaceful. Then the inevitable happened. I entered perimenopause, and my period became irregular. Some cycles lasted thirty days, others twenty. Sometimes I'd skip a period or two altogether. With my period behaving like an ambivalent Victorian suitor who drops his visiting card rarely and on no discernible schedule, I could not time my SSRIs. My doctor convinced me to overcome my trepidation and try a low-dose estradiol patch to combat my shifting moods. The patch, however, did not provide the instant and profound relief I was used to. More troublingly, the use of unopposed estrogen—estrogen taken alone—is associated with an increased risk of endometrial and uterine cancer. This risk can be eliminated by adding progestin, but that's been associated with an increased risk of breast cancer. Furthermore, progestin has a marked negative effect on mood, especially in women with PMS or PMDD. Since the only reason I was wearing the patch was to ameliorate my low moods, I was not about to add a medication that would make me depressed and possibly give me cancer.

And then things took a turn for the worse. I found myself in a state of seemingly perpetual irritability. I seethed, I turned that fury on the people around me, and then I collapsed in shame at my outbursts. These alternating states of anger and despair came far more frequently than before, and made me feel hopeless. I couldn't seem to find pleasure in my life, or even contentment. I saw the world through a sad and dingy scrim. I knew there was light and love on the other side, but I couldn't manage to lift the grimy curtain of my unhappiness.

My husband, who had been dealing with my vicissitudes of mood for years, seemed finally to be exhausted by them. We fought, and we seemed to take far longer to recover from our altercations. Or perhaps that's more of my despondency talking. Perhaps he was no less patient than before, but my depression made me newly terrified that he would once and for all pack his bags and leave me alone with my ugly self.

It was in this state of mind that I stumbled across James Fadiman's book.

Before becoming a writer, I was a federal public defender and law professor with a particular interest in criminal justice reform. For many years, I taught a seminar called The Legal and Social Implications of the War on Drugs at the UC Berkeley

School of Law, and was a consultant to the Drug Policy Alliance, an organization dedicated to the reform of U.S. drug laws. However, though I have experience and expertise with drug-policy reform issues, I knew very little about psychedelic drugs. I had never taken LSD, and my experience with other hallucinogens began and ended in my freshman year of college, with a pleasurable but somewhat disconcerting few hours spent languidly spinning on a tire swing after consuming a very small quantity of psilocybin in the form of "magic mushrooms."* I have always been too afraid of enduring a terrifying bad trip or suffering lasting psychiatric harm to experiment further. But microdosing seemed different, less frightening. The doses Fadiman discussed were *sub*-perceptual, so small that there was no possibility of any kind of hallucination, positive or negative. Not so much going on an acid trip as going on an acid *errand.*

The individuals whose reports Fadiman presented in his book experienced "joy and gratitude," increased focus, better mood. I wanted that. They reported rarely losing their tempers, becoming more fun to be with. I really wanted that. They experienced that most seductive and elusive thing: a really good day. I needed that! None reported any negative experiences, but, then, the book was hardly a thorough research study. It provided, however, a glimmer of hope. With reservations, of course.

There has never been an officially sanctioned study of microdosing. The closest thing to research is Fadiman's anecdotal data collection, assembling reports from individuals who reach out to him. There is, however, a tremendous amount of data on LSD. Before the drug was criminalized, it was thoroughly studied. Thousands of doses were administered in therapeutic and research settings, with very few negative effects. LSD has a very

---

*Or maybe the mushrooms weren't magic at all. I didn't hallucinate, and who wouldn't become dizzy spinning on a tire swing? It's possible that all I ate was a handful of dried shiitakes dipped in cow manure.

low toxicity level and a large safety range.* This means that even massive doses are not physically dangerous. Microdoses have no discernible biological effects at all.

I contacted James Fadiman and received a memo entitled "To a Potential Self-Study Psychedelic Researcher." The document makes clear that it is not meant as an encouragement to engage in illegal activity but is, rather, a set of cautions and procedures designed to minimize harm, should you engage in illegal activity without the encouragement of James Fadiman.

The protocol is simple. To participate in the international self-study group on the effects of sub-perceptual doses of LSD on normal daily functioning, a "self-study psychedelic researcher" is to take microdoses of LSD on repeating three-day cycles. The suggested dose is ten micrograms, one-tenth or less of what a person would have to take in order to experience an altered state of consciousness. The idea is to take a dose so small that you don't actually feel anything unusual. Or at least nothing immediately tangible. On Day 1 of every cycle, participants are to take ten micrograms of LSD. They are to keep to their normal schedules of work, leisure, meals, coffee, naps, exercise, and social life. They are instructed to monitor mood, physical strength, symptoms, productivity, and the ease with which they do their work, and to "write a few notes about how [the] day went." On Days 2 and 3, participants are to take no LSD, but merely to continue monitoring and noting.

I read Fadiman's memo, I reread his book, I researched, and I considered. The idea of becoming a "self-study psychedelic researcher" felt ridiculous. I am the mother of four children. I am, to use my children's gibe, "totally basic." I wear yoga pants all day, I post photos of particularly indulgent desserts on Instagram. I am the mom surreptitiously checking her phone at Back

*The safety range is the span of difference between a therapeutic dose and a toxic one. If the safety range is narrow, then someone can easily overdose.

to School Night, the woman standing behind you in Starbucks ordering the skinny vanilla latte, the one getting a mammogram in the room next to yours, the one digging through her too-full purse looking for her keys while you wait impatiently for her parking spot. I am a former attorney and law professor, a law-abiding citizen. A nerd. If a cashier hands me incorrect change, I return the excess. I don't cheat on my taxes, don't jump the turnstile in the subway, don't park in handicapped spots. I write and lecture on the criminal justice system; I don't regularly commit crimes.

But I was suffering. Worse, I was making the people around me suffer. I was in pain, and I was desperate, and it suddenly seemed like I had nothing to lose. I decided to try a one-month experiment. I would follow James Fadiman's protocol, taking a microdose of LSD every three days. I would carefully track the results, keeping notes of the effects. Because I am a writer, I would write these notes up in a form that might be useful not just to myself or to Fadiman, but to others curious about the potential therapeutic uses of microdosing. I would also use this month to learn more about psychedelic drugs and to think deeply about what brought me to try something so unusual, so desperate. A single month out of fifty years. What harm—or what help—could there be in that?

A Really Good Day

Day 1

....

Microdose Day

Physical Sensations: Heightened awareness.

Mood: Excited. Nervous. Delighted.

Conflict: Who, me? Even the idea seems absurd.

Sleep: Hard time falling asleep. Woke up early.

Work: Astonishingly productive, lost track of time.

Pain: My shoulder—frozen for the past year and a half—is killing me.

Today I took my first microdose. My senses are ever-so-slightly heightened, a feeling all but unappreciable, so perhaps it's psychosomatic, though that word carries little meaning when anything that might be happening to me right now has inevitably to do with the interaction of mind and body. I feel a tiny bit more aware, as if my consciousness is hovering at a slight remove, watching me tap the keys on my keyboard, rub my ankles together, sip a mouthful of tea and swallow it. The trees look prettier than usual; the jasmine smells more fragrant.

It suddenly occurs to me that I feel *mindful,* a feeling I have tried to achieve through meditation, though I always come up with zip. I am finding it a little bit easier to notice both my thoughts and my body moving through space. Though, even as I write this, I fear the sensation has passed.

Even more thrillingly, for the first time in so long, I feel happy. Not giddy or out of control, just at ease with myself and the world. When I think about my husband and my children, I feel a gentle sense of love and security. I am not anxious for them or annoyed with them. When I think of my work, I feel optimistic, brimming with ideas, yet not spilling over. There's nothing hypomanic about this mood. My mind is not racing. I feel calm and content. Surely, the results cannot be evident so quickly? This is, in all likelihood, nothing more than the placebo effect. But even if it is all in my mind, even if the mood passes, I am grateful for this respite.

When I woke up this morning, I crept out of my house to the place where I hid the little cobalt blue dropper bottle that contains my microdose of diluted LSD. Careful not to hold it up to the light (LSD degrades when exposed to ultraviolet light— ironic, considering all the black-light posters users have stared at while feeding their heads), I shook the bottle a few times, filled the dropper, and carefully deposited two drops under my tongue.

This was certainly not the first time I had tried an illegal drug, though I have never been what you would call a regular drug user. I smoked marijuana a few times in high school, a dozen or so times in college, once or twice as an adult, and then not again until I was prescribed medical marijuana (I live in California), first to end my dependence on the sleeping pill Ambien and then to ease the pain of a frozen shoulder. I have used MDMA six or seven times.* In college, I tried cocaine twice, and those mushrooms that purported to be magic once. All together? More than some people my age, less than Presidents Obama and Bush.

Nor am I an avid user of legal recreational drugs. I don't like the taste of alcohol, and am too readily susceptible to its effects, so even when I'm not taking psychiatric drugs I rarely drink.

---

*Stay tuned. You'll read more about how and why I've used MDMA later on in the book.

Though I've certainly been mildly intoxicated, I remember being inebriated only twice: once in high school, when I threw red wine up on the shoes of a boy I liked (he drove me home, helped me up the stairs to my bedroom, muttered an awkward excuse to my mother, and disappeared from my life), and once in college, when I was convinced to try a beer funnel (I threw that up, too). Tea is my stimulant of choice, and on a workday I can go through a pot or two before noon, when I stop in order not to spend the night wide awake.

I have never purchased drugs from a drug dealer. Whatever illegal substances I've ingested have been passed to me at a party or given to me by friends. When I decided to try the protocol, despite living in Berkeley, a place I'd always assumed to be the psychedelic capital of the world, I had no idea how one would go about buying the drug. Should I wander down to People's Park and hit up one of the dealers who ply their trade among the homeless teens? How would that go?

"Hey, lady, smoke, shake?"

"Why, yes! Do you happen to have lysergic acid diethylamide? And do you take Visa?"

Having dismissed the possibility of a street hand-to-hand, I found myself in yoga class one morning, staring at the grubby-footed young woman on the mat next to mine. Her sweat-stained Interstate 420 T-shirt was a good sign, but then I noticed the Tibetan mandala tattoo on her ankle. How can you trust someone who inscribes permanently on her body something specifically designed to symbolize the transitory nature of the material world? I couldn't buy drugs from an idiot, especially a dirty one.

It then occurred to me that, like all middle-aged women in the Bay Area, I have a healthy supply of gay male friends, most (though by no means all) of whom are childless. Surely, they still knew how to party! Or at least maybe knew someone who knew someone who knew how to party. I started calling.

Unfortunately, it turns out that the gay men of my acquaintance no longer jet around from one circuit party to the next, but, instead, spend their weekends in the same domestic torpor as I do. Binge-watching episodes of *Orange Is the New Black* is the closest they get to criminality. My former-stoner friends were similarly useless. The guy who used to grow hydroponic weed in his dorm room closet? He's the third-grade room parent, his only remaining allegiance to the counterculture the Darwin fish bumper sticker on his Prius.

I was at a loss, so though Fadiman stresses the importance of discretion, I began tentatively bringing up the subject of micro-dosing in conversation. If the response was familiarity or even curiosity (or really anything other than befuddlement or disgust), I'd mention that I was looking for a reputable (or at least not entirely disreputable) source. After some time, an acquaintance told me that he had heard a story about an elderly professor who had been microdosing with LSD for years. He didn't know the professor's name or anything about him, but he'd pass a message along to the person who had told him about the professor. Maybe that person would reach out to the professor on my behalf. The entire tale had the ring of the apocryphal, and I had little faith that anything would result from this attenuated game of telephone with someone who I wasn't sure even existed.

I continued my fruitless quest. I even momentarily considered trying to log on to the dark web, but since I am only marginally more technologically savvy than my mother, who has yet to figure out how to turn on her cell phone ringer, I realized that with my luck I'd probably end up soliciting drugs directly from the DEA homepage. I only ever got as far as Googling LSD and finding endlessly threaded message boards where eager seekers were told by more experienced keyboard shamans that when they were truly ready the drug would come to them. Obviously, these guys were high. I gave up.

About a week later, I received a message from my acquaintance. The possibly mythical professor was sympathetic to my predicament. Moreover, he was nearing the end of his life and no longer had use for his remaining LSD. He would send it to me. The story seemed preposterous, but two days later, I opened my mailbox to find a brown paper package covered in brightly colored stamps, many of them at least a decade old. The return address read "Lewis Carroll." Inside the package, wrapped in tissue, was a tiny cobalt blue bottle. On a scrap of white paper, printed in sans-serif italics, was the following note:

Dear Fellow resident of Berkeley,

Because of a request from an old friend, you will find 50 drops of vintage quality in the small bottle. Take in two drops portions (5 mcg per drop).

Our lives may be no more
Than dewdrops on a summer morning,
But surely,
It is better that we sparkle
While we are here.

L.C.

Weird. Very, very weird. And yet also kind of adorable. And freaky. I was ready, and it had come to me.

My first order of business was to test the drug. When I began flirting with the idea of trying the protocol, I ordered an LSD test kit. Without the security of the FDA, I wanted to make very sure that what I was taking was actually LSD and not some toxic substitute. Far too often, what is sold on the street as one drug is something else entirely. For example, as the precursor chemicals to MDMA (commonly known as Ecstasy or Molly) become harder to find, hundreds of new psychoactive substances, some of which are very dangerous, are being synthesized and sold under the name. According to the DEA, the vast majority of what is currently being sold as Molly is in fact something else, often a synthetic cathinone (known as bath salts), methamphetamine, or most likely a combination of a variety of substances, some benign, some very dangerous. My eldest child attends Wesleyan University, where a group of students ended up in the hospital after consuming what they had been told was pure Molly. The kids suffered respiratory distress, and at least one of them nearly died. It took six shocks with a defibrillator and an intubation to save that young man's life. It appears that what the kids took was not MDMA but AB-Fubinaca, a synthetic cannabinoid commonly known as "Spice" or K2, which is far more dangerous. Similarly, toxic substances have been sold as LSD, leading in at least a few cases to death. I was not about to consume a drug without testing it first, no matter how cute a note it came with.

From where did I order this testing kit, you might wonder? I already told you I'm too nervous for hand-to-hand purchases and too inept to log on to the dark web. I got my LSD testing kit from the Internet's largest purveyor of toilet paper, half-hour dramas, and discounted books. That's right, I bought it on Amazon. And it qualified for Prime two-day shipping!

Squinting at the fine print on the box through my reading glasses, I read through the directions twice—I didn't want to make any mistakes. I delicately squeezed a single drop from the cobalt blue bottle into the opening at the top of the test kit and squeezed the rubber sleeve, which broke the thin glass barrier between the drop and the testing solution, allowing them to mix together. The solution was meant to turn bright lavender in the presence of LSD, but I saw only the faintest shade of purple. I reread the directions. Stared again at the solution. Was it even purple I was seeing so very faintly, or was it my imagination? Suddenly I realized what the problem was. LSD is effective at infinitesimal doses. A single drop of pure LSD would contain a massive amount of the drug. For this reason, LSD, even in its liquid form, is always diluted. "Blotter acid," for example, the most common way LSD is sold, is a piece of paper, generally decorated with some kind of design, soaked in a diluted solution of LSD and perforated into little squares. One single confetti-sized square is designed to contain the standard dose—approximately one hundred to one hundred and fifty micrograms of LSD.* If a single drop of Lewis Carroll's solution contained a mere five micrograms of LSD, it had to have been so vastly diluted that it would barely register on the testing kit. After an hour of Web surfing (there seem to be a limitless quantity of Web sites offering information about psychedelic drugs, including how to test them), I made a decision to have faith that the contents of Lewis Carroll's bottle would not make me grow either very big or very small. Or kill me.

I took the drug, and went on to have a really good day.

---

*Or at least that's what it says on the Web and in the thirty-two books about psychedelics I bought and neurotically pored over in anticipation of beginning this experiment because I am a good student and an anxious nerd and I like to do my research before taking anything resembling a risk. I haven't ever actually seen a tab of acid in person. According to DEA data from confiscated samples, the actual range of LSD on blotter is from thirty micrograms (if your dealer's a cheapskate) to a hundred and twenty.

Day 2

....

Transition Day

Physical Sensations: Normal. A little draggy because of lack of sleep.

Mood: Grumpy at beginning of day, but by end of day productive and content.

Conflict: Even when irritable, I didn't argue with anyone.

Sleep: A sleepless night.

Work: Not pouring out like yesterday, but a solid day's work.

Pain: Intense shoulder pain during the night.

This morning, when I woke up, I thought, "Oh, it's you." Not the new-and-improved me of yesterday, who was effortlessly cheerful and affectionate with her children and husband and who wrote more in a single day than she usually does in a week. Just plain old me. About the second day, Fadiman's protocol notes, "Many people report that the second day effects are as positive or even better than the first day." For once in my life, would it have killed me to be like everyone else?

Perhaps I did not immediately experience the typical positive second-day results because I was exhausted from a long night of sleeplessness and pain. I have been in pretty much constant pain since last spring, when I was felled with frozen shoulder, a disorder in which the capsule of the shoulder becomes inflamed and stiff, resulting in excruciating pain,* especially at night. Frozen shoulder comes on without warning and for no reason, and can last up to three years. It is debilitating and dispiriting, and it's surely part of the reason for my current state of anhedonic desperation.

The symptoms of frozen shoulder are worst at night, and it has been a very long time since I got a decent night's sleep. The pain keeps me from falling asleep, and wrenches me awake when I roll over. I have tried everything to relieve this pain, from physical therapy to acupuncture, ibuprofen to opioids.† In fact, nothing provided any relief until a doctor suggested I try medical marijuana. I resisted the idea at first. I have no interest in recreational drug use; I didn't and don't want to get "high." But the doctor reassured me that I could purchase marijuana devoid of intoxicating effects. It is the chemical tetrahydrocannabinol (THC) in marijuana (or "cannabis," as the bright young people at my local dispensary prefer to call it) that causes the feelings and mental effects we associate with the drug. Cannabis also contains a related but structurally different isomer, cannabidiol, or CBD. CBD has pain-relieving properties, and acts as an anti-seizure agent, but it doesn't make you high. Since the decriminalization and popularization of medical marijuana, high-CBD strains have been engineered that all but eliminate THC.

I followed the doctor's advice and tried the high-CBD cannabis; though the relief was by no means complete, it did substantially decrease my pain, if only at night, when I allowed myself

---

*Two sentences and I've used the word "pain" three times. That about sums it up. Frozen shoulder hurts like a motherfucker. Worse than labor, worse than dental work.

†The term "opiate" generally refers only to those morphinelike substances found in opium (i.e., morphine, codeine, and thebaine). The newer and more inclusive term "opioid" refers to opiates, semi-synthetics (e.g., heroin, oxycodone, hydrocodone, etc.), and synthetics (methadone, fentanyl, etc.). Because this distinction can be distracting and confusing, I'm going to use the term "opioid" exclusively.

to take it. How ironic. Addictive and dangerous opioids, fatal at high doses and yet freely prescribed by physicians,* did nothing to alleviate the pain of my frozen shoulder, but cannabis, still illegal under federal law and in many states, worked.

When I taught my seminar on the drug war, I began every semester by writing the question "What is a drug?" on the whiteboard. I divided the board into sections—medicine, drug, food— and then had students brainstorm, calling out every substance they could think of and debating where to place it on the chart. Coffee, which is a stimulant, is a food. What about a caffeine pill? Or nicotine? Are they medicines, foods, drugs? Oxycodone, an opioid alkaloid synthesized in part from the poppy, is a medicine. Heroin, an opioid derivative of morphine, also synthesized from the poppy, is a drug. Do these differentiations make any sense at all?

America did not always make such distinctions. In fact, for the first hundred years, citizens of this country were at liberty to alter their consciousness with any substance they pleased. Thomas Jefferson planted poppies in his medicinal garden at Monticello and may have used opium—supposedly to treat chronic diarrhea, but perhaps also for fun. The man was hardly a model of propriety. Only in 1875 was the first drug law passed, in San Francisco, and even that did not prohibit a drug but prevented a specific use: the smoking of opium in Chinese opium dens. It was an attack on emigrants from China, who smoked their opium, leaving the more typical American opium user, a middle-aged, white, Southern woman, to tipple from her bottle of laudanum (opium combined with alcohol) in peace.

During that time and up through the early twentieth century, opioids and cocaine were readily available and frequently used. The Sears Roebuck catalogue, the amazon.com of the time, fea-

---

* And are probably what made Rush Limbaugh go deaf, though they can't be blamed for the fact that the only voice he's ever been able to hear is his own.

tured kits with syringes and vials of heroin or cocaine, complete with handy-dandy carrying cases. Cocaine was the official remedy of the Hay Fever Association, and bartenders dropped it into shots of whiskey for a little added boost. Coca leaf and kola syrup were combined with cocaine to create what became, unsurprisingly, the most popular drink in the world. In fact, it wasn't until 1929 that Coca-Cola became free of the drug, thereafter relying solely on caffeine to invigorate its customers.* Bayer pharmaceutical ads from the period advertise both aspirin and heroin. Mothers were urged to lull their cranky babies to sleep with the aid of tinctures containing all manners of opioids, including morphine and heroin. Opium, cocaine, and their derivatives were injected, granulated and sprinkled on open wounds, drunk and otherwise ingested by anyone who could afford them.

As a result of these patent medicines, addiction to opioids was at an all-time high at the turn of the last century. In 1900, a remarkable 2 to 5 percent of the population was addicted to these drugs. Only in 1906, when the Pure Food and Drug Act required manufacturers to start listing the ingredients of their products on the labels, did rates drop, perhaps because people became aware of exactly what it was that was hushing their babies so effectively.

But even then there was no particular stigma against drug use. Eighty percent of addicts were upstanding citizens, employed, with families and dependents. They thought no more of taking their laudanum or cocaine than we today think of having a glass of wine with dinner. The list of notable narcotic users includes Dr. William Stewart Halsted, the "Father of Modern Surgery," one of the founders of Johns Hopkins Hospital, who first discovered that cocaine could be used as an anesthesia on his patients, and then took to enjoying its other effects on himself.

*They took most of the coke out of Coke in 1903, but it took them a further twenty-six years to perfect the process and entirely rid the coca leaf of its psychoactive substances.

The first federal drug law, the Harrison Narcotics Tax Act of 1914, was ostensibly a regulatory act that required physicians to purchase a license to dispense narcotics, and to keep records of their prescriptions. However, because it prevented the prescribing of narcotics solely as a treatment for addiction without another underlying ailment, all of the upright individuals who were addicted but not otherwise ill suddenly found themselves bereft of legal sources. Some kicked their habits, but many others chose alternative paths. Dr. Halsted, for example, after a traumatic period of cocaine withdrawal, switched to legal morphine and heroin, which he used for the remainder of his life, all the while enjoying a prosperous and successful medical career.

Harking back to the good old days of ubiquitous drug addiction is a ridiculous way to make yourself feel better about having received a package of illegal drugs in your mailbox and embarking on a project that will strike many as lunatic. If I'm honest, the project seems crazy to me, too. I wouldn't do it if I wasn't desperate. Though I had not considered it before, I think it's likely that the fact that marijuana—which, like LSD, is listed on Schedule I of the Controlled Substances Act "with no currently accepted medical use and a high potential for abuse"—helped my frozen shoulder, when dangerous and yet legal drugs did not, influenced my decision to try microdosing. It may be the one time pot has actually been the gateway drug that Nancy Reagan said it was.

However, when I started Dr. Fadiman's protocol, I stopped using even the small amount of cannabis that was helping to soothe my shoulder pain. I didn't want to confuse any results. Moreover, the consequences of mixing drugs, even nontoxic drugs, can be unpredictable.

When I woke up after my pain-filled, sleepless night, even before I got out of bed, I reached for my laptop with the arm attached to my good shoulder, and reread Dr. Fadiman's protocol. This time I noticed something I had missed: the protocol can cause sleep disturbances. He writes, "Some people take something to get to sleep at their regular time." This is something I have to figure out how to deal with.

Still, I have too many children to indulge in early morning self-pity. I flung back the covers and dragged myself downstairs. It wasn't until I was in the kitchen, drinking my first cup of tea and ushering my kids out the door to catch their various buses and rides, that I noticed that I had managed much more easily than usual to shrug off my bad mood, even if my shoulder hurts too fucking much to shrug.

Something is happening. Whether it is all in my head remains to be seen.

Day 3

....

Normal Day

Physical Sensations: None.

Mood: Irritable, depressed, anxious.

Conflict: Picked a fight with my husband.

Sleep: Another bad night.

*Work: Weirdly productive considering my
    crappy mood.*

Pain: Ugh.

I know the protocol has a purpose, that the two days off are designed both to prevent me from developing a tolerance to the LSD, and to provide the experience of periodic "normal" days so I can better assess the quality of my mood on the Microdose and Transition Days, but it's the first Day 3 of the cycle, and I already hate it. Once again, the pain in my shoulder woke me in the middle of the night. I miss the peace of yesterday afternoon, the peace that allowed me to wince in pain and then remind myself that frozen shoulder never lasts longer than a year or two. Three, tops. Today, rather than consider the therapeutic effects of time, I grumble that it's already been a year, I cannot handle two more, and even after the shoulder thaws, there usually remain residual restrictions in movement. Today I have lost perspective. No. I *have* perspective. I have the perspective that, as bad as my pain is, worse is the humiliation of suffering an ailment whose risk factors are primarily being over forty and being a woman. As if turning the big 5-0 wasn't bad enough, now I am forced to spend my nights tossing and turning from what the Chinese call "fifty-year shoulder." George Clooney is fifty-five. Does he have to put up with this shit?

Last night, as I lay in bed trying to force myself to sleep, I felt an all-too-familiar sensation, one that I'd naïvely hoped the microdosing would short-circuit. I felt like I was crawling out of my skin. I tossed and turned, flinging my limbs around, groaning with frustration. My stomach began to roil, and I suddenly remembered the story I'd read recently in the Hypochondriac's Bible (aka the Tuesday Health section of *The New York Times*). A woman experiences a heart attack differently from a man. Her symptoms aren't limited to the left side of her chest and her left arm. Instead of chest pain, she may experience a sense of fullness. I felt full! Also empty. Or maybe neither. I certainly felt *something*. And my stomach hurt, another symptom. I was sweating, too.

It's wrong to say I was sure I was having a heart attack, but I definitely considered it a possibility.

What kind of a wretchedly irresponsible idiot was I, taking an illegal drug, especially one so widely considered to be dangerous? I am a mother, for God's sake! How could I even consider taking these risks? My mind jumped ahead to when EMTs would be strapping me to a gurney, asking, "Ma'am, are there any drugs you are taking that we should know about?" and me, in the midst of my heart attack, being like "Funny you should ask. Have you ever heard of microdosing?"

The reason I didn't use as many drugs as so many of my college contemporaries was that I was afraid not just of losing control but of losing my mind or my life. Of all the drugs on offer, LSD was the one I was most terrified of. I believed LSD to be on a par with heroin and methamphetamine, or perhaps even more dangerous. Lying in bed last night, I felt that fear overwhelm me. I tried to breathe, to remind myself that I had carefully researched the drug before beginning this experiment. In my mind, I ran through everything that I had learned.

Though I don't consider myself a gullible person, and though my work in drug policy reform has made me more familiar than most people with the way drugs have been represented and misrepresented throughout history—with some harms downplayed, others exaggerated—before beginning this experiment I had swallowed without question all the stories I had heard about LSD. I believed that people who took LSD experienced lifelong "acid flashbacks" that prevented them from leading normal lives. I believed they flung themselves off the roofs of buildings under the illusion that they could fly. I even believed a rumor I'd heard in high school, that a person who uses LSD more than seven times inevitably becomes psychotic. I was flabbergasted when I met my husband and he told me he'd dropped acid nine times. He's pretty much the least psychotic person I've ever met. In fact, he's almost disturbingly sane.

Those fears, I told myself sternly as I felt around in my wrist for my pulse,* are not borne out by the facts. Whatever I and so many others have heard, in the nearly eighty years since the drug was first synthesized, at least twenty million Americans and many more millions of people around the world have used LSD, to very little ill effect.

Moreover, the Swiss research chemist who first synthesized the drug, and who consumed it and other hallucinogens frequently throughout his life, including microdosing during his last decades, lived to be 102 years old!

When he discovered LSD in Basel in 1938, Dr. Albert Hofmann was employed by Sandoz Pharmaceuticals, a company

---

*As if I have the faintest idea what the difference between a normal and an abnormal pulse is.

founded in the middle of the nineteenth century that was, among other things, one of the earliest producers of saccharin, the sugar substitute beloved of little old Jewish ladies the world over. (My grandmother kept a pill dispenser of saccharin on her kitchen table, and another in her purse, to guarantee ready access to calorie-free Sanka that tasted vaguely like aspirin.) Hofmann was the lead Sandoz researcher investigating ergot, a fungus that had visited periodic plagues of madness and misery on medieval cities. During the Middle Ages, ergot would infest grain stores, leading to widespread outbreaks of ergotism, commonly known as St. Anthony's Fire, named for the order of monks devoted to treating its victims. Victims of ergotism suffered two different forms of the illness. The gangrenous form caused full-body blistering and the rotting away of limbs. The convulsive form caused seizures, delusions, and death.

In small doses, ergot also causes uterine contractions, and was thus a common, if dangerous, abortifacient.* All of this made the compound very interesting to chemists like Hofmann, whose work involved altering chemicals to make them useful in treating disease. Hofmann worked with the ergotamine molecule, synthesizing subtle variations in search of one with medicinal applications. As he worked, he numbered his variations. The two diluted drops I placed under my tongue two days ago were his twenty-fifth variation, LSD-25.

When Hofmann first created this iteration of the chemical and tested it, he found that it had a uterine contracting effect, but not as much as other ergot compounds he had synthesized. He noticed that the lab animals tested with LSD-25 became highly excited, but since he was focused on discovering a substance that would stimulate circulation and respiration, that effect held no interest for him. He put LSD-25 in the metaphori-

---

*The morning-after pill for medieval women who preferred a gangrenous, raving demise to a baby. There are days when I can totally empathize.

cal cupboard along with LSD-1 through 24, and moved on with his ergot research, eventually producing an ergot alkaloid known as Hydergine, which improved circulation and cerebral function and is still used in the treatment of dementia and Alzheimer's.

Years later, for no reason that Hofmann could explain, he felt called to return to his experiments with LSD-25. In his book *LSD, My Problem Child,* Hofmann said he experienced "a peculiar presentiment—the feeling that this substance could possess properties other than those established in the first investigations." It might simply have been a scientist's instinct; it might have had something to do with the laboratory animals' unusual reaction to the compound. Hofmann, however, believed that something more mysterious drove him to return to that particular variant. It was as if the drug wanted to be found. Believe that or not, five years after first synthesizing LSD-25, Hofmann did so again.

As he worked with the compound in his laboratory, Hofmann began to feel dizzy and restless. Then he began to hallucinate. He wrote, "I perceived an uninterrupted stream of fantastic pictures, extraordinary shapes with intense, kaleidoscopic play of colors."

Assuming correctly that he'd accidentally ingested the chemical, and intrigued by those fantastical and vivid images, Hofmann decided to try the drug again, this time in a controlled experiment with a verified dose. Three days later, in the company of a group of lab assistants, he stirred 250 millionths of a gram (250 micrograms) into a beaker of water and drank it down. This is approximately twice what became the average dose for a "trip."

Within half an hour, Hofmann began again to experience the same hallucinatory symptoms, but with a disturbing intensity. He asked one of his assistants to accompany him home, and they made the curious decision, which Hofmann attributes to its being wartime and his having no car, to ride their bicycles. This was, it turned out, a bad idea. According to Hofmann, "Everything in my field of vision wavered and was distorted as if seen in a curved mirror." When his research assistant helped him into his room, things became even worse. "A demon had invaded me, had taken possession of my body, mind, and soul. .... I was seized by the dreadful fear of going insane. I was taken to another world, another place, another time. My body seemed to be without sensation, lifeless, strange. Was I dying?"

The very question I had asked myself, after taking 4 percent of the dose he had taken!

And yet Hofmann's research assistant found that he was in no physical danger. "Pulse, blood pressure, breathing were all normal." Then things changed. Hofmann stopped panicking and began to "enjoy the unprecedented colors and plays of shapes that persisted behind my closed eyes." The day after that dizzy bicycle ride and its aftermath, Hofmann was himself transformed. "A sensation of well-being and renewed life flowed through me."

Thus was launched the era of human experimentation with LSD. Sandoz made the drug available to scientists for traditional analytical research as well as for more unusual experiential experiments. In the materials that accompanied the drug, Sandoz suggested that psychiatrists who took the medication might gain insight into the minds of their patients. LSD could help them understand what it was like to be insane.

From the 1930s through 1968, when the United States and other governments criminalized LSD and effectively terminated research, scientists throughout the world experimented on thousands of volunteers, both healthy individuals and the mentally ill. They tried LSD on alcoholics and catatonics, on schizophrenics and depressives, and, most notably, on themselves. Many LSD researchers became their own subjects. It's easy to understand why. How many of us have enough willpower to turn away from a "sensation of well-being and renewed life"? Not so much chasing the dragon as reaching for the cuddly kitty of contentment.

During the heyday of LSD research, scientists published more than a thousand research papers and dozens of books. They held symposia and conferences to discuss and compare their findings.

The outcomes were overwhelmingly positive, though some scientists did report subjects who had negative experiences. Some people experienced "bad trips," which caused them distress. A few researchers, notably Timothy Leary and Richard Alpert, abandoned established modes of scientific study for incense and mantras and *The Tibetan Book of the Dead*—a disturbing development, not to the researchers themselves, but to those who paid their salaries. But in none of those experiments did anyone die or suffer serious injury.

In fact, contrary to what I believed before I began my preparatory research, contrary to what the vast majority of people probably believe, LSD is, as drugs go, safe. In terms of morbidity, it's a lot more like marijuana than heroin. According to a thorough review of the drug's pharmacology published in 2008 in the peer-reviewed journal *CNS: Neuroscience & Therapeutics,* "There have been no documented human deaths from an LSD overdose."

Chill *out*! I told myself, in an attempt to stem the tide of panic. Do you imagine that, having taken a fraction of the dose of a drug that tens of millions of people have consumed, you will be the first ever to die? You, Ayelet, are not that special.

Surprisingly, haranguing myself proved useless in alleviating my anxiety attack, so I pulled out my research notes and pored over a report of a 1972 incident in which eight people were admitted to San Francisco General Hospital after taking a massive quantity of LSD, the highest reported dose ever consumed by humans. This group of partiers had snorted lines of what they believed was cocaine but what was actually LSD. This is an astonishing dose. Recall that all it takes to trip is a tiny amount diluted on a dot of blotting paper. The huge overdose made them terribly sick. When they arrived at the hospital, they were vomiting, had hypothermia, and showed signs of internal bleeding. Five slipped into comas; three needed to be intubated to breathe. And yet, within twelve hours, they had all completely recovered. It's taken me longer to get right after a Pilates class.

In evaluating how toxic a substance is, scientists attempt to determine its median lethal dose (known in scientific parlance as "LD_{50}"). LSD is psychoactively powerful; minute dosages, starting at a millionth of a gram, produce noticeable effects. And yet, even a dose of two thousand micrograms, two hundred times the dose I took, twenty times the typical "tab," causes no discernible biological side effects at all. The fact that there has never been a documented death from LSD overdose makes it impossible to determine its human LD_{50} with absolute assurance, but Hofmann, extrapolating from animal studies, estimated that it must be hundreds of times the typical dose. A textbook entitled *Haddad and Winchester's Clinical Management of Poisoning and Drug Overdose,* published in 1990, reports the LD_{50} to range from 0.2 mg/kg to more than 1 mg/kg.* I weigh about fifty-eight kilograms, which means that, to be having an LSD-caused heart attack, even in that volume's very conservative estimation, I would have had to ingest at least 11,600 micrograms, not ten. I wasn't dying. But what about my mental health? In my quest to feel better, was I risking permanent psychic injury?

One of the first American researchers into the effects of LSD, Dr. Max Rinkel, a psychiatrist at the Massachusetts Mental Health Center, reported that healthy subjects (notably his colleagues, on whom he experimented) experienced marked personality changes while under the influence of LSD. Some became withdrawn, even exhibiting autistic behaviors. Others became manic. Some became suspicious and hostile; others experienced deep ecstasy. Rinkel characterized these personality changes as mimicking schizophrenia or psychosis. Once the drug's effects wore off, however, so did these changes.

Over the course of eighteen months between 1966 and 1968, when recreational use of the drug was at its peak, a survey of doctors and hospitals in Los Angeles found that at least forty-one

---

*Michael W. Shannon et al., *Haddad and Winchester's Clinical Management of Poisoning and Drug Overdose.*

hundred people had experienced acid trips disturbing enough that they sought a doctor's help. The majority of their adverse reactions were merely transitory anxiety or depression, but there have been reports of more serious problems.

No phenomenon causes me more anxiety than the specter of "LSD psychosis," generally defined as a reaction to the drug that is prolonged, lasting days to months, or one that requires hospitalization. According to the research, however, the majority of individuals diagnosed with LSD psychosis have a history of psychiatric illness, have taken a substantial cumulative amount of the drug, and have histories of polydrug abuse. The first category could theoretically apply to me. I have a history of PMDD and a misdiagnosis of bipolar disorder. My emotional pain is the very reason I started down this path. Neither other element is present in me, however, and, like the song says, two out of three ain't bad.

Still, in a 1984 paper, Dr. Rick Strassman, a research physician for the University of California, Davis, wrote, "There are occasional reports of severe and prolonged reactions occurring in basically well-adjusted individuals."* He cited a study from the 1970s in which two young women were admitted to psychiatric hospitals weeks after taking average doses of LSD. According to the authors of that study, both women were "normal" before trying the drug, and both ended up profoundly depressed, and in one case allegedly homicidal. (She said she wanted to kill her mother, but, then, what twenty-one-year-old woman doesn't?) After multiple treatments with ECT (electroconvulsive therapy), the two girls recovered and were discharged.

And yet Strassman, after a thorough review of this study and others, concluded, "It appears that the incidence of adverse reactions to psychedelic drugs is low, when ... patients are carefully

---

*Rick J. Strassman, "Adverse Reactions to Psychedelic Drugs. A Review of the Literature."

screened and prepared, supervised, and followed up, and given judicious doses of pharmaceutical quality drug." His conclusion is in line with other, more recent research, as well as what mid-twentieth-century scientists found.

One of the most important things the early LSD pioneers discovered is that the personality of the researcher *administering* the drug had a profound effect on the experience of the patient. If the examiner was cold and distant, the subject occasionally became hostile, even paranoid. The subjects of a warm and gentle researcher almost universally experienced feelings of love and joy. What are the implications of this finding in terms of my administering the drug to myself? No one is meaner to me than me. I was probably being cold and distant with myself when I hit the dropper!

In response to this discovery, researchers articulated the concept of "set and setting" in influencing subjective drug experiences, not just of LSD but of all drugs. Set refers to the subject's own subjective mental state. How stable is she? What does she think she will experience? Setting is the environment in which she takes the drug. If the environment is threatening and chaotic, or clinical and cold, she's more likely to have a negative experience. If the environment is safe and supportive, she is more likely to have a meaningful, positive experience. Not, for example, a sweaty bed freak-out in the middle of the night.

Though I'd much prefer to undertake this experiment in an official setting, supervised by psychiatrists and using pharmaceutical-grade LSD, I don't have that option. The last decade has seen a renaissance in research into the effects of psychedelic drugs, including LSD, but microdosing is not being researched by anyone in the world. Though some might be in the early planning stages, there are at this time no studies going on, double-blind or otherwise. Dr. Fadiman's collection of notes from experiments like my own is the closest approximation to a study out there. It's the Wild West, and I'm running my own saloon.

I reminded myself that Dr. Fadiman has collected hundreds of reports, and though a few individuals have experienced some anxiety while microdosing, no one has ever lost her mind. Nor could anyone lose her mind from such a dose. Not even me.

I put aside my notes and took a few deep breaths. I was not dying of a heart attack. My preparation for this month-long experiment had been as thorough as possible. I did my research and took as many precautions as I could. There is risk, certainly, but so is there with any medication or drug. As a point of comparison, according to a thorough review of the literature by Pro-Publica, more than three hundred people in the United States die every year from taking acetaminophen (that's *Tylenol*) and another forty-four thousand end up in the emergency room. Compared with this, LSD seems almost harmless.

Those stories I heard about people flinging themselves off the roofs of buildings, convinced that they can fly? Those are urban legend, not fact. And what about suicides? According to the 2008 literature review, "The incidence of psychotic reactions, suicide attempts, and suicides during treatment with LSD . . . appears comparable to the rate of complications during conventional psychotherapy." There have been reports of people falling while on LSD, some fatally, but most likely because of disorientation and confusion. The myth of the flying tripper probably began with television host Art Linkletter's twenty-year-old daughter, Diane, who committed suicide in 1969. Her father, perhaps unwilling to admit or confront her history of depression, was convinced that an experience with LSD six months before had caused her to jump to her death. He became a committed anti-drug campaigner, helping to spread the myth that people on LSD jumped off buildings to their deaths.

In fact, a recent study published in the *Journal of Psychopharmacology* found that psychedelic use is correlated with *lower* rates of suicidal thinking and suicide. According to researchers, "Lifetime classic psychedelic use was associated with a 19% reduced likelihood of past month psychological distress, a 14% reduced likelihood of past year suicidal thinking, a 29% reduced likelihood of past year suicidal planning, and a 36% reduced likelihood of past year suicide attempt."*

Given all the evidence of its safety, why is LSD so maligned? It's most certainly because of the way, in the 1960s, LSD came to be associated with youthful rebellion and social upheaval. When Timothy Leary, a psychologist and former Harvard lecturer and early researcher who advocated widespread recreational LSD use, told the children of the middle class to "Turn on, tune in, and drop out," they did, terrifying their parents. People were horrified to see their children protesting the war in Vietnam, joining in the civil-rights movement, smoking pot, and taking LSD. White America began to view their country as a fractured and scary place. They latched on to drugs, and especially LSD, as a symptom of the problem.

But I'm not my grandmother, clutching my pearls as I sip my saccharin-flavored Sanka and fretting about the bright and shining youth of America's transformation into a bunch of dirty hippies. I am confident that this drug is safe at a dose far higher than the near-homeopathic one that I'm taking.

I took a few more deep breaths and finally drifted off to sleep. First thing in the morning, I picked a fight with my husband.

One of the reasons that I started this experiment was that I had come to feel, even in moments when my mood was fine, a faint sense of peril, as if I were perpetually at risk for a setback that could trigger an outburst. My temper felt like an angry bullmastiff, kept in check by a frayed muzzle. After my brutal night, the mastiff slipped the leash.

My husband is out of town again. He travels often, as do I, but this year it's been out of control. In the months since September 1 of last year, we have spent 103 days apart. If things go as planned, before September rolls around again, we will have

---

*Peter S. Hendricks et al., "Classic Psychedelic Use Is Associated with Reduced Psychological Distress and Suicidality in the United States Adult Population."

spent a total of 195 days and nights apart. More than half of the year.

We have been married for over twenty years, and our marriage in a very real way defines not just my personal life but my career. A decade ago, I wrote an essay in which I credited my happy marriage to the fact that, though I loved my kids, I wasn't *in* love with them. If a good mother is one who loves her children more than anyone else in the world, I wrote, then I am a bad mother, because I love my husband more than my children. In some ways, my career has been built not on my dozen books or the many other essays I have published, but on the outsized response to that essay.

The morning of the essay's publication in the *New York Times* Modern Love column, my e-mail inbox was inundated with angry responses. Then I went ahead and made things worse by going on *Oprah* to defend myself against the mob of angry mommies. In the decade since, I have never given an interview, a reading, or a lecture in which that essay hasn't been brought up at least once. To be fair, that's mostly my own fault. A few years after I published the essay, I wrote an entire book, *Bad Mother: A Chronicle of Maternal Crimes, Minor Calamities, and Occasional Moments of Grace,* about the destructive impulse of mothers to castigate each other and ourselves.

Because I have become so thoroughly identified with the topics of motherhood and marriage, the prospect of experiencing a rough patch in my marriage terrifies me. Though I know all marriages experience ups and downs, when we are in a low period I panic, imagining the sanctimommies of the Internet gleefully reveling in my unhappiness. (Okay, yes, I'm probably being paranoid, but I bet at least a few people would gloat.)

This patch has been rough. Really rough. I cannot decide whether the continued separations are part of the problem or if they are what has kept us from permanently fracturing. When apart, we fight only rarely. Mostly, we stay in close touch, texting

and talking, consulting on every issue, and sending gooey emo-
jis. Hearts. Smiley faces with hearts for eyes. But lately, when we
are together, we bicker. Worse than that, we fight. We yell, we
cry, we collapse and promise it'll never happen again. And then
it does, over and over.

I've been desperate for my husband to come home to help me
take stock of my protocol. More than anyone, he can evaluate my
state of mind and judge if there's been a noticeable change. I am
also eager to talk to him about the mild perceptual differences
I'd noticed in the hour or so after I first took the microdose, the
way my senses seemed slightly enhanced, like I'd been bitten by
a radioactive no-see-um. Unlike me, my husband has experience
with typical doses of LSD. I knew he would be able to give me
insight on that aspect of the experience. Also I missed him.

The fact that I have been waiting so impatiently for him
to come home makes the argument we had on the telephone,
usually our happy place, even more painful. After I woke up
wretched from my sleepless night, I called him. I shouldn't have,
because from the very beginning I was gunning for a fight.
Nearly as soon as he picked up the phone, I began complaining
about our shared workspace.

A couple of months ago, my husband had an idea. The inspiration for this idea is one of the things we fought about, but,
because I have vowed to stop imputing bad motives to the people I love, I will present his side of the argument as fact, without picking apart ulterior motives or launching into a digression
about whether or not Freud was right about the role of the
unconscious in directing behavior.

Not long ago, my husband surprised me with a couch. He
placed it in a corner of the studio we share (really his studio,
which he allows me to squat in), and moved his own workspace into the middle of the room. He says he bought the couch
because I hadn't been using the studio and he was trying to lure
me back. He expected me to recline on the couch, laptop in my

lap, and immerse myself with a newfound focus. But the couch is too narrow, the arms are too hard; I can't get comfortable on it. Moreover, with his workspace now in the middle of the room, I feel crowded. Crowded *out*.

This morning, when I called him, I suddenly and for no particular reason launched into a familiar litany of complaints. There's so much I don't like about his studio! I complained about the couch and the light and about how I feel crowded and pushed out. It was neither the first, the tenth, nor the one hundredth time he's heard me bitching about this. Is it any wonder he got frustrated with me?

"How many times do we have to have this fight?" he asked. "You should just get an office of your own."

That really infuriated me. Little postage-stamp offices rent for a thousand dollars a month in the lunatic Bay Area real estate market.

"So we'll spend a thousand dollars a month," he said. "It's worth it."

"We don't have an extra thousand dollars a month!" I yelled.

When I am angry, I do stupid things. I hang up the phone (oh, how much more satisfying that used to be when it could be done with a furious bang!). I Google phrases like "The effects of divorce on children." I check real-estate listings for one-bedroom apartments within walking distance of our house that we could trade off living in while the other is on duty as that week's custodial parent. After I engaged in these customary behaviors, I began, also as is typical, to berate myself. The whole fight was my fault. It's always my fault when we fight, because my husband is easygoing and cheerful, and I am a bitch. If it weren't for me, we'd never fight. I'm an awful wife, a terrible partner. How can he stand me when I can't stand me?

The problem with self-blame is that it launches a vicious cycle. It makes me despondent, and when I am despondent I lash out at my husband. Which makes me feel worse. Which makes me lash out. Which makes me feel worse. And so on and so forth, with the sharp threads of my shame spiral screwing a hole right through our relationship.

The cognitive behavioral therapist I have lately been seeing tells me that conflict is a dynamic. Couples react to one another in an infinite, closed loop, and thus one person is no more culpable than another. She insists that my self-reproach is a barrier to happiness, both my own and ours as a couple. Even though I trust her insight, I cannot seem to change my behavior or my thought patterns. Just articulating the thought that blaming myself is bad for my relationship is really nothing more than another round of self-reproach. If *my* self-flagellation is the source of our conflict, isn't it necessarily true that I am the problem lurking at the heart of my family, like a flaw in the center of a diamond?

Day 4

....

Microdose Day

Physical Sensations: Energized and activated.

Mood: Terrific.

Conflict: None.

Sleep: Better, though I woke early.

*Work: Found myself so effortlessly in the flow I
     didn't even notice time passing.*

Pain: Significantly less than in days past.

I was so very glad to wake up this morning. First of all, I slept
better than I have over the last couple of days, perhaps because
by last night the LSD was completely out of my system. Most
important, however, today is once again Day 1 of the protocol
cycle: Microdose Day! I don't know if it was my eagerness or the
LSD that made me so cheerful, but, one way or another, today
was an absolute delight. A series of annoyances did nothing
more than make me shrug. My kids dawdled over breakfast and
were late to school. I missed the deadline for booking a flight,
and ended up having to pay a higher fare. Then the dog knocked
my arm while I was sipping from my teacup, causing me to
splash Earl Grey all over the pages of the book I was reading.
She looked at me guiltily, waiting, I expect, for me to scold her.
Instead, I scratched her ear.

"It's all right, Mabel," I said. "Shit happens."

Shit happens? When have I ever uttered those words in a tone other than ironic?

I decided to call my mother and spread some of my good cheer around. Poor Mom. She's been going through her own hell. She lost four close friends this year, and had a knee replacement that went horribly awry, made worse by an incompetent wound specialist whose unnecessary and traumatic surgery resulted in her being infected with MRSA. Add this to an unsatisfying marriage, and it's a wonder she can get up in the morning.

The specter of my mother's unhappiness, even when uncomplicated by health issues or grief, haunts me. I wonder how much my search for contentment is motivated by fear of her example? I certainly have no fear that my marriage will be as painful as hers has been. My husband is loyal, loving, and expressive. My husband and I fight, but not with the same fervor as my parents, or anywhere near as frequently, even during this last, terrible year.

My mother's work, too, has been a series of compromises and intermittent disappointments, from the moment my father encouraged her to drop out of graduate school and marry him. The tragedy of her life is that she abandoned a field that gave her joy. My mother is so obsessed with art and architecture that visiting Frank Lloyd Wright's Fallingwater is for her a pilgrimage as spiritually uplifting as the Hajj. My mother has always said that her decision to leave school was a function of the times. In 1963, at age twenty-three, she felt like an old maid, she cared for my father, and she believed that her only choice was to give up her career aspirations and become a wife and mother. In recent years, she has wondered to me whether there was more to it than that. My father's proposal, delivered as a joke in a telegram— "I'm pregnant. Come marry me"—came at a moment of vulnerability. Newly enrolled in school, and living with her brother and his wife, who had only recently married, she was feeling like a third wheel, but too nervous to strike out on her own. Had that telegram arrived only a few months later, once she was better established, she doubts she would have married my father.

When I was in high school, my mother made the decision to go back to graduate school, but not in art history. She is sensible, fiscally responsible. She chose a professional degree that was more likely to lead to reliable employment. Unfortunately, though she was a skillful hospital administrator and excelled at her job, I know she found it less satisfying than architecture, her first academic and professional love.

I am in many ways like my mother. Like her, I am competent and reliable. Like her, I'm a little bossy.* Like her, I do my best to help, even when that requires sticking my nose someplace it doesn't belong.

There's a story my husband tells about me, how, late one night in Los Angeles, we were driving up a nearly deserted street when we saw a car pulled half on the sidewalk, its doors gaping open. A man and a woman were struggling beside the car. I screamed at my husband to pull over. Before he had even rolled to a stop, I was out of our car and reaching out a hand to the woman.

"Do you need help?" I asked her.

"Yes!" she said.

Her husband shouted, clawed at her, but I grasped her hand in mine and yanked her free. Then I pushed her into our car and jumped in behind her. I was eight months pregnant.

That is definitely something my mother would have done. I'm proud of helping that woman. I'm proud that, like my mother, I have tried to integrate public service into my career and my life. And yet the characteristics I share with my mother, even the most positive ones, have always worried me. Competent, reliable, and helpful far too easily topple into pushy and critical (as my children would attest). In thinking about my relationship with

---

*Okay, more than a little. A lot bossy.

my mother, I realize that that anxiety has colored—even damaged—my relationship with her. My own insecurity and self-loathing have somehow become all knotted up with my feelings toward her. Fearing our similarities has made me occasionally ungenerous with her, overbearing when I should be compassionate, distant when I should be engaged. I'm always willing, even eager, to help and advise her, but before today I rarely just listened to her, without judgment.

The ease with which I was able today to express compassion and concern without trying to push a solution on her is surprising. I wonder, is it possible that the LSD is making me a better listener?

Day 5

....

Transition Day

Physical Sensations: None.

Mood: Started out activated, but calmed down.

Conflict: At first a little prickly, but nipped it in the bud.

Sleep: Woke early but felt well rested.

Work: Worked well. Not in the flow, but not struggling, either.

Pain: Almost none!

Today, though I woke up feeling a little irritable, I managed to assert control before losing my temper with the kids or flaming anyone on the Internet. Impulse control? Me? Can this really be happening?

My persistent failure to control my impulses is one of the main reasons I keep trying different therapies. I want to increase the time between psychological trigger and reaction. I need only as long as it takes to take a single breath, enough of a hesitation to activate my superego and soothe the immediate agony of id. A moment to stop and ponder the question: what is the sensible reaction to this provocation, not the most pleasurable?

Having grown up in a family of yellers, I am far too prone to top-volume reactions to provocation. My mother yelled at me; I yell at my kids. I've always thought it was merely a conditioned response, but I have lately come to realize that I do it because I enjoy it. The yell, the angry e-mail, the snarky tweet, the sarcastic comment, all provide a momentary release of tension that feels really good. It is like the joy of scratching an itch until it bleeds. The pain is the point. It erases the irritation. For a moment. But then the itch returns, worse than before, and soon you're wearing long pants in August because you've got scabby legs.

On the first day of this experiment, when I felt I was noticing the world around me in more detail, I had an idea that the microdose of LSD might be slowing me down in the best possible way. I hoped that, as it heightened my ability to pay attention to my surroundings, it might also help me become capable of resisting the impulse to act. Isn't that exactly what mindfulness promises? By paying attention, we will increase our self-control. We will find ourselves able to stop and think.

This morning, when I managed, despite feeling irritable, not to blow up at anyone, I began to believe that, though it's obviously too early to tell, it's at least possible that my hopes will be realized. The question, or at least one of them, is how.

I turned to a psychopharmacologist to find out what is going on in my brain when I consume the microdose. He told me that LSD is an agonist, a stimulator, of the 5-HT2A serotonin receptor. Antidepressants also act on 5-HT receptors, including 5-HT2A, but they work by inhibiting the reuptake of serotonin, causing it to remain in synapses longer. Because serotonin is one of the neurotransmitters thought to be most closely linked with feelings of well-being and happiness, the theory behind SSRIs is that having serotonin sit around longer, with your synapses marinating in it, makes you feel better. By contrast, when a psychedelic drug stimulates 5-HT2A receptors, that leads to the stimulation of brain-derived neurotrophic factor (BDNF), which my psychopharmacologist friend described as "like Miracle-Gro for your brain. It stimulates growth, connections, and activity." A psychiatric researcher described the neurological effects of LSD to me this way: "By activating the 5-HT2A receptor, you increase the transmission of glutamate." Glutamate is the neurotransmitter most responsible for brain functions like cognition, learning, and memory. Though they're talking about two different substances in the brain, the two doctors are essentially saying the same thing. BDNF and glutamate are interrelated. Psychedelics enhance neuroplasticity, the ability of the brain to grow and change, by increasing the level of BDNF in the brain and by increasing glutamate activity.

Can this enhanced neuroplasticity, this stimulated growth and connectivity, be what's causing me to be less impulsive? Rather than slowing me down, can it be making me more reflective and thus better able to control my anger? Can that be what's making me feel better? Two Swiss researchers at the Neuropsychopharmacology and Brain Imaging Research Unit at the University Hospital of Psychiatry in Zürich published a paper in 2010 that suggests that this is possible. In "The Neurobiology of Psychedelic Drugs: Implications for the Treatment of Mood Disorders," Franz X. Vollenweider and Michael Kometer reviewed forty years of LSD, psilocybin, and ketamine research in the context of "modern concepts of the neurobiology of psychiatric disorders." They concluded that psychedelics may well be useful in treating mood disorders, depression, OCD, and anxiety. A British feasibility study published in the *Lancet* in the spring of 2016 found that psilocybin not only reduced depressive symptoms but also anxiety and anhedonia.*

What we call hallucinogens or psychedelics are three different kinds of chemicals. Two are plant-derived: psilocybin and mescaline (which occurs in a number of cactus varieties, including peyote). The other is LSD and other derivatives of ergot. These

---

*Robin L. Carhart-Harris et al., "Psilocybin with Psychological Support for Treatment-resistant Depression: An Open-label Feasibility Study."

three types of chemicals act on the brain in the same way, and thus can be grouped together. All three produce their hallucinogenic effects by stimulating 5-HT2A. This stimulation leads to "a robust, glutamate-dependent increase in the activity of pyramidal neurons, preferentially those in layer V of the prefrontal cortex." The "stimulation of the postsynaptic 5-HT2A receptors on a subpopulation of pyramidal cells in the deep layers of the PFC leads to an increase in glutamatergic recurrent network activity." For those of you for whom, like me, all that neurological stuff reads like a lecture by Charlie Brown's teacher, Miss Othmar ("wah wah waaaah waah wah"), let's just go with Miracle-Gro for the brain.

Hallucinogens increase the interaction between serotonin, BDNF, and glutamate, which can result in people's developing a new perspective on things, including their own problems. Treatment with psychedelics reduces anxiety and improves the mood of patients facing death, as researchers at Johns Hopkins, UCLA, and NYU have recently shown. All three institutions have been or are currently engaged in psilocybin studies on volunteers with end-stage cancer, with astonishing results.* Patients dosed with psilocybin in a pleasant environment accompanied by two researchers providing comfort and support underwent spiritual experiences that didn't just make them feel better, but transformed the way they thought about their illnesses, and allowed them to confront death without fear. It gave many of them the "good death" we all hope for. Other recent research with psilocybin has shown that it relieves cluster headaches,† and aids in the cessation of smoking.‡

---

*See American College of Neuropsychopharmacology, "Active Ingredient in Magic Mushrooms Reduces Anxiety, Depression in Cancer Patients."

† See https://clusterbusters.org/.

‡ R. A. Sewell, J. H. Halpern, and H. G. Pope, Jr., "Response of Cluster Headache to Psilocybin and LSD"; Matthew W. Johnson et al., "Pilot Study of the 5-HT2AR Agonist Psilocybin in the Treatment of Tobacco Addiction."

Incidentally, when I asked a few people with firsthand knowledge why current researchers choose to use psilocybin rather than LSD in their studies, they told me that the sheer quantity of LSD research that was carried out in the middle of the last century would have actually made it a more logical substance to test—there was so much good data out there, it didn't really make sense to start from scratch—but LSD simply has too much political baggage. Its reputation, though unearned, is terrible, and most researchers have made a calculation that federal approval would be less likely for studies that proposed dosing subjects with LSD. Psilocybin is relatively unknown; moreover, it's a naturally occurring substance, which makes people more comfortable with it. Also, the effects of psilocybin last approximately six hours, not the ten or so of an LSD trip. Even psychiatric researchers want to make it home for dinner.

Among the only researchers currently using LSD in a therapeutic context is Peter Gasser, a Swiss psychiatrist who trained in the therapeutic use of psychedelics in the late 1980s and early '90s, when such research was sanctioned in Switzerland. His work, ongoing, uses doses of two hundred micrograms of LSD as a tool of psychotherapy. He, like the psilocybin researchers, has seen notable results in increased well-being.

In a study at the Imperial College in London,* researchers discovered that a single dose of LSD "produced robust psychological effects; including heightened mood but also high scores on the PSI, an index of psychosis-like symptoms. Increased optimism and trait openness were observed 2 weeks after LSD and there were no changes in delusional thinking." They concluded that, although psychedelics like LSD produce disturbing psychosis-like symptoms during the period of intoxication, in the long term they "leave a residue of 'loosened cognition'... that is conducive to improved psychological wellbeing."

*R. L. Carhart-Harris et al., "The Paradoxical Psychological Effects of Lysergic Acid Diethylamide (LSD)."

Another recent study, using fMRI machines to track the brain's response to LSD in healthy volunteers, found that the drug creates a kind of hyper-connectivity in the brain, allowing unrelated and usually discrete regions to communicate with one another.* It also appears to affect the default mode network (DMN), a network of regions in the brain active during wakeful rest or daydreaming. The DMN is involved in a variety of things, including self-reflection and remembering the past and imagining the future. LSD, at least in a dose large enough to make you trip, causes your DMN to become disorganized, which leads to ego dissolution, the sense that you are one with the world.

Basically, stimulating serotonin receptors loosens you up cognitively, which makes you happier.

Flush with my newfound understanding of neuroplasticity and neurobiology, I posed a simple question to Dr. David Presti, a professor of neurobiology in the department of molecular and cell biology at UC Berkeley and the author of the textbook *Foundational Concepts in Neuroscience: A Brain-Mind Odyssey*. "Is the small amount of LSD I'm taking making my brain more neuroplastic, and is that why I'm less irritable?"

Presti, an expert in the neurochemistry of drugs, said, "Sure, we can say these chemicals bind to serotonin 2A receptors and they activate glutamate circuits and they induce nerve growth factors, but we really just don't have a clue how all that connects with what is happening in the psyche."

Deflated, I sighed. But he reached out an encouraging hand. The important thing, he told me, is not necessarily what is going on inside my brain, but that I feel better. Presti believes in a more "globally integrated" theory of the brain than some of the other neuroscientists I consulted. He's far more interested in experience and anecdote, in what I'm *feeling,* than in attaching a specific receptor to my mood. He was very encouraging about my

---

* Enzo Tagliazucchi et al., "Increased Global Functional Connectivity Correlates with LSD-Induced Ego Dissolution."

experiment, far more than my friend the psychopharmacologist who, while curious, was clearly made anxious by the prospect of someone consuming without supervision a substance that has not been professionally tested. Presti said, "I really think there's something going on with microdosing. I think when people do get around to researching it, it's going to be relatively easy to demonstrate positive effects that are better than conventional antidepressants, which are awful." About antidepressants Presti said, "They have all kinds of side effects, and we have no idea, really, what they're doing. They cost a lot of money and they're marketed with all kinds of flimflam."

Was he actually saying that microdosing was either as safe as or perhaps even safer than conventional antidepressants? I asked him, incredulous.

"Oh, absolutely."

I am a rationalist who likes firm and clear explanations, and I was so excited to think I might have found one. Neuroplasticity! BDNF! Glutamate! Synapses and neurons and all sorts of things measurable by fMRI machines! But the brain does not give up its secrets so easily. For the time being, and perhaps forever, I'm going to have to accept not knowing exactly what is going on in my brain. As difficult as that is, I was comforted when Presti reiterated what I had learned, that psychedelics are not physically harmful to the body for most people, even at massive doses. He told me that he has absolute confidence in the safety of my project. It is, at least in the view of that one particular neurobiologist, perfectly safe. I tucked that thought away for the next time I felt like I was having a heart attack in the dead of night.

Day 6

....

Normal Day

Physical Sensations: None.

Mood: Excellent.

Conflict: None.

Sleep: Woke up in the middle of the night, but fell back to sleep eventually.

Work: The words took some time to flow.

Pain: More or less the same as before I started the protocol.

Feeling good will make a woman do strange things; today I called my father. The call with my mother a couple of days ago went so well I figured, hey, you're already experimenting with illegal hallucinogens; why not do something really wild?

When I talk to my father, it is less of a conversation than a monologue, or a series of mini-lectures. Kind of like attending a one-man TED conference at the Hebrew Home for the Aged. Today's topics were, as ever, "Soviet History: The Stalin Era," "Zionism and Trotskyist Theory," and "Lincoln vs. McClellan: Whose Fault?" Or something like that. I admit I might have zoned out a few times during the call. What made today so unusual was that, instead of quickly losing patience and inventing an excuse to get off the phone, I hung in there. I stayed on the line. I heard the animation and even delight in my father's voice as he gave me a detailed digest of his most recent haul from the Fort Lee Public Library. This is how he makes himself happy, I realized. Anyway, what did you expect? You call a telephone psychic, you get artful guesses and vague insights. Call Daddy and you get the Second Battle of Bull Run.

My father and I have always had a difficult relationship, but now, when I look back, I realize that it is my own expectations—my ideas about the father I need, the father I wish I had—that have been the source of the longing, disappointment, frustration, and ultimately anger that have characterized my feelings about my father for so long.

The futility of my expectations was made comically clear to me a couple of years ago, after my father somewhat mysteriously handed me a stack of microcassettes. They were recordings of his psychotherapy sessions, made during the early eighties with a New York City psychologist named Albert Ellis. I didn't know what to make of this odd gift, what message they might contain, what he was trying to tell me by giving them to me. For a long time I didn't listen to the tapes; I was too annoyed. *You want to tell me something?* I would imagine saying to him. *Try talking!* But sometimes I could not help wondering about what might be recorded on those microcassettes. All the feelings he had never expressed. His feelings about himself, his marriage. His feelings about managing his bipolar disorder. Most of all, his feelings about *me.* Maybe on those tapes I might hear the voice of a man who thought and wondered and cared about his daughter. The voice of the father I had always wished for, had always hoped, against hope, might be hiding in there, under there, somewhere.

Finally, at the urging of a friend, I sat down and listened to the tapes—six hours, representing two months of sessions with one of the most prominent psychologists of the day. So what did they talk about, my dad and the great Dr. Ellis? His feelings, worries, and cares? The people he loved? The personal and professional ramifications of his mood disorder?

Nope.

What they talked about, in great detail, was the history of communism, class struggle, and the kibbutz movement. They never got around to Abraham Lincoln.

When I was little, I used to wish my father could be more like Shimon.

Shimon is an old friend of my parents. He lives in Israel— where I was born. He and his wife have two daughters, on whom he dotes. Even before my conscious memory of him begins, there are stories in my family of the particular affection Shimon showed for me, and of how eagerly I looked forward to seeing him. Shimon is expressive, warm, even effusive. I could always feel, from the time I was a little girl, how much he enjoyed my company. The last time I saw him, a couple of years ago, he remembered having visited our apartment in Jerusalem when I was a toddler. He said that I brought a little chair into the living room, sat down in front of him, and regaled him with my firm opinions on all manner of subjects. He no longer recalled what I had said, but he did remember how much he'd enjoyed listening to me. I have no memory of that particular moment, of course, but I have the clearest sense memory of Shimon's dry kiss on my cheek, of the warmth of his big hand, missing the tip of one finger, enfolding my little one. We moved from Israel back to Montreal before my third birthday, and after that I saw Shimon only rarely, but whenever I did, I would feel a rush of excitement, as if something that had gone missing a long time ago was about to be returned to me.

In my mind Shimon was always old, though he can't have been more than forty-two or -three the first time I sat on his lap. On that last visit, in 2014, he was ancient, but his eyes still sparkled with pleasure when I walked in his front door. He cracked walnuts for me with his trembling yet still-strong hand, placing the nut meat in my palm just like he did when I was seven years old. I am a middle-aged woman, and I had not seen Shimon for more than twenty years. As I sat there eating the nuts he cracked for me, I felt beloved.

How many other Shimons have there been over the years, older men whose company and attention I have eagerly sought, who listened when I set my (little) chair down in front of them? My high school English teacher Mr. Bennett. Derrick Bell, my constitutional law professor. John Cillag, a Hungarian gentleman with whom I struck up a conversation in a Budapest museum while researching my novel *Love and Treasure;* afterward, we corresponded by e-mail, met for coffee, and he was kind enough to read drafts of the book and offer helpful suggestions. A wise and gentle educator named Tom Little, head of Park Day School in Oakland for thirty-eight years before his untimely death in 2014.

And Dr. James Fadiman.

After he sent me the memo outlining his protocol, I asked Dr. Fadiman if he'd be willing to talk to me, not really expecting him to agree. I figured he was inundated with e-mails from people like me, people seeking a solution to some problem or a resolution of some pain. But he sent me his telephone number, and one evening, after I'd settled the kids for the night, I called him.

Fadiman's voice is deep and avuncular, and when he is smiling you can hear it. We ended up talking for a long time, and not just about the intricacies of microdosing. We talked about my moods and the troubles in my marriage. There was something in Fadiman's voice and manner that made me feel I could confide in him, ask him for advice, seek and possibly earn his approval.

A couple of weeks later, at Fadiman's invitation, I drove down to Palo Alto to attend a lecture he gave on the topic of psychedelic research and mental health. After the talk, I went up to the stage to say hello. I was a little tentative, not wanting to intrude or impose. I didn't know if he would be as eager to meet me as I was to meet him.

Fadiman is a youthful seventy-six, hair still mostly brown, with sleepy eyes and a trim brown beard, only lightly threaded with silver. The moment I told him my name, his face lit up with the smile I had heard over the phone, and he gave me a warm, fatherly hug.

During that long first phone call of ours, in the course of which I had confided more to Fadiman than I've confided to my father in my whole life, he asked me why I thought I was drawn to microdosing, what I thought I was looking for. My answer at the time was "the ability to manage my moods and enjoy my life," but now it seems to me that maybe a more accurate answer might have been: "This."

If so, then it's probably the sad truth that nothing, not even Dr. Hofmann's magical "problem child," can give me what I'm looking for. I'll never have the father I've hoped for, wished for, needed all my life. But today, for whatever reason—thanks maybe to Albert Hofmann, or Jim Fadiman—when I called my father and settled in for the usual lecture, I didn't get impatient. I didn't get annoyed. I hung in there through the intricacies of the Molotov-Ribbentrop Pact (or maybe it was the Great Purge), thinking, *Look, this is the father you got, and he's the only father you have. Might as well let the man talk.*

Day 7

....

Microdose Day
Physical Sensations: Activated.
Mood: Giddy.
Conflict: None.
Sleep: Slept well.
Work: Amazing.
Pain: Didn't notice any.

I'm feeling good today, perhaps a little too good. I am happy and cheerful, but my words are tumbling out faster than I can control. This feels a little like hypomania, that energetic state of mind that can be productive and pleasurable, but can also lead to risky, impulsive behavior. Though I'm not experiencing any delightful yet troubling euphoria, I am certainly disinhibited. This afternoon, I found myself telling the physical therapist who was working on my shoulder all about my experiment. I have, since I began taking the microdose, been so circumspect, confiding in only one or two very close friends. Yet here I was, gushing to a virtual stranger about microdosing and how it was making me so productive and happy. Ironically, one of the things about which I waxed poetic was how much less impulsive I've been. I have been feeling a certain unfamiliar control, I told her. I'm still getting triggered by the kids, the dog, the husband, the Internet, but for the last couple of days I have felt as though there is a little room around these triggers, space for me to decide how to react, instead of just reacting. But of course there I was, lying on a table, supposed to be breathing deeply and silently, and instead babbling on like a psychedelic twit.

My work, however, went beautifully.

Albert Hofmann, discussing his first planned LSD experience, wrote, "There was a change in the experience of life, of time. But it was the most frustrating thing. I was already deep in the LSD trance, in LSD inebriation, and one of its characteristics, just on this bicycle trip, was of not coming from any place or going any place. There was absolutely no feeling of time."

I'm taking a tiny fraction of what Hofmann did, and I haven't tried to ride my bike, but I can say with some authority that a change in the experience of time isn't exclusive to bike riding while on a massive dose of LSD. Today, as on the two prior Microdose Days, I became so immersed in my work that I didn't notice time passing. Getting lost in work, what's known as "flow," is one of the most exciting things about the process of creating. Conceived by the Hungarian psychologist Mihaly Csikszentmihalyi, flow is the state of "intense emotional involvement" and timelessness that comes from immersive and challenging activities. Flow can happen when you are creating art or computer code or when you are scaling a mountain. It's a gift that arrives rarely, when you are most focused and present.

It is its elusive nature, I believe, that makes flow so compelling. I remember learning about operant conditioning as a college freshman in my Intro to Psychology class. If a rat pushes a lever and gets kibble every time, it will soon grow sated. But if the kibble drops only occasionally, and on no discernible schedule, the rat will keep pushing the lever long after she otherwise might have stopped. Creative flow is the artist's kibble. Having experienced it once, you want it again, and the fact that it doesn't always happen makes it all the more precious and tantalizing.

You keep coming back to the desk (or the easel or the instrument), day after day, in the hope that the gift might suddenly reappear.

I am hardly the first person to find a psychedelic drug useful in inspiring flow. Since prehistory, people have ingested mind-altering substances as creative inspiration. These substances, from peyote to iboga to soma and ayahuasca, have inspired works of art that attempt to describe both the mystical and the mundane—though, in the case of ayahuasca, I am told the state of creative flow usually alternates with less welcome flow at either end of the digestive tract.* Aldous Huxley, the English writer and philosopher and author of *Brave New World*, deserves the credit for instigating or at least popularizing the use of psychedelic substances as part of the creative endeavor in the Western world. In his book *The Doors of Perception*, a profoundly influential work of psychedelic literature, Huxley narrates his experience of taking mescaline. About the potential creative value of psychedelics, he writes, "To be shaken out of the ruts of ordinary perception, to be shown for a few timeless hours the outer and the inner world, not as they appear to an animal obsessed with survival or to a human being obsessed with words and notions, but as they are apprehended, directly and unconditionally, by Mind at Large—this is an experience of inestimable value to everyone and especially to the intellectual." Huxley used LSD, even going so far as to have his wife inject him with the drug on his deathbed. He did not, however, believe that LSD and other psychedelics should be widely available. Their use, he felt, should be limited to those engaged in artistic, intellectual, or mystical endeavors.

Most of us are well aware of the legacy of psychedelic experimentation in music and art. We know Lucy's in the sky with

---

*You might not consider any work of art worth that particular price of admission, but I've been known to risk diarrhea for a dish of ice cream.

diamonds and the piper's at the gates of dawn. What's less well known is that a variety of scientists and technologists have used LSD as a catalyst for innovation. For example, Francis Crick, co-winner of the 1962 Nobel Prize in Medicine for the discovery of the structure of the DNA molecule, reportedly experimented with LSD while working on the problem. Though he never confirmed the rumors, friends insist that he told them he actually conceived of the double-helix shape during an LSD trip.*

The biochemist Kary Mullis, co-winner of the Nobel Prize in Chemistry in 1993 for his work on the polymerase chain reaction (PCR) technique, was, unlike Crick, frank both about his use of LSD and about how using the drug helped him in his work. He is widely quoted as having said, "Back in the 1960s and early '70s I took plenty of LSD. A lot of people were doing that in Berkeley back then. And I found it to be a mind-opening experience. It was certainly much more important than any courses I ever took." In a BBC documentary, Mullis further stated, "What if I had not taken LSD ever; would I have still invented PCR? I don't know. I doubt it. I seriously doubt it." Steve Jobs attributed his creative genius in part to LSD, considering his experience using the drug to be, according to the journalist John Markoff, who interviewed Jobs for his book *What the Dormouse Said: How the 60s Counterculture Shaped the Personal Computer Industry*, "one of the two or three most important things he had done in his life."

In an interview with CNN, a Cisco engineer named Kevin Herbert comfortably discussed his use of LSD as an aid in solving intractable engineering problems. He told the reporter, "There was a case where I had been working on a problem for over a month, and I took LSD and I just realized, 'Wait, the problem is in the hardware. It's not a software issue at all.'"

---

*Presti, whom I trust implicitly, doubts this story. But it's such a good one! Couldn't we just pretend it's true?

Jim Fadiman was himself one of the early researchers into the link between psychedelic drugs and creativity. As an undergraduate at Harvard, he studied with Richard Alpert, a young, charismatic psychology professor who, along with Timothy Leary, was an early proponent of both the study and the use of psychedelic drugs in the United States. After he graduated from college, Fadiman met up with his professor on a balmy spring evening in Paris, at an outdoor café. Alpert shook a small pill from a glass bottle into the palm of Fadiman's hand and changed the course of his life.

The drug was psilocybin, and it caused Fadiman to realize that "there was something about human interaction that [he] had been missing." Fadiman had what he describes as a classic mystical experience. "I realized I was more than myself, more than Jim Fadiman. My personality was only one part of who I am." When Fadiman and I had a chance to sit down and discuss the ramifications of this mystical experience on the course of his life, he smiled and said, "How ya gonna keep 'em down on the farm after they've seen Paree?"

In the wake of that experience and others that followed, and inspired by a letter from the draft board delineating the courses of action available to young men of military age during the Vietnam War, Fadiman enrolled as a graduate student in psychology at Stanford. He was, he told me, unhappy about getting a degree in a subject that no longer interested him just to avoid the war. While leafing through the course catalogue in search of classes more inspiring than those in his own department, he came upon a course called Human Potential, taught by a professor of electrical engineering named Willis Harman. His interest piqued, Fadiman tracked Harman down in his office. He asked if he could take the class, but was informed that it was already oversubscribed.

"I've taken psilocybin three times," Fadiman said.

Harman stood up, walked across the office, and closed the door.

Harman could not, in the context of Stanford, be open about his psychedelic experiences, but Fadiman could. Harman hired him as his teaching assistant.

Fadiman's dissertation was titled "Behavior Change Following (LSD) Psychedelic Therapy," but its true topic was much more far-ranging. He was interested in understanding the nature of creativity itself, and whether psychedelic drugs could inspire and enhance it. Fadiman became a fellow at the International Foundation for Advanced Study, run by Harman, a privately funded research facility. The "facility" was no more than a suite of offices above a beauty parlor, but it had a USDA permit to perform clinical studies of psychedelic drugs. Stanford and its surrounding areas were then, as now, home to innovators in aeronautics, engineering, and the nascent field of computers, and Harman, Fadiman, and their colleagues wanted to see if psychedelics could enhance creative problem-solving in professionals in those highly technical fields.

They recruited senior research scientists from different local companies as subjects, and asked them to bring with them to the sessions at least two different problems on which they had been working without success for at least three months. These subjects were executives at Hewlett-Packard, fellows at the Stanford Research Institute, architects, and designers. Among them were the people who would design the first silicon chips, create word processing, and invent the computer mouse.

Fadiman and his colleagues administered one-hundred-microgram doses of LSD to the subjects and guided them through the next hours as they puzzled over their intractable problems.* The subjects worked on their problems and took a variety of psychometric tests. The results were striking. Many of the subjects experienced flashes of intellectual intuition. Their performance on the psychometric tests improved, but, more important, they

---

*Incidentally, Harman, Fadiman, and their two colleagues designed the protocol for the experiment while themselves on an LSD trip.

solved their thorny equations and problems. According to Fadiman, "A number of patents, products, and publications emerged out of that study."

In the spring of 1966, Fadiman had just given a dose of LSD to four participants in his seventh research group when he, like other researchers around the country, received a letter from the Food and Drug Administration notifying him that the status of his LSD experimental drug exemption had been changed. This change in status resulted in the immediate termination of his research permit. Fadiman read the letter, and then glanced at his colleagues. "I think we got this letter tomorrow," he said. Their research subjects had started to trip, and they had better things to do than worry about the FDA.

All together, twenty-eight scientists, artists, and innovators participated in these guided LSD experiences at the International Foundation for Advanced Study. What Fadiman finds most fascinating about the study is something that he realized only in retrospect. Though the participants went on to do groundbreaking work throughout Silicon Valley and farther afield, making critical discoveries, founding major corporations, and fundamentally changing the world, none underwent any profound mystical experience during the experiment that caused them to change their lives. Fadiman theorizes that this is because of the way LSD operates on the brain. The drug provides a remarkable clarity of focus. It inspires transformation not globally but in the object of your intention. If, for example, you take the drug in a psychotherapeutic set and setting, you will focus on personal issues and may gain insights relevant to your emotional life. If you take the drug anticipating a spiritual experience and in a spiritually encouraging environment, you may have a transcendent mystical experience that causes you to re-evaluate your place in the universe. If, however, you focus on a specific intellectual problem, it is there that your insights will reside. This theory is fascinating, and deserving of further research, but though Fadiman and Harman published the results of the study, their officially sanctioned research ended that day.

Authorized experimentation with LSD and other psychedelics by scientists, engineers, inventors, and artists ended when the drug was criminalized in the late sixties, but underground experimentation continued, albeit on a lesser scale. Similarly, recreational use of the drug continued. According to U.S. government surveys, between four and five hundred thousand new users of LSD self-report every year, even though the drug has been illegal for decades. Certainly, use continued in some form in Silicon Valley; it has surged in popularity in recent years.

I discussed the use of psychedelics in Silicon Valley as a tool to enhance creativity and problem solving with Tim Ferriss, investor, entrepreneur, and best-selling author of *The 4-Hour Workweek*. When I asked Ferriss why he thinks psychedelics continue to be used by tech entrepreneurs, he attributed it to an obsessive focus on innovation, combined with a drive to achieve. Silicon Valley is, he said, "an ecosystem that rewards achievement incredibly well, but it is oftentimes devoid of appreciation on a personal level." He described sitting at dinner with half a dozen company founders, each worth hundreds of millions of dollars, "and they're more miserable than anyone you've met."

People in tech are researchers and problem solvers, Ferriss said. They search for solutions to their problems, both professional and personal. It makes sense that, when trying to resolve both their personal unhappiness and their periodic creative impasses, they would notice the early research on psychedelics and the anecdotal evidence of current users. They are all hackers at heart, trying to expand the computing capabilities of their own gray, lumpy wetware so that they can be the next Steve Jobs.

There is also, Ferriss told me, a third driver to this experimentation. "You have in general a very socially liberal agnostic or atheistic community. For those people, there's still an innate or intellectual drive to find something bigger, greater. Psychedelics are a tool to explore the mystical or religious in private."

I'm not looking for anything big or great. I just want to take greater pleasure in my life. I want to work better, be a more patient and supportive mother and wife. I have so very little interest in mysticism and religion. God's got enough on Her plate without having to meddle in my hallucinations.

Day 8

....

Transition Day

Physical Sensations: None.

*Mood: Almost euphoric. Happy with my work,
    life, family. A really good day.*

Conflict: None.

Sleep: Fell asleep easily. Slept seven hours.

Work: Cooking along.

Pain: Mild.

It's been over a week now, and either this experiment is working
or the placebo effect is a mighty force. I feel so good I don't care
which of those is true. No, that's not true. I do care, because if it's
purely a placebo, then I could get the same effect without committing a crime. Though the quantity of LSD in my little cobalt
blue bottle is minuscule, under both California and federal law
I could be arrested and charged with possession. I could face a
one-to-three-year sentence in state court and up to a six-month
sentence in federal court. Obviously, this would not be good;
redheads look terrible in orange. Oh, and I'd miss my kids and
my husband. Still, all things considered, I have been remarkably
blasé about the criminality of this experiment, even though I
know that mere drug possession is prosecuted in this country
with the same vigor as drug trafficking. Our jails and prisons are

full of people whose only crime was to possess drugs; a shocking number of them were caught not with heroin or methamphetamine or another drug of addiction, or even with LSD, but with marijuana. More than 40 percent of arrests for drug possession in this country are for a drug that 19.8 million of us have used in the past *month*.

The war on drugs has resulted in a massive increase in the size of our prison population. According to the Sentencing Project, a nonprofit organization dedicated to sentencing reform, fully half of federal prisoners are serving time for drug offenses, and "the number of drug offenders in state prisons has increased thirteen-fold since 1980." The vast majority of these are neither violent offenders nor kingpins but low-level offenders guilty of doing little more than what I did yesterday.

And yet I am so little at risk of prosecution that I am not only taking LSD but writing about it. Why? Because the sad fact is that my race and class make prosecution less likely.

As Michelle Alexander, author of *The New Jim Crow*, told me, "The war on drugs and the war on crime are the most recent manifestation of an impulse to punish, control, and exploit poor people of color which will surface repeatedly in our country until we are willing to face our racial history." Our interminable drug war has from its inception set its sights firmly on the poor and the brown. The first drug laws, the anti-opium laws of the 1870s, were directed at Chinese immigrants, never mind that the country was full of white middle-class laudanum addicts, tippling from their dropper bottles all day long. Early in the next century, support for the laws criminalizing cocaine was ginned up by claims that "drug-crazed Negroes" were destroying white society and murdering white women. Southern senators, unperturbed by their wives' opioid addictions, believed that cocaine made black men superhuman, even that it made them immune to bullets. When the first drug czar, a man named Harry Anslinger, wanted to criminalize marijuana, he appealed to people's biases against immigrants from Mexico, claiming that the drug made Mexicans sexually violent. William Randolph Hearst jumped on this bandwagon, warning again and again in the pages of his newspapers about the dangers of the Mexican "Marihuana-Crazed Madman." This demonization continues today.* White people are five times as likely to use drugs as African Americans, yet African Americans are incarcerated for drug offenses at ten times the rate of whites.† The racism of the drug war has been the single most important driving factor in the ever-escalating incarceration of people of color in the United States.

When I was an attorney, I experienced this arbitrary and unjust system firsthand. Though I practiced in the federal courts and should have been dealing only with large-scale drug conspiracies and offenses, I represented many defendants, most of them people of color, who faced draconian sentences for relatively minor offenses. One in particular stood out from the rest. My client, an undocumented immigrant from Mexico, was charged with the distribution of methamphetamine. A man of compromised intellect, he had been hired by a local drug dealer to schlep a box of methamphetamine from one place to another. The dealer, however, turned out to be a DEA confidential informant. My client was looking at a sentence of more than fifteen years, with a ten-year mandatory minimum.

In the federal system, sentences are not left to the discretion of judges. They are calculated in accordance with the Federal Sentencing Guidelines, promulgated by the United States Sentencing Commission. Before the Sentencing Guidelines, a defendant's sentence depended in large part on the judge to whom his case was assigned. End up in the court of a judge with a

---

* As anyone who's seen coverage of a Donald Trump rally can attest.
† See http://www.naacp.org/pages/criminal-justice-fact-sheet. Another shocking statistic from the NAACP: "African Americans represent 12% of the total population of drug users, but 38% of those arrested for drug offenses, and 59% of those in state prison for a drug offense."

capacity for empathy and you might walk away with probation. Be assigned a hard-ass and you might spend the rest of your life in jail. And guess whom the hard-asses were most likely to punish? Race and class bias were rampant under that system. By removing judicial discretion, the Sentencing Guidelines and the mandatory minimum sentences for drug crimes passed by Congress were intended to rid the system of sentencing disparities. Instead of a judge's individual assessment of a case, a crime, or a defendant, the Sentencing Guidelines and mandatory minimums require that charges and sentences be determined primarily by a single factor: the quantity of drugs bought or sold.

Back when I was a young federal defender, I carried with me a thick book, the *Federal Sentencing Guidelines Manual,* in which every federal crime was assigned a point value. (It was around six hundred pages and weighed about as much as a brick of cocaine with a street value of twenty-seven grand.) The point value for drug crimes was determined by consulting the "Drug Quantity Table." The box of methamphetamine carried by my client weighed at least three kilograms, which carried a "Base Offense Level" of 36. The back half of the book contained adjustments for things like "Role in the Offense" and "Acceptance of Responsibility" (pleading guilty). The chapter on criminal history added points for every prior offense. Among the first things I did with every client was to add up the points of his crime and his criminal history, and then flip to the back page of the book, to a table that calculated exactly what sentence he could expect to receive. My client in the methamphetamine case had no criminal history at all, so his Base Offense Level was not adjusted higher for that. Still, because of the sheer quantity of the drugs in the box he had carried, he was subject to a sentence of between 188 and 235 months.

This systematized approach to sentencing is certainly rational. There should be consistency in sentencing; a defendant's future should not depend on how the judicial assignment wheel is spun.* However, the idea that nothing about my client's personal situation could make an impact on his sentence was infuriating. Here was a man who was of such limited intelligence that years ago he would have been called mentally retarded. He was set up by a wily, sophisticated informant who had purposely packed the box with enough drugs to trigger the massive penalty. What justice would be served by sentencing my client, who was a danger to no one other than himself, to more than fifteen years in jail?

Moreover, the Sentencing Guidelines and mandatory minimums have failed to accomplish their stated goals. True, they removed judicial discretion from the federal system, but there has been no reduction in bias. All that's happened is that the bias of jurists with sufficient experience and, at least theoretically, wisdom to be appointed to the bench, has been replaced with that of prosecutors, who now determine, via their charging documents, what sentence a defendant faces. We have saved the system from the perils of the personalities of individuals appointed by the president and confirmed by the U.S. Senate and turned it over to the personalities of ambitious young lawyers, many of them right out of law school, and many of them perfectly incubated examples of wealth and privilege.

Things have improved somewhat since I was in practice. In 2005, the Supreme Court, in a case called *United States v. Booker*, ruled that the guidelines were not mandatory but advisory, and that judges can depart from the calculations if they so choose, though these departures still have to be "reasonable." The Fair Sentencing Act of 2010 made changes to the mandatory minimum laws that might have allowed the judge in my client's case to consider factors that could have mitigated his sentence, though the bulk of that law applies to crack cocaine, not meth-

---

*In some jurisdictions, including the one in which I practiced, a literal wheel was spun to determine court assignments.

amphetamine. But back when I was taking my client's case to trial, the judge had no discretion at all. Her sole job after the determination of guilt or innocence was to do some arithmetic and apply the sentence required by the answer.

We had had an excellent entrapment defense. I had assembled a mountain of evidence against the informant, a vicious and loathsome man with a history of entrapping first-time offenders, none of whom had ever committed crimes before he encouraged them to do so. My client had no criminal record, and was found by the government's own expert witness to have an IQ of approximately 85, significantly below average. I was confident that I was going to win, so confident that when the assistant U.S. attorney called me the afternoon before trial, and asked me what I would have settled the case for had he initially offered a plea different from the Sentencing Guidelines range, I said, "Nothing more than two phone counts."

A phone count is courthouse jargon for the offense of using a communications device in the commission of a crime. The maximum statutory penalty is four years. My client spoke to the informant a number of times over the phone. Those calls were recorded. If he were charged with communication crimes rather than with drug distribution, though the Sentencing Guidelines sentence would still be determined by the quantity of the drugs at issue in the case, the sentence would be capped at four years for each phone count. If my client pled guilty to those two counts, the judge would have no choice but to sentence him to a maximum of eight years instead of the fifteen to nearly twenty he was looking at.

The AUSA said, "Plead now, tonight, and you can have your two phone counts."

I said, "Did I say two? I meant one."

"I'll give you two. Take it or leave it."

I faced a terrible dilemma. If I won at trial, my client would not go to prison. If I lost, he'd spend at least fifteen years in jail, and perhaps closer to twenty. Moreover, even if I won, he would still be facing detention and deportation for entering the country illegally. He could even have been prosecuted for that offense. The AUSA was offering my client eight years. After eight years, you have something of a life left to you. Your children are still children. After fifteen or twenty years? What and who remains?

Today, with the benefit of age and experience, I wish I had refused the deal. But I was young, I was scared, this was Orange County, and my client was an undocumented Mexican immigrant. Juries from notoriously conservative Orange County were not sympathetic to the people they called "illegals." It was, of course, my client's decision, but his intellectual capacity was profoundly diminished. He would do whatever I told him to do.

It was evening by the time I made my decision. The judge had stayed at work late to hear the plea. We stood in the temporary quarters of the Federal District Court, a grim, windowless, modular portable. The judge began the plea colloquy. She asked me if I had represented my client to the best of my ability, if I supported his decision to take the plea, if the law supported the plea. My voice shook as I affirmed each element, and I started to cry. By the end I could barely speak. My client put his arm around my shoulders. Facing eight years in prison, *he* comforted *me*.

Afterward, as I walked through the dark night to the parking lot, a car pulled up next to me. The window glided down. From inside, the judge called my name.

"There's something I want you to know," she said.

Having just been yelled at by my boss for breaking down in court, I braced myself for more criticism.

"There are some things," she said, "that are worth crying about."

Her window slid up and she rolled away.

Day 9

....

Normal Day

Physical Sensations: None.

Mood: Calm and content.

Conflict: None.

Sleep: Decent night's sleep.

Work: Productive.

Pain: Minor.

My husband comes home today, finally. I've been missing him terribly. To pass the time until his plane landed, I went out to his studio to work.

We live in a house built in 1907 by a Berkeley physician who practiced in a miniature consulting room on the first floor. My husband renovated a derelict shed in the yard as his idiosyncratic studio, with a desk tucked into a dark, windowless nook, the light blocked by a tall bookcase. For a while, I worked in Dr. Schaeffer's former office, my desk abutting the hand-washing sink, my ink cartridges and red pencils in the long instrument drawers. The room was dark; its windows were hidden beneath eaves. Wainscoting, stained nearly black, crawled up the walls. A heavy bookshelf ran the entire circumference of the ceiling, a leather strap keeping the books in place. Very cool. I hated it.

From the moment I moved into that office, I loathed the

gloom, the dark wood, the heavy window shades, the decrepit, original, Victorian-style light fixtures. I couldn't bear to work in there, but neither could I bring myself to spend money renovating the space. I had sold my first book, and two more in the same mystery series; I taught a seminar every year at the law school and did consulting work; but even so I earned a fraction of what I had as an attorney. Though I never articulated the feeling, or even really recognized it, I didn't believe that the approximation of a career I had cobbled together justified the expense of a renovation.

Then my husband began traveling more for work, and the business of his business, which I had always handled in order to feel I was participating in the economic life of our family beyond the pittance I earned, became too much for me to manage on my own. He hired a part-time assistant to help book his travel, deal with his correspondence, and do all the things that were taking up the hours of my day that I was supposed to spend writing. I happily turned Dr. Schaeffer's dreary consulting room over to the assistant, and wandered with my laptop out to cafés, to work surrounded by people and pastry—an ideal environment, I insisted, for an extrovert with an addiction to sugar.

This lasted until my wrists and elbows started to ache. I needed a more ergonomic arrangement than Starbucks could provide. My husband invited me to set up a desk in a corner of his studio in the backyard. This system, though not ideal, worked for years. He keeps vampire's hours, sitting down to work at around eleven at night and working until dawn burns out his eyeballs and sets his heart aflame. I work in the mornings, once the kids leave for school. On the rare occasions when we were both in the studio at the same time, we enjoyed one another's company. We sat back-to-back, each listening to the other clicking away on the keys. My husband claimed he could tell from the tempo of my tapping whether I was working or surfing the Internet, and thus he kept me disciplined.

But something about his space bothered me, too. My desk faced a wall, something my husband enjoys but I despise. I could roll my chair back to look out the window, but still I felt claustrophobic. I am, it seems, a poor workman, and I blamed my tools for my creative frustrations. After a while, I just stopped going out to the studio to work.

The couch that my husband bought recently to make me more comfortable has only made matters worse. His workstation, now in the middle of the room to make way for the couch, takes up all the available floor space. Then there is a matter of the stuff: the obsolete audio equipment, the mid-century radios, the reel-to-reels, the three or four or eleven eight-track players, the turntables, speakers, tuners, and amps. And let's not forget the dolls, models, and figurines. The studio is adrift in bits and oddments that lend it a distinctive personality. That personality, a charming and delightful one, is my husband's. Aside from a few photos of the children, a row of books on the bottom of one of the bookcases, and a bulletin board on which I can tack up notes and images for the project I am working on, there is nothing of mine in the studio. Though he's welcomed me in, I feel like a girlfriend who's been given a drawer in a bachelor pad bathroom.

Today I had, as ever, a hard time getting comfortable enough in the studio to focus. I lay on the couch, my feet up on a pillow. Unsurprisingly, I dozed off.

When I woke, I gazed at the furnishings in the office, so charmingly expressive of my husband's iconoclastic personality. Then I looked around my little corner with its sad, few things. I leapt up, ran out to the storage shed, and found an empty cardboard box. I shoved all of my things into the cardboard box, tossed the box into the back of the shed, and surveyed the space. Without my few objects trying to assert a partial dominion, the studio felt like it belonged entirely to my husband. It felt right.

I sat down on the couch and happily got to work, my mood profoundly altered. I don't need to share my husband's studio.

I can work anywhere. On a couch in the corner of the room, at a table in a café, in the library. I am nimble and free from the constraints of needing to have a room of my own. According to her nephew who penned a biography, Jane Austen didn't require an elaborate, secluded space: "She had no separate study to retire to, and most of the work must have been done in the general sitting-room, subject to all kinds of casual interruptions." If *Pride and Prejudice* could be produced under such circumstances, only a pretentious fool with an overly precious sense of her own importance would demand a place of her own, free of vintage eight-track players, in which to write.

Day 10

....

Microdose Day

Physical Sensations: Weirdly conscious that one of my eyes sees better than the other.

Mood: Wonderful. Happy. Content. Another really good day.

Conflict: None.

Sleep: Seven hours.

Work: Wonderfully productive. I see why some people microdose as a substitute for Adderall.

Pain: Much less.

It's surprisingly difficult to squeeze precisely two drops of liquid into one's own mouth. I have to do it in the mirror, and even so there's a certain fraught quality to the experience, as I am terrified of accidentally ingesting too much. I must have looked frazzled when I came into the house this morning, because one of my kids gave me a suspicious look.

"What are you doing?" he said. "Where were you?"

"Um, just, you know," I mumbled, fishing for time, "taking a walk."

"Why?"

"It's supposed to, like, improve my mood or something." I winced. Why was I sounding like a fourteen-year-old whose mother notices her red eyes ("I was, like, riding my bike behind a bus or something")?*

"Good," he said. "Walk longer." Ordinarily, that's just the kind of sass that might put a damper on my mood, but not today, Satan!

"Very funny," I said. "Anyway, I don't think it works like that. More isn't necessarily more. In fact, in this case less is more."

But by then he had already lost interest and wandered into the kitchen in search of breakfast.

It feels a little uncomfortable to be keeping this experiment a secret from my kids. From the very first time our kids asked about drugs, while listening to the radio ("Dad, when he says he gets 'high with a little help from his friends,' he doesn't mean high like on drugs, does he?"), my husband and I have tried to be forthright. ("Yes, he means high on drugs.") We talk about which drugs have a high potential for abuse and injury, and how to avoid those perils, and we also talk about which drugs are relatively safer. We try to be very clear about the risks and rewards of drug use.

All of this frank talk inevitably invites questions about our own drug use. My husband and I have always operated on the principle that, though we don't owe our children an answer to every one of their questions, when we do choose to say something, we owe them the truth. If the kids ask us if we've done a certain drug and we don't feel that they're old enough to understand the answer or even if we just prefer not to say, we'll tell them that. Otherwise, we grit our teeth and fess up. We never lie.

I'm surprised, frankly, that so many parents do. Or perhaps it's not lying. Perhaps it's collective amnesia. A number of years ago, we were dropping off our kids at sleep-away camp and bumped into an old college friend of mine. His son is older than my kids, and was already applying to college. I asked if his son was look-

---

*This is an actual excuse I once gave my mother after, I believe, the first time I smoked pot.

ing at Wesleyan, our alma mater. God forbid, my old friend told me. The school has such an intense drug culture!

I laughed. It was so clearly a joke. Wesleyan might be notorious for it, but all schools have drug cultures, including the Ivy League institution his child ended up attending. I know of at least one person whose child came home from Harvard with a heroin addiction. True, my old college friend was particularly sensitive because he was in law enforcement, but hadn't the two of us been at the same parties? I was not much of a drug user, so my mind was not so addled that I forgot who was there. (Hint: *he* was there!) As I recall, he imbibed a lot more freely than I did. Maybe that's why he couldn't remember.

That was hardly the first moment of parental hypocrisy or convenient amnesia around drugs I have encountered. Many Gen X and Y parents, no matter how little their joint-rolling expertise harmed their careers and personal prospects, are racked with anxiety when it comes to their children and drugs. How many parent meetings have I sat through, listening to earnest educators explain how we can best help our children stand up to "peer pressure"? As if all our children are weak-willed moral midgets, unable to resist the drug-pushing Svengalis of the eighth grade. Every once in a while, someone will have the temerity to wonder if a few kids might be smoking pot not because they're bullied into submission, but because they think it's fun. That person will usually be roundly shouted down. That person is usually my husband or me.

Because we believe that the refusal to be honest will eventually hurt our children, my husband and I have adopted a harm-reduction strategy when it comes to issues like drug use. Harm reduction is defined as a set of practical strategies and ideas aimed at reducing negative consequences.* The basic tenets of

*The best-known example of a drug-related harm-reduction policy is a needle exchange program, in which drug users are provided with clean needles so they do not share dirty ones and thus expose themselves and others to potentially fatal

harm reduction when it comes to drugs are that drug use is a fact of contemporary life, that drugs can be dangerous, and that it is possible to minimize the harm. Harm reduction is not incompatible with disapproving of drug use, but it is incompatible with denying that drug use exists.*

The truth about drug use is so much more complicated than we want to believe. It's certainly more complicated than our drug education programs allow. Take, for example, Project D.A.R.E. (Drug Abuse Resistance Education), the most popular drug education program. For twenty-five years, D.A.R.E. persisted in miseducating children that all drugs, from marijuana to methamphetamine, were similarly dangerous; all drugs would destroy their brains and lives. Numerous reputable studies proved that the "facts" D.A.R.E. was pushing were both inaccurate and ineffective. Research showed that children who participated in D.A.R.E. programs actually experimented with drugs at *higher* rates. This makes sense. A seven-year-old hears that the demon weed will sizzle his brain and thinks, *I'll never do drugs!* A cynical fourteen-year-old hears the same message, notices that her cousin the pothead just graduated magna cum laude from Harvard, and dismisses not just the misinformation about marijuana, but everything else the D.A.R.E. program has to offer. It was only in 2009, with its funding sources at risk, that D.A.R.E. finally adopted a science-based approach, focusing on honesty, safety, and responsibility.

Recognizing the context in which teenagers live is critical to helping them make good choices. And the context in which

---

diseases. According to the World Health Organization, needle exchange programs "substantially and cost effectively reduce the spread of HIV among intravenous drug users and do so without evidence of exacerbating injecting drug use at either the individual or societal level." Dr. Alex Wodak and Allie Cooney, "Effectiveness of Sterile Needle and Syringe Programming in Reducing HIV/AIDS Among Injecting Drug Users."

*If you listen closely, you can hear the sound of my children's play dates and prom dates shriveling up and blowing away.

our children live is one in which drugs are a constant presence. According to a 2014 study funded by the National Institute on Drug Abuse (NIDA), more than half of high school seniors report having tried illegal drugs.* And these are self-reports! The figure might even be larger, because people tend, if anything, to under-report illegal activity.† Forty percent admit to having used an illegal drug in the previous year, and 25 percent in the previous month. The rates of alcohol use are even more striking. Fully 68 percent of seniors say they have tried alcohol. Given these numbers, a parental policy exclusively focused on abstinence is not only deluded but dangerous.

Most people are familiar with Mothers Against Drunk Driving's "Contract for Life," in which the child agrees not to drive drunk but to call for a ride, and the parent agrees to provide the ride without judgment or consequence. This is a classic harm-reduction model. None of us wants our children to abuse alcohol or drugs, but even less do we want them to fear our wrath so much that they take a ride that ends up killing them. Studies show that the flexibility in thinking that allows your teens to learn is what also causes them to be more likely to engage in an unknown risk (drunk driving, possibly dying) than a known risk (being yelled at by Mom). It's as though the very thing that makes them smarter must first make them stupid. My husband and I feel that the best way to combat this stupidity is with information.

Giving kids accurate information about drugs is particularly critical right now, because we are currently experiencing a dramatic increase in opioid use. This is hardly surprising, given the massive amount of advertising dollars pharmaceutical companies have invested in these drugs. More than a decade of intensive marketing and overprescription of painkillers like Oxycontin, Percocet, and Vicodin has led to skyrocketing use and abuse rates.

---

*Sara Bellum, "Real Teens Ask: How Many Teens Use Drugs?"
† Teenagers are really good liars. Especially to their parents.

It's important to recognize that these drugs aren't in and of themselves evil. They are invaluable for treating acute pain. The morphine I was given immediately after my Caesarean sections helped alleviate what otherwise would have been intolerable agony. Moreover, opioids, if taken under proper conditions and without adulteration, aren't particularly physically harmful. If you take opioids in appropriate doses and don't mix them with alcohol, you will not die. When opioids are given for limited periods of time to deal only with acute pain, such as the pain of surgery or the pain of dying of a disease like cancer, addiction is generally not an issue. To the dying, addiction is irrelevant, and for those dealing with acute pain, once the pain resolves, so generally does the need for the drug.* Only rarely does a patient become addicted after just a few days of opioid use.

It is when these drugs are prescribed over the long term for chronic pain that problems occur. There is a growing consensus that there is little evidence that opiods are reliably useful in dealing with chronic pain.† Patients report that the drugs become increasingly ineffective over time.‡ Moreover, with prolonged use, the risk of addiction rises.

The CDC believes that the best way to stem the tide of opioid abuse is to reduce the number of "unnecessary prescriptions" by physicians. Though on first blush this seems sensible, it ignores the fact that the rise in heroin use is not so much a result of the overprescription of opioids but of overprescription *followed by prohibition*. When patients are no longer able to receive prescriptions for the opioids on which they have become dependent, when pills are reformulated to make them more difficult to abuse, or when pills become prohibitively expensive, patients start searching for alternatives to stave off withdrawal. That's when

---

*Wilson Compton and Nora Volkow, "Major Increases in Opioid Analgesic Abuse in the United States: Concerns and Strategies."

† Charles F. von Gunten, "The Pendulum Swings for Opioid Prescribing."

‡ Pauline Anderson, "Scant Evidence for Long-Term Opioid Therapy in Chronic Pain."

they discover heroin, a cheaper and more potent way to get the same kind of high. According to the CDC, the numbers of people who report using heroin has doubled in the last decade.* Heroin is, next to tobacco, the most addictive drug we know of. According to the National Institute on Drug Abuse, nearly one-quarter of the people who use heroin end up becoming dependent.†

This has led to a dramatic increase in overdose and death.‡ In particular, the fatal heroin overdose rate, which was stable throughout the early years of this century, has gone through the roof. Heroin is produced and distributed by criminals operating outside of any regulatory system and, unlike prescription opioids, is not regulated for potency and purity. Fatal overdose is thus far more likely. Recently, for example, heroin dealers have begun lacing their product with easily obtainable fentanyl, a highly addictive synthetic morphine alternative that is thirty to fifty times as potent as pure heroin. The results have been catastrophic.

My older kids go to college on the East Coast, and we spend part of the year in New England, which is ground zero for the heroin epidemic. In the increasingly likely event that one of my kids witnesses an overdose, I want them to know that they must immediately dial 911. I don't want them to follow the fatal course of action of so many other frightened teens, desperately immersing an overdosing friend in a tub full of ice water, or dumping the person in a hospital parking lot, to expire in a pool of his or her own vomit.§

---

*Rose A. Rudd et al., "Increases in Drug and Opioid Overdose Deaths—United States, 2000–2014."

†"DrugFacts: Heroin," accessed June 27, 2016, at https://www.drugabuse.gov/publications/drugfacts/heroin.

‡According to the National Institute on Drug Abuse, between 2001 and 2014 there was a sixfold increase in the number of deaths from heroin overdose; deaths from overdose of prescription drugs tripled ("Overdose Death Rates" at drugabuse.gov).

§This was the fate of a twenty-four-year-old from Wilmington, Delaware, named Greg Humes, whose tragic death has inspired many parents to turn to harm reduction instead of insisting on an abstinence-only approach to drug education.

I have recently changed the message I give my kids when it comes to stimulant drugs such as methamphetamine. My kids tease me that my three phobias are rats, sharks, and methamphetamine. As disgusted as I am by rats (even the cute ones my eldest keeps as pets), as confident as I am that I will be chomped in half by a Great White if I so much as paddle in the ocean, the street drug known as "crank," "ice," or "crystal" has, for years, really scared the shit out of me. When I was a federal public defender, I had a client with cardiomegaly and congestive heart failure caused, according to his cardiologist, by repeated exposure to methamphetamine. I used to tell my kids that methamphetamine is so toxic that it would kill them, and so addictive that a single experience with the drug could lead to dependence. It was only while researching this book that I realized I'd been inadvertently lying to them.

We're going to take this next part slow, because it's going to contradict everything you think you know about meth. It certainly contradicted everything I thought I knew. What I learned was so hard for me to believe that I had to read and reread the studies several times. I asked Dr. Carl Hart, a Columbia University neuropsychopharmacologist and the country's pre-eminent researcher on methamphetamine,* the same questions so many times that eventually he got sick of repeating himself and stopped answering my e-mails.

Here goes:

Stimulant drugs like methamphetamine are dangerous. According to the Drug Policy Alliance, "Increased or prolonged use of methamphetamine can cause sleeplessness, loss of appetite, increased blood pressure, paranoia, psychosis, aggression, disordered thinking, extreme mood swings and sometimes

---

*In 1998, Dr. Hart became the first African American tenured professor of science in the history of Columbia University. In 1998. I'm typing that twice because otherwise you'd probably think it was a misprint.

hallucinations."* There is some evidence that it causes long-term cognitive harm. A 2010 study found that methamphetamine users performed worse than nonusers on tasks associated with daily functioning (dealing with finances, communicating, managing medications and transportation).[†]

However (and here's where you're going to start hearing things that will surprise you), the extent of this impairment seems to be less dramatic than we've been led to believe. According to Dr. Hart, though long-term effects have been observed, cognitive functioning of meth users generally falls within the normal range.[‡] We hear a lot about the deleterious effects of the drugs, Dr. Hart says, because researchers studying drugs like methamphetamine or crack cocaine tend to view any and all differences, no matter how small, as clinically significant. This, he says, is a reflection of bias, not of fact. Researchers see effects from drug use because they anticipate seeing effects from drug use.

And what about those negative behavioral effects of stimulant use? The crimes and violent outbursts? These do occur, though Dr. Hart insists that the dangers associated with stimulants are over-reported in the media. The evidence shows that antisocial behavior associated with methamphetamine is less common than we think, and more likely to be a function of circumstances such as poverty, trauma, and the presence of a criminal marketplace than of drug-fueled rages.[§]

The most damaging physical effects of stimulant use appear to be tied to their effects on sleep. According to Dr. Hart, "Low to moderate doses of amphetamine can improve mood, enhance

---

*"Methamphetamine Facts," accessed April 20, 2016, at http://www.drugpolicy.org/drug-facts/methamphetamine-facts.

[†] Brook L. Henry, Arpi Minassian, and William Perry, "Effect of Methamphetamine Dependence on Everyday Functional Ability."

[‡] Carl L. Hart et al., "Is Cognitive Functioning Impaired in Methamphetamine Users? A Critical Review."

[§] Carl L. Hart, Joanne Csete, and Don Habibi, "Methamphetamine: Fact vs. Fiction and Lessons from the Crack Hysteria."

performance, and delay the need for sleep. Repeated administration of large doses of the drug can severely disrupt sleep and lead to psychological disturbances, including paranoia."* It's sleep deprivation, not crack or meth, that makes some people crazy.

What about meth mouth? We all know what that looks like, we've seen the photographs! The pretty white girl with blond hair and blue eyes, turning before our eyes into a haggard crone with a mouthful of snaggly brown stumps. Methamphetamine restricts salivary flow, leading to xerostomia—dry mouth—which, if left untreated, can cause tooth decay. But so do all stimulants, including Adderall! Adderall and other stimulants are among the hundred most prescribed drugs in the United States, and yet we don't have an epidemic of "Add mouth." One of my kids has ADHD and has a prescription for Vyvanse, an amphetamine that works just like Adderall. Not only can this child finally sit still through a test, but he has gloriously sparkling teeth, a function of his profound commitment to dental hygiene—the best, according to his dentist, of any teenager she's ever treated. According to Dr. Hart, "The physical changes that occurred in the dramatic depictions of individuals before and after their methamphetamine use are more likely related to poor sleep habits, poor dental hygiene, poor nutrition and dietary practices."† As hard as it is to believe, "meth mouth" is a myth, a function of media sensationalism.‡ Some even theorize that the hype around meth mouth is actually an expression of horror at the loss of white privilege, a warning that if whites are not careful they will descend into "white trash."§

---

*Hart, Csete, and Habibi, "Methamphetamine: Fact vs. Fiction."
†Ibid.
‡T. Linnemann and T. Wall, "'This Is Your Face on Meth': The Punitive Spectacle of 'White Trash' in the Rural War on Drugs."
§"Given the weak evidentiary basis for epidemic and diagnosis, I offer a preliminary interpretation that the meth epidemic is constructed as symptom and cause of White status decline, with dental decay the vehicle for anxieties about descent into 'White trash' status" (Naomi Murakawa, "Toothless").

The addiction rates of stimulants are high, but not as high as those of heroin or nicotine, and most people who take methamphetamine will never become problematic users. Research* shows that the number of users of methamphetamine who go on to develop an addiction to the drug is 17 percent.[†] Yes, you read that right. Only 17 percent of people who use methamphetamine end up addicted to the drug. But here's the thing. A rate of addiction of 17 percent is *high*. It only sounds low because the drug warriors and their media mouthpieces have led us to believe in the "one and done" myth. We've been told that a single dose of methamphetamine, a single puff of a crack pipe, a single injection of heroin, is enough to make an addict. But that's simply not true in the vast majority of cases. Had we not been exposed to an aggressive campaign of misinformation that led us to expect something like a 99 percent addiction rate, we would be able to recognize that it is a very big deal if nearly a fifth of methamphetamine users and nearly a quarter of heroin users become addicted. Instead, we see those numbers and are confused.

From now on, when I talk to my kids about methamphetamine, I'm going to stop doing a Google image search for "meth mouth." Instead, I'm going to be candid with them about the drug's high potential for abuse ("If you and nine friends try meth together, one or even two of you could end up addicted") and about its negative effects. I'm also going to tell them what I always tell them about drugs: one of the worst "side effects" of drug use is arrest. If you are arrested for using drugs, our system can come down on you like a ton of bricks. Though of course my

---

* Megan S. O'Brien and James C. Anthony, "Extra-Medical Stimulant Dependence Among Recent Initiates."

[†] Dr. Hart believes even that figure is exaggerated. In a report prepared for the Open Society Institute, he writes, "Less than 15 percent of those who have ever used the drug will become addicted." (Hart, Csete, and Habibi, "Methamphetamine: Fact vs. Fiction.")

children share a quality that makes it unlikely that they will be arrested: they're white. When they're walking down the street, they will probably not be stopped and forced to turn out their pockets. Their black friends, however, face a very real risk of this.

In addition to providing my kids with accurate information and having in place a system of consequence-free party pickups (made especially easy now with the advent of Uber and Lyft), our family harm-reduction policy has, since the incident at Wesleyan University when the group of students nearly died taking a drug they thought was Molly, included stocking a cupboard with drug testing kits, so if the kids try Molly or another club drug they can be sure they aren't inadvertently taking poison. We also stock their bathroom cupboard with condoms, though recently one of our daughters has taken over this role, becoming a member of Berkeley High School's "Condom Club," distributing condoms to her friends. She's a little Johnny Appleseed, but with johnnies.

All this frank talk about risks and rewards can make a parent uncomfortable, even afraid. Abandoning the question of whether my kids use drugs, and focusing instead on minimizing the chances of their being hurt by drugs, feels sometimes like abdicating responsibility. But it isn't. It's actually a hell of a lot of work. You can't just say, "Don't smoke pot!" You have to go out and do the research. You have to explain to your kids that some studies have shown that marijuana can affect the developing brain in negative ways, so they should put off smoking pot for as long as possible.* You have to explain to them that alcohol is even worse for their brains than marijuana.† All this can be exhausting. So here's an alternative: print out a copy of *Safety*

*K. L. Medina et al., "Neuropsychological Functioning in Adolescent Marijuana Users: Subtle Deficits Detectable After a Month of Abstinence." For a thorough review of research on marijuana and youth, see Seth Ammerman, Sheryl Ryan, and William P. Adelman, "The Impact of Marijuana Policies on Youth: Clinical, Research, and Legal Update."
†L. M. Squeglia, J. Jacobus, and S. F. Tapers, Ph.D., "The Influence of Substance Use on Adolescent Brain Development."

First: A Reality-Based Approach to Teens and Drugs, a thoughtful, research-based harm-reduction guide for teens, parents, and educators, written by Marsha Rosenbaum, Ph.D., and published by the Drug Policy Alliance.*

A harm-reduction approach to parenting need not be permissive. My kids know how I feel about the risks and rewards of drug use. They know that there are drugs that I hope they will put off using until they are older (marijuana and alcohol), drugs I hope they will use only when they are older and under very circumscribed conditions (MDMA, psychedelics), and drugs that I hope they never use (methamphetamine, cocaine, heroin).

But what about this experiment of mine? Although having a harm-reduction policy means that I don't lie to my kids about drugs, it doesn't require me to discuss anything I don't feel comfortable sharing. I get to decide what I tell them about my own life. Though I have to admit that it feels dishonest, I'm not ready to be open with them about this. For now, I'm going to stick with "taking a walk."

*At http://www.drugpolicy.org/sites/default/files/DPA_SafetyFirst_2014_0.pdf.

Day 11

....

Transition Day

Physical Sensations: None.

Mood: Nice.

Sleep: Woke up way too early.

*Work: Trouble focusing at first, but eventually
   got down to it.*

*Pain: Is it the microdose, or is my shoulder just
   finally starting to unfreeze?*

I woke this morning at dawn after having fallen asleep too late. I tried to force myself to go back to sleep. I snuggled up to my husband, laid my head on his chest, and felt his heart beat against my cheek. Antoine de Saint-Exupéry once wrote, "Love does not consist of gazing at each other, but in looking outward together in the same direction." Bullshit. When I gaze at my husband, when I feel his body along the length of mine, I feel a deep, contented joy, a warmth that begins in my belly, spreads out to my limbs and through the top of my skull. If that's not love, what is?

I kissed him softly so that I didn't wake him, and slipped out of the darkness of our bedroom, through the quiet hall, downstairs to the kitchen. Though the cacophony of a house full of children is one of the delights of parenthood, I am coming to love the early hours of the morning, when I wake to a silent house. So used to being a grump in the mornings, so used to clutching mightily to every last shred of sleep, I find it a pleasure to sit silently at my kitchen table, drinking a cup of tea, with the dog resting her chin on my lap as I scratch her ears while I read the paper or check my e-mail.

Still, despite the delight I'm taking in this early morning solitude, I am worried about how little I'm sleeping. Though the protocol warns that some people require a sleep aid, I am loath to get back into a habit I worked so hard to kick.

Some of my earliest memories are of lying beneath my scratchy polyester quilt, my head balanced on a pillow at once lumpy and hard, staring at the blades of yellow street light slicing between the slats of the mini-blinds that inadequately covered my window. I fought hard to keep from looking at the glow of my flip clock, but the numbers would drop with an audible flop, reducing one by one the possibility of getting enough accumulated minutes of sleep before the radio buzzed static and KISS-FM.

That lasted my entire life, until I discovered Ambien. That's when everything changed. I would climb into bed and pop a pill, and the lights would go out with a snap. Sometimes the metaphorical lights went out even before the actual ones. My husband, coming in from work at 3:00 or 4:00 a.m., would find me, lights blazing, glasses on, book in hand, snoring away.

I loved that drug so much, even if some of the side effects were, well, disconcerting. Jet lag rendered me impervious to the effects of a single Ambien pill, so when I was traveling I would often allow myself a second one, and sometimes, my judgment impaired, even a third. It turns out there's a reason the correct dosage is five to ten milligrams. The following text stream, reproduced verbatim, illustrates what happens when you take thirty milligrams:

You love m me right?

YES

Our kids are goog. We did ik

Okay, Ambien typing

If I die too ire il be ins rigyra

Put screen away

Sex in nit sir. Very sky adequate

Stop. Turn off phone and you will be
asleep in 5

You talk me. Before you I was
imonible. Now in on accordion
monorail

HONEY TURN OFF YOUR PHONE
NOW

Income home tomorrow

Please, darling. I am begging you. If
you love me, turn off your devices,
pick up your book, and read. Screens
activate

Hiccups

Bad enough sending such gobbledygook to my husband, but
once I took two Ambien on a red-eye to London and decided that
a very beautiful and accomplished actress friend would make
the ideal wife for my husband and stepmother for my kids in the
event that the plane plummeted into the Atlantic. I texted her a

long set of unfortunately too-coherent instructions on how she should go about taking my place.

Worse than making me a late-night idiot, Ambien made me depressed, though I did not recognize this correlation until I finally stopped taking the drug. Only in retrospect did I appreciate how much gloomier I was the day after I'd taken an Ambien. It also played havoc with my memory. This, too, took a while to realize, masked as it was by the fact that since having children I have experienced an overall decline in memory. For years I blamed my failure to remember simple events—whereas once I'd effortlessly memorized long mnemonics for things like the Rules of Evidence—on pregnancy brain, or lactation fuzzies, or on the myriad distractions of a large family, but now I realize that Ambien was at least partially at fault. Short-term memory loss is a recognized side effect of the drug. Even worse, studies show that, though Ambien might actually help in the consolidation of long-term memories, that effect is true only for bad experiences.* Ambien, which makes you forget everything else, actually sharpens your recall of unpleasant emotions and events. Like I needed any help with that.

The six years I relied on Ambien were the first six years of my youngest child's life, and I have heartbreakingly few memories of that time. Worse, those I do have are all too often unhappy. What if that period of my life was characterized not only by the unhappiness and mood swings that I recall, but also by periods of contentment, even joy, that I have lost like digital photos on a crashed computer? What if Ambien has warped my perception of the extent of my unhappiness, causing me to forget happiness and remember only misery? Wouldn't that almost be sadder than never having been happy at all?

Kicking the Ambien habit was hell. I lay in bed night after night, rolling from side to side, flinging the covers off, pulling

---

*Erik J. Kaestner, John T. Wixted, and Sara C. Mednick, "Pharmacologically Increasing Sleep Spindles Enhances Recognition for Negative and High-Arousal Memories."

them back up, longing for a pill, my Nightly Roll Call of Anxieties studded with entries like "You'll never sleep again" and "You're a pathetic drug addict." I felt like I was trying to break free from an addiction, though my doctor had promised me that Ambien was not habit-forming. Even now, when I search for research on the topic, I am reassured that he was correct—when, that is, the drug is used correctly. But how non-habit-forming can a non-habit-forming drug be if the non-habit-forming drug has you forming a habit where you're taking enough to form a habit?

Indeed, my experience with Ambien doesn't rise to the level of the accepted definition of drug dependence. I did not experience a "preoccupation with a desire to obtain and take the drug, and persistent drug-seeking behavior."* But, then, I always had a prescription bottle in my medicine cabinet, refilled automatically through the mail every three months. I ran out of toilet paper more often than I ran out of Ambien. On the rare occasions when my pharmacy failed me, I experienced a pang of concern, but that was immediately remedied by a call to my doctor. A heroin addict with a bucket full of dope on her nightstand wouldn't need to engage in "persistent drug-seeking behavior," either.

The problem is that the "correct" way to use Ambien isn't how most of us use it. Supposedly, Ambien is intended for occasional insomnia. A night here or there, once in a rare while. But when I was taking the drug, it was my every-night companion. My regular midnight snack. I only rarely took more than the recommended dose, but I was less apt to skip a pill than I ever was when I was taking birth control. Though my evidence is only anecdotal, most Ambien devotees I know are like I was, using Ambien regularly, not occasionally, because their insomnia is regular, not occasional.

My campaign to kick the drug was two-pronged. First I substi-

---

*From World Health Organization Expert Committee on Drug Dependence (Twenty-eighth Report, 1993) definition of drug addiction. WHO Technical Report Series 836.

tuted medical marijuana as a nighttime medication (though only briefly); then I turned my bedroom into as close an approximation of a sensory deprivation tank as I could achieve without passing my nights in a soundproof pod full of salt water.

I took the concept of "sleep hygiene" to a level of neurosis that only others who spend their nights frantically calculating the mounting hours of their sleep deficits can appreciate. I turned off the heat in our bedroom, chose a fan for its cooling and white-noise properties, and eliminated all sources of light. Tiny squares of black vinyl electrical tape cover every single LED light. All of this has left our bedroom darker and quieter than a womb, and a hell of a lot colder.

In that black, freezing, white-noise-filled room, I generally sleep almost as soon as my head touches my (three) pillows. But what about on the all-too-many nights when I'm out on the road? This is not a neurosis that travels easily. I do my best, turning the heat down and the air conditioning up. I travel with a pack of black Post-its that I stick over all LED and other indicator lights, including the insanely bright strobes that are a feature of hotel smoke detectors. I put a rolled-up towel in front of the door to block the light from the hallway. I wear earplugs. Actually, now that I'm taking stock, everything I do to try to get some sleep in a hotel is also an exact recipe for how to die successfully and obliviously in my room should the hotel I'm staying in catch fire. That's a thought to help me drift off next time I hit the hay in a Radisson.

I know that the precautions that I have taken against insomnia have only served to acclimate me to an absurd ideal. I've made myself soft. If I really wanted to cure my sleeplessness, I would take away all these crutches and teach myself to fall asleep in a hot room, on a hard, lumpy mattress covered in prickly sheets, beneath an unshaded skylight—the exact state, in fact, of my childhood bedroom. Surely, the fact that I'm no longer a discontented preadolescent wearing a padded bra and a huge chip on her shoulder would militate against the discomfort. But, honestly, who really wants to find out?

Moreover, even before I began the microdose protocol, though I would generally fall asleep with little difficulty, I often popped awake at 4:00 a.m. Sometimes I think I should make regular 4:00 a.m. plans with my other perimenopausal friends. We could do something productive with our wakefulness, like play mah-jongg or renovate derelict apartments for homeless families, instead of tossing and turning on our sweat-soaked sheets, Googling the side effects of hormone patches and bio-identical hormone creams, and "accidentally" kicking our blissfully sleeping spouses.

Still, though I am staying up late and waking up early, I'm not feeling the effects of the resulting sleep deprivation as much as I would have expected. But even this concerns me. Needing less sleep can be a warning of the onset of hypomania. I should be tired, and if I'm not, that might itself be a problem. The prospect of the protocol's causing either hypomania or a return to insomnia is really starting to worry me. And, of course, that worry is keeping me up at night.

Day 12

....

Normal Day

Physical Sensations: None.

Mood: Fine.

Conflict: None.

Sleep: Perfectly fine.

Work: Productive.

Pain: Minor.

Today I decided to risk repetitive stress injury and work at a café. The café had free Wi-Fi, but I was halfway through my morning before I realized that I had not once bothered to go online. How strange. Who am I?

I am usually so addicted to the Internet that I can't be productive unless I turn off my laptop's Wi-Fi, and even then I keep my phone at the ready just in case of emergency. If, for example, the barista swirls the face of Jesus into the foam of my cappuccino, I need to able to get the photo up on Instagram right away, so pilgrims can attend before the bubbles dissolve.

But today hours passed before I even remembered that I had close at hand a means of escaping the responsibilities of work. Can this be the microdose? If so, it's an unanticipated outcome. I experienced a similar phenomenon when my psychopharmacologist prescribed Ritalin, but that class of drugs made me anxious and irritable. (By "irritable" I mean that they made me scream obscenities at my husband, blare my horn at cars that I felt were lingering at stop signs, and fling various objects across the room.) But though today I was focused, I was not at all irritable. I felt calm and composed. Almost unnervingly so.

My highest hope for this experiment is that it will result in my experiencing more days like this. I have always been excitable, impulsive, and easily agitated. There is no quality I admire so much and possess so little as equanimity.

Is equanimity a characteristic of intelligence, or does it seem so because we associate rationality with intellect? Certainly, that isn't true of brilliance. The genius of fantasy is often mercurial and tumultuous. "We of the craft are all crazy," Lord Byron said. "Some are affected by gaiety, others by melancholy, but all are more or less touched."

I came upon that quote years ago, when I was diagnosed with bipolar disorder. I read it in a book by Kay Redfield Jamison, a professor of psychiatry and an expert on manic-depressive illness, who is a fellow traveler. Her memoir *An Unquiet Mind* provided me with the comfort of shared experience, but it was her book *Touched with Fire: Manic-Depressive Illness and the Artistic Temperament* that I loved. In that book I learned that my diagnosis didn't doom me to a life of somnambulant, drug-induced torpor alternating with ill-tempered irritability. Or at least not necessarily. All I needed to do was figure out how to harness my "heightened imaginative powers, intensified emotional responses, and increased energy" and I might, like Jamison herself, join the ranks of genius. Like the poets Robert Lowell and Anne Sexton, like Emile Zola and Virginia Woolf, like Georgia O'Keeffe and Jackson Pollock, I might be "touched with fire."

Except that all too often Jamison's geniuses were consumed by the fires they set. Moreover, my work, though more "serious" now than it was when I was writing books with titles like *A Playdate with Death,* is no *Café Terrace on the Place du Forum* or

"She Walks in Beauty." My talent, such as it is, does not merit the emotional price paid either by me or by the people I love. I can't simply dismiss my lack of equanimity as a necessary evil, the flip side of creativity. I must try instead to find it.

About an hour northwest of where I live, nestled in a little glen in the hills of Marin, is the Green Gulch Farm Zen Center. I've driven by it dozens of times on my way to the coast. Every Sunday, the Zen Center hosts a public meditation and dharma talk, a lesson in Buddhism, followed by lunch. Their mission is "to awaken in ourselves and the many people who come here the bodhisattva spirit, the spirit of kindness and realistic helpfulness." Equanimity is one of the four core practices of Buddhism, along with Loving-Kindness, Compassion, and Sympathetic Joy. Buddhism teaches that you can intentionally create equanimity in your body by relaxing and letting sensations wash through you. You can create equanimity in your mind by letting go of negative judgments and treating yourself and others with loving acceptance. You learn how to do all this through meditation. My favorite.

My first experience with meditation occurred when I was pregnant with my second child and frazzled from caring for his older sister. I was lured to that class (and have been lured since to yoga classes, meditation circles, TM mantras, and mindfulness iPhone apps) by the promise of increased happiness, decreased pain, improved memory and cognitive function, and a longer, more satisfying life. I sat in a middle-school classroom that smelled of pencils and feet and, at the behest of the instructor, practiced imagining a lotus blooming above my head, dropping its petals one by one. This was in the early era of the Internet, when it was not so easy to search out photographs of things we'd never seen before, and it was years before I realized that my "lotus" was actually a chrysanthemum. Lotuses have eight petals, chrysanthemums 1,327. This might explain why I got so bored.

I have been taught by a whole variety of experts how to meditate, but, rather than sit calmly, noticing my thoughts, I usually have an internal meditation monologue that goes something like this: *You're thinking again. You can't even shut off your mind for five minutes. Now you're thinking about thinking. Stop berating yourself for thinking! Why are you so full of self-loathing, so inept and incompetent, that all you can do is criticize yourself when you meditate? What the fuck is wrong with you?* And on and on until the timer finally goes off.

One of the very few things I can say with confidence about the practice of meditation is that no one's guru has ever given them the mantra "What the fuck is wrong with you?"

Whenever I manage to meditate more than three days in a row, I consider attending one of Green Gulch's Sundays. Once, I even explored the possibility of going there for a three-day retreat. However, Green Gulch is a "scent-free community," and I have curly hair. I am, apparently, not so desperate for equanimity that I am willing to tolerate a day without my regular leave-in conditioner.

Also? The city in which I live is full of meditators of all shapes and kinds. In my experience, though the vast majority of them are models of empathy and equipoise, there is nobody as hostile as a hostile Berkeley Buddhist. He may brim over with bodhisattva spirit, but he'll still snake your parking spot in the lot of the Berkeley Bowl.

Still. Here is a practice that claims it can help me achieve what I seek. Wouldn't it be more admirable to commit to that practice, scent- (though hardly odor-) free as it may be, than seek equanimity in a medicine dropper full of Schedule I? Perhaps I should do both. I will try for the rest of the month of the protocol to meditate for ten minutes every day. On my own. Just me and my conditioner.

Day 13

....

Microdose Day

*Physical Sensations: About ninety minutes after
    dosing felt nauseated. Diarrhea. Passed (ha!)
    in a couple of hours.*

Mood: Happy.

Conflict: None.

*Sleep: Woke up super early, got up and read,
    then fell back asleep and slept in.*

*Work: Productive, though never lost track of
    time.*

Pain: No improvement, but no worse either.

This morning I woke up with a calm appreciation for my life.
What is this feeling? It feels too placid for joy, too serene for
bliss. Is it contentment?

For the first time since I began the protocol, I slept late, waking only when my husband did. The fog had already burned off
when he flung open the blackout curtains and opened the bedroom window. Sun filled the room, and I could smell the earthy
musk of the massive redwood tree outside our window. This tree
is why we bought this house, or, rather, the ancient rosebush
that once twined itself around the trunk and bloomed high in
its branches, its white blossoms like fairy lights amidst the dark-
green needles.

When I was five months pregnant with our second child, we moved to Berkeley from Los Angeles. We rented a house from a pair of academics on sabbatical in China, figuring that it would take us no more than a couple of months to find a house to buy. The rental house was up the block from where we live now, and the morning after we arrived we wandered down the street and saw the tree. I'd never seen such a thing, flowers blooming hundreds of feet in the air. The rose's gnarled vine was covered in peely bark and as thick around as my arm, and before climbing the redwood, it swooped over the path to the porch, dipping down so that it almost brushed the top of the head of anyone who walked up the steps. The rest of the yard was wild, thick with undergrowth and piles of dirt.

The house, an old Berkeley brown shingle in the Arts and Crafts style, was under construction. As we stood, staring up at the tree, a workman came out of the front door.

"Excuse me!" I called to him. "Is this house for sale?"

He shook his head and pointed across the street. The man who lived there, he explained, was renovating the house for his sister-in-law.

We continued on our way, only slightly disappointed. Berkeley is full of beautiful old bungalows, redwood trees, and wild rosebushes. We were sure we'd find another one easily enough.

Unfortunately, we arrived in town at the beginning of what became a permanent real-estate boom. We saw dozens of houses, and made three or four offers, our price range creeping higher and higher, into a zone so unrealistic that it seemed pointless to worry about it. We were so far above what we could afford, what difference did another ten thousand make? And yet every house we bid on ended up selling for an amount far more than the ridiculous figure we'd offered.

Meanwhile, my belly was growing, and the professors were due back from China. We were getting desperate. So desperate that we made a flyer, begging for a place to live. We took a photograph of ourselves, me with my big belly, my husband looking pensive, our two-year-old daughter with her mop of ringlets. "Sell us your house!" we scrawled on the photo. We made a hundred copies and slipped them under doors, hung them on the community bulletin boards of taquerías and cafés, and pinned them to lampposts. My husband's brother, humiliated (their last name is an uncommon one, and he's popular around town), called us and asked, "Have you two completely lost your minds?" A few years later, when he found himself with a pregnant wife and a rental about to expire, he behaved no less irrationally. Bay Area real estate is far more likely than a bad LSD trip to drive you to psychosis.

All that time, we watched as the renovation of the house down the block progressed. Old plumbing was torn out. Electricians' vans came and went. Then, one day, our real-estate agent called to tell us that there might be a house in the neighborhood for sale. A man had been renovating a house for his sister-in-law, but she had just been forced to take a job in another city. We met our Realtor at his office, and he walked us around the corner to the house with the crazy rose vine.

When our Realtor called him, the owner of the house wasn't ready to sell. He wanted to finish the renovation first—call back in a few months, he said. But we didn't have a few months. We offered more than he asked, more than we could afford. Still he said no. And then, one day, I stood beneath the blooming redwood tree, my shirt riding up over my bulging belly, and burst into tears. I begged him to sell us the house right away, as it was, unfinished. He shifted uncomfortably from foot to foot, he gazed up at the white roses peeking through the needles of the redwood tree, and then, finally, he shrugged his shoulders and agreed. It was hormones that made me cry (and panic), not manipulation, but I'd be lying if I said I wasn't glad that the tears worked.

We immediately set about finishing the renovation so that

we could move in before the professors' return. The work was supposed to be done before I gave birth, but even though our very considerate baby held on for a full two weeks beyond his due date, the contractors were still finishing the kitchen when I went into labor. In the early stages, my midwife told me and my husband to take a walk to move things along, and we wandered down to the house. I stepped into the kitchen and saw that the workmen had installed not the slab of dark-green granite countertop we'd spent an afternoon carefully selecting at the warehouse but instead something pink and speckled.

"What're you gonna do?" the contractor said with a shrug. "It's already in. You'll get used to it."

"Are you kidding me?" I said. Then a contraction hit. I crouched down, my belly rippling. I moaned, rocking back and forth. The contractor and his men stared. The contraction passed and I stood up.

"Pink!" I shrieked. Another contraction followed hard on the first, and I crouched down again, groaning.

"Go to the hospital!" the contractor said, not realizing that I was about to put *him* in the hospital.

Through my contraction, I gasped, "I will never get used to pink granite!"

The contractor begged me to leave. He promised that by the time the baby was out of my womb the mistake would be rectified. Fortunately for him, it took a full two days and a C-section for my son to move out of his rental in my uterus. When I wandered back into the construction site, the baby hanging from a sling, the offending pink granite had been replaced with dark green. Like tears, sometimes being scary will get the job done. Rocking back and forth to keep the baby asleep, I gazed around the kitchen and shrugged. Granite is granite, I thought. Eight years later we tore it out, recycled it, and replaced it with zinc.

The spring after we bought the house, we waited for the roses in the redwood to bloom. April passed, then May, then June. In

July we called a tree surgeon, who climbed into the tree and told us that the rose vine was dead. It was an ancient rose, planted alongside the redwood in 1907, when the house was built, but it had bloomed for the last time the previous spring.

Though I don't believe in God and I don't believe in fate, I am superstitious. I knock on wood; I don't walk under ladders. I have no explanation for this behavior. It overtook me relatively late in life, after I met my husband, who, despite being an eternal optimist, is the one who taught me to throw salt over my shoulder and mutter the phrase *"kene-ahora"* to avert the evil eye. Neither of us really believes in this stuff, but we're both uncomfortable if we forget to utter the magic words. I think in my case the simple fact is that I have no confidence in the permanence of my good fortune. I don't believe I deserve it, so I'm terrified it will be taken away.

Given this, how could I see the death of the very thing that had attracted us to the house as anything but a harbinger of bad luck?

"It's an omen," I moaned, staring up at the dead vine.

You won't be surprised to hear that my husband was unperturbed. It means something, he said, just not what you think. The rose attracted our attention. It drew us to the house where we were meant to raise our family. There's no reason for it to bloom anymore. It's done its job, and now it can die.

We planted another rose, but we haven't let it take over the redwood. It turns out that the vine was choking the tree. Once the tree surgeons had cut the dead rose loose, the redwood began to thrive, growing new and healthier branches, reaching ever higher into the sky. Today the needles shimmer in the late-morning light, and because I am seeing things in a new way, I notice what I have missed on virtually every other morning of the last eighteen years. It is beautiful.

Day 14

....

Transition Day

Physical Sensations: None.

Mood: Woke up crabby, then everything changed.

Conflict: None.

Sleep: No more than six hours, despite trying hard to sleep for longer.

Work: Not as productive as yesterday, but not too bad.

Pain: A little bit in the night.

Today's epiphany: What if mood is a *choice*? What if I've just been too lazy to be nice to my family? I know this is simplistic. I know that over the course of my life I've felt no more able to control my storms of irritability than I've been to control the weather, but today it feels possible. When I first woke up, I was my usual pre-microdosing self: grouchy and tired, resentful of a world designed for people who like nothing better than to spring ecstatically out of bed, meditate for an hour, and salute the sun as it rises. If I had my druthers, I would loll in bed until noon with only the newspaper and a cup of tea for company. (Oh, to be a resident of Downton Abbey, with a silver bell to summon servants in whispering slippers bearing trays of tea and buttered toast!) After a few predictable moments of grumbling and longing (married ladies are meant to breakfast abed), I thought to myself, It's really not that hard to be nice, even at six-thirty in the morning.

My tread was light as I came downstairs. When my kids straggled in from their bedrooms, their faces creased with sleep, their noses buried in their phones, I greeted them with affection and good humor. This is bare-bones parenting; it should be the norm. And yet generally in the morning, if I even manage to haul my ass out of bed, all I can manage is a periodic grunt from my perch at the kitchen table, hunched over my tea and *The New York Times*. But today, as I placed my children's (serially prepared, because God forbid people in the same house should eat the same thing in the morning) breakfasts before them with a cheerful clatter, I told them each how much I loved them. I cracked a few jokes. I reminded one that because we both had restless nights we needed to be on alert for low moods caused by sleeplessness.

As I attempted to weave a French braid into my teenage daughter's hair, and planted a kiss on her cheek, she said, "Oh my God, who even *are* you today?"

When I was seven years old, I had a recurring dream that featured a bucolic glen in the woods populated by sweet-tempered animals, including a fawn. (I think I might recently have seen *Bambi*.) Everything about the dream was lovely: The flowers bloomed; the sun filtered prettily through the canopy of trees. The animals' fur was soft, and they were all eager to be petted. The velvet-nosed fawn was the gentle leader, beloved by the other animals, admired by visitors to the glen. Only I knew that the fawn was actually evil, a demon hiding behind thickly lashed chocolate eyes.

Night after night, I woke up from this dream crying and calling for my mother. Half asleep, she would stagger into my room, comfort me, and settle me back to sleep, the way I do with my own children when they have night terrors. One night, on her way out of my bedroom, she walked into the door, hit her head, and fell to the ground with a crash. My father came running, there was noise and confusion, and then they were gone. I assume he whisked her back to their bedroom. I lay in my bed convinced that the fawn had attacked my mother, knocking her soul out of her body and taking its place.

Who even are *you?* I would think when I looked at my mother. But I knew who she was. She was the fawn.

I can't remember if it was days, weeks, or months that I lived with the grim certainty that my mother was not my mother at all, but really just the evil fawn in human form. I do remember that I wasn't always afraid or worried about the changeling. Sometimes it could even be a comfort. My mother would yell and I would think, "Oh, that terrible, terrible fawn," and recall with longing my real, true mother. Missing her allowed me to be less wounded by the angry fawn who sometimes took her place.

As I skipped around the kitchen this morning, dispensing kisses and cracking jokes in silly voices, the thought crossed my mind that my children might wonder if some mystical or extra-terrestrial creature had not invaded their mother's body and replaced the moody bitch who normally dwelled inside it.

My daughter, after I'd planted yet another noisy kiss on her cheek, rubbed her face and said, "You are being so *annoying*! What is *wrong* with you? Did you put, like, LSD in your tea?"

Day 15

....

Normal Day

Physical Sensations: None.

Mood: Good at first, but then it all went to hell.

Conflict: It definitely feels like some people are more annoying than they need to be, and some of those people live in my house.

Sleep: Eight solid hours. Overslept.

Work: My first unproductive day.

Pain: Moderate discomfort.

Even though it happened nearly two weeks ago, even though last week I achieved some real peace by boxing up and putting away the few things I kept in his studio, and even though my husband and I had been getting along so well since his return, we used our hour in couples therapy this week to rehash our argument about his studio. At least, that's how things started. But after more than twenty years of marriage, our arguments inevitably devolve into the meta. We might begin by arguing about whether or not I should rent my own office, but almost immediately we find ourselves fighting about whose fault it is that we are fighting, who fights fair and who doesn't, whether this fight is the same as those that came before, what's really going on underneath it all.

This time was no different. Almost as soon as we described our argument to the therapist, I told her that the real problem wasn't whether or not we should share the studio.

"The real problem," I said, "is that he's angry at me."

"I am not!" my husband insisted.

I ignored him, and continued talking to the therapist. "He's sick of dealing with my moods. And who can blame him? It's my fault things have been so hard between us recently."

He said, "I wish you'd stop saying that."

"It's okay. You're right to blame me. I blame myself."

My husband turned to the therapist. "I don't blame her. Can you please help her understand that?"

"Do you love your husband?" the therapist asked me.

"Do I love him?" I said. I couldn't believe she'd asked such a stupid question.

"Yes. Do you love him?"

"More than anything in the world."

"So why do you threaten to leave me when we fight?" my husband said. "Why do you pack your bags every time we have an argument?"

It's true. If an argument becomes intense, I will often start flinging clothes into a bag. Sometimes I'll even walk out the door and drive around for a while, before coming home chastened and sorry. Not so different from the child who puts a sandwich in her backpack before loudly announcing that she's running away forever. Having watched my parents struggle within the confines of their marital strife, I respond to crisis with a desperate, if fleeting, desire to escape. This behavior drives my husband wild. A child of divorce, he cannot bear to be left, even if he should know by now that I always come back. It triggers his fears of abandonment.

"You can't do that anymore," the therapist told me. "You can't threaten to leave. It's cruel."

"Here's the thing," I said. "It's because I love him that I should do him the favor of leaving him. He'd be better off without me."

My husband flinched.

"I should leave him, but I won't," I continued, speaking to the therapist, not to my husband.

"Are you saying you want to leave him?" she asked.

"Of course not! It would make me absolutely miserable to be without him. I'll never leave him."

"Because it would make you miserable."

"No! Don't you get it? My misery isn't the point. I deserve to be miserable. What I really want is for him to be happy, and I know he'd be infinitely happier without me."

"So you threaten to leave because you think that's what's best for him?"

"Exactly. But here's the problem. I can't trust him."

My husband cast his eyes to the heavens.

"He has terrible taste in women," I continued. "He's attracted to the neurotic and broken. He specializes in fruitlessly trying to fix the unfixable. I'll never leave him, because there's no *point* in leaving him. He'll just go out and find someone even crazier than me." If I died, he probably wouldn't marry my actress friend, the one to whom I thoughtfully provided comprehensive Ambien-fueled instructions on how to take my place. He wouldn't be into her, because she has her shit together.

"For God's sake," my husband muttered.

The therapist said, "Do you believe him when he says he loves you?"

"Of course! Didn't you hear what I said? It's his love that's the problem! It's proof of his terrible judgment." Using the logic of Groucho Marx: "I don't care to belong to any club that will have me as a member." Unassailable!

"Say it," she said. "Tell him you know he loves you."

I turned to my husband. "I know you love me, even though loving me is a terrible mistake."

The therapist shook her head. "Just tell him you know he loves you. Leave off the rest of the sentence."

I tried again. "I know you love me because your problem is that you are only attracted to awful women."

"Try again."

"I know you love me, but you shouldn't."

"Try again."

"I know you love me, but I don't deserve it."

"Again."

It took about a dozen attempts before I finally managed, sobbing, to bite off the rest of the sentence and let the five words hang in the air.

"I know you love me."

My husband's eyes filled. He pulled me close. I collapsed in his arms, crying so hard I soaked his shirt.

The hour was up.

He cried, he told me after, because it made him so sad to see how hard it was for me to say those five words.

Since then, all day long, I've been saying them lightly, almost as a joke.

"I know you love me," I said in the car coming home from therapy.

"I know you love me," I said when we walked up the stairs to our porch.

"I know you love me," I said as we cooked dinner together.

"I know you love me," I said as we made love.

Every time I said the words, I finished the sentence silently in my head. But maybe that's just today. Things might look different tomorrow. Tomorrow, after I dose, maybe I won't need to finish the sentence at all. Or, better yet, maybe "I know you love me" will finally feel like a complete sentence.

Day 16

....

Microdose Day
Physical Sensations: Stomach upset.
Mood: Tired but good spirits.
Conflict: None.
Sleep: Average.
Work: Productive.
Pain: Some minor pain.

I spent the afternoon with Jim Fadiman in Santa Cruz, at his modest work retreat, a small, unrenovated apartment with a million-dollar view of the Pacific. The surfers were out, bobbing and paddling through the swells, as seagulls pinwheeled through the sky. The view of crashing surf is so compelling that Fadiman has had to turn his desk to face the wall in order to accomplish anything. Maybe I should stop kvetching about feeling claustrophobic facing a wall in my husband's studio and pretend that I have to sit that way because there is something behind me so breathtakingly beautiful that I could not do a lick of work if I faced the other direction.

Fadiman uses the apartment as a private space to work, away from the distractions of home and, presumably, of his wife of many decades, Dorothy, a documentary filmmaker. Together they have two daughters, both of whom are grown. He speaks of them fondly and with charming paternal pride.

His bookshelves are stuffed with many of the same volumes that I've been accumulating in my own psychedelic library: Hofmann's *LSD, My Problem Child,* Tom Shroder's *Acid Test,* Ram Dass's *Be Here Now,* and Henri Michaux's *Miserable Miracle.* I wonder if, when his daughters were young, their reactions to the books were the same as my children's, a puzzled frown, a rolled eye, a sniff that somehow manages to encompass both disgust and curiosity.

In addition to having a similar library, Fadiman drives the same car as I do, a silver Prius—which, to be fair, is the least coincidental of coincidences. We live in the Bay Area. I once parked my car in a row of half a dozen identical ones in the parking lot of my local Whole Foods.* Still, same books, same car, same psychedelic interests.

Over Chinese food at his favorite local restaurant, Fadiman told me the story of his life, from the time the government shut down his research and derailed the career for which he had been trained at Harvard and Stanford, until his recent work collecting narratives of microdosing. He is the most companionable of conversationalists. Even when talking about his own life, he makes room for questions and opinions. For a man who does so many interviews and speaks in public so often, he seems uninvested in listening to the sound of his own voice. He asks questions in a nonjudgmental way that encourages confidences. He seems trustworthy and, above all, *interested.* Though, honestly, how do I really know that? I've only interviewed the man a few times. Maybe his daughters complain that he monopolizes the conversation and never evinces any interest in what they have to say. For all I know he might have given them a box of tapes of himself droning on to his therapist about forced collectivization in the Ukraine.

---

*Frustrated at never being able to figure out which silver Prius was mine, I put a second Obama sticker on the bumper, because having only one made it indistinguishable from the rest. I suppose, if I really wanted to make it easier to find, I'd slap a National Rifle Association sticker on it.

Fadiman told me that when the International Foundation for Advanced Study shut its doors, he began a career as a successful management consultant, working for companies like Lockheed, Dow Chemical, and Foster's Freeze on human resources issues. He cofounded the Institute of Transpersonal Psychology, now known as Sofia University, focused on integrating concepts of spirituality and transcendence with emotional and personal development. He published textbooks and even a novel. He was invited frequently to lecture on the topic of his early psychedelic research, but he was not part of the psychedelic underground, not a member of any of the groups of sixties "psychonauts" who continued to experiment with various mind-altering drugs. He wrote, he taught, he lectured, and he worked.

And then, in 2008, Fadiman was invited to Chicago to give a lecture about the history of psychedelic research. There he met a woman he refers to as "Madeline," whose narrative of microdosing he included in *The Psychedelic Explorer's Guide*. Madeline worked, took care of her children, was a partner to her spouse, all while consuming tiny doses of LSD. She had been regularly microdosing with LSD for years, taking the drug on average six days out of every month, sometimes more if she was working on "a project requiring extraordinary focus." Madeline came to microdosing on her own, without guidance, but eventually she learned what Fadiman had already, that Albert Hofmann himself had regularly microdosed for the last decades of his long life.

Fadiman found out about Hofmann's novel use of the drug from one of his neighbors in Santa Cruz, a man named Robert Forte. According to Forte, Hofmann believed that, had Sandoz Pharmaceuticals been willing, they could have brought to market a version of LSD in a small dose that could have competed with stimulants like Ritalin and Adderall. Imagine a world where frazzled school counselors call parents to say, "Listen, we really think you need to put your kid on LSD." Terence McKenna, an ethnobotanist and psychedelic lecturer, also reported that

Hofmann had informed him that he made a regular practice of microdosing—particularly, Hofmann apparently said, when walking among "tall trees."*

After meeting Madeline, Fadiman learned about another individual who was interested in experimenting with microdosing. It was then that he decided to put together a protocol that would both maximize the safety of the practice and encourage some kind of tracking of experiences. Noticing that people reported that the day after microdosing was often even better than the first day, Fadiman developed the three-day model. The third day, what I call "Normal Day," is not, Fadiman says, strictly necessary. It does, however, provide a recurring set point to better evaluate the effectiveness of the experience. It also reduces the chances of developing a tolerance to the drug.

There are others who believe there are good reasons for taking a break from regular microdosing. Tim Ferriss, for example, sounds a word of caution about the practice. "There is very rarely a biological free lunch," he told me. His concern stems from the fact that LSD and other psychedelics are serotonin receptor agonists, meaning they activate serotonin, much as SSRIs such as Prozac do, though the mechanism is different. Ferriss believes that it's certainly possible that, like SSRIs, low-dose psychedelics can make people feel better, but he worries that they might also have an impact on the brain's own serotonin production in some as-yet-unanticipated manner. Ferriss's concern with microdosing is that extended use might cause tolerance to develop and endogenous production of serotonin to be thrown out of whack. However, when I raised this concern with a psychopharmacolo-

---

*Interestingly, research shows that walking in nature, especially among tall trees, reduces anxiety and depression as effectively as SSRIs (Rachel Hine, Carly Wood, and Jo Barton, *Ecominds: Effects on Mental Wellbeing, an Evaluation for Mind* [London: Mind, 2013]). The Japanese even have a name for this: *shinrin-yoku,* or "forest bathing." Their Ministry of Health encourages it as a stress reliever; to my knowledge, they've yet to weigh in on the added benefit of a tiny dose of a psychedelic drug.

gist friend, though he agreed that it was possible, he downplayed the risk. This is not, he said, a problem unique to LSD microdosing. David Presti agreed: "Whatever risk there is, is likely to be less than those associated with antidepressant medication use for extended periods of time." Presti pointed out that there is evidence that over the long term SSRIs themselves actually deplete serotonin, and yet those for whom antidepressants are effective are rarely discouraged from taking them for extended periods. Still, the specter of tolerance and of long-term effects on serotonin production makes Normal Day seem like a good idea, even if it's my least favorite day of the protocol. And my kids', although they don't know why.

Since the 2011 publication of Fadiman's book, he told me, he has received approximately three hundred requests for his protocol. Of those, he has received back fifty reports of varying length and specificity. The reports have been sent in from all over the world. The majority of people microdose with either LSD or psilocybin, but he's received reports from people using other psychedelic drugs, including ayahuasca, iboga, and even a plant called Syrian Rue. Fadiman showed me a heaping cardboard box of documents, and said he had another just like it at home in Palo Alto. Some people write long narratives; others create charts and track specific behaviors and characteristics. Some keep elaborate journals. Some, like me, do a combination. Fadiman is not quite sure what to do with all these personal and idiosyncratic reports. It's difficult to compare the very different documents and the experiences they recount in order to draw any real conclusions. But he's trying at least to summarize the data.

I asked Fadiman if he had received any reports of negative reactions, either emotional or physical, to microdosing. He told me that, of those who have sent in reports, two people stopped the protocol mid-month, one because of extreme fatigue on Days 2 and 3 (Transition Day and Normal Day), and one because of what Fadiman describes as "an abrupt change in life situation." He advised two others to stop when they reported negative reactions, and discouraged the experimentation of a person with bipolar disorder and sleep issues. We can't know what number of the three hundred or so people who solicited the protocol but failed to follow up with a report attempted microdosing. It seems likely to me that at least some might have failed to follow up because they had a bad experience and chose not to continue with the full thirty days.*

Other than those few negative experiences, the reports Fadiman has received back are overwhelmingly positive. People described a series of benefits, which Fadiman separates into four categories: emotion, intellect, relationships, and physical. Emotional benefits included reductions in anxiety, elevations in mood, increases in equanimity, and feelings of being open, accepting, and happier. Intellectual benefits included improved focus, the ability to sustain creativity for longer stretches, and more effective problem-solving. People reported that their relationships improved. They didn't have as many conflicts with the people in their lives, and some claimed to be more likable, more popular with colleagues and friends. I found the physical benefits Fadiman collected oddest of all. One woman insisted that her painful, irregular periods became less painful and grew more regular. Some people reported gradually finding themselves more willing to exercise and eat well. When I heard this, I joked to Fadiman that if he were to figure out some way to market the protocol as a weight loss tool he'd never have to worry about money again. Too bad I've not experienced that effect

---

*In an odd coincidence, on the way home from Fadiman's house, I just happened to be listening to an episode of a podcast called *Reply All,* in which a producer and one of the hosts attempted their own weeklong microdose experiment, with decidedly mixed results. They initially experienced some benefits, but soon became anxious and uncomfortable about keeping the protocol a secret from their colleagues. If my kids are suspicious of my newfound good spirits, I can only imagine how quickly grown podcast employees might catch on. One of the producers became more animated than normal, even hypomanic. He also managed, one day, to take a double dose, which meant he was out of the range of the sub-perceptual and into the perceptual. He did this on a day when he was taking a long and dull road trip. Set and setting, people—they're everything when it comes to drug experimentation.

myself. I'm not exercising any more than before—though, come to think of it, I'm not indulging as often as usual in things like Dolly's Naughty Cream doughnuts. Perhaps that's because of the slight stimulating effects of the microdose, though that wouldn't explain why this effect sustains through Transition Day and Normal Day. However it's working, I'm eating fewer doughnuts though I'm managing to maintain my muffin top.

There were other unusual results reported to Fadiman. One individual claimed to have quit smoking after a five-year pack-a-day habit. Six cycles of the protocol was all it took, and the positive behavior sustained for eight months and counting. Another stopped smoking marijuana. Three stopped using Adderall. An individual with Parkinson's disease reported that, though symptoms of the disease continued unabated, the person felt much less depressed than before attempting the protocol. Someone else passed a driver's test after failing twice before. A stutterer experienced gradual but noticeable alleviation of symptoms. Most of all, a lot of people had a lot of really good days.

Fadiman considers his project to be a form of crowd-sourced field research, similar to a Phase Two clinical study, attempting to determine if the drug at this dose level provides any benefits. But what's missing, of course, is a Phase One clinical study, to assess safety. Fadiman feels that the established safety of LSD and psilocybin at much more significant doses makes this less of a concern. I'm conservative and anxious by nature, and though I'm not worried enough not to do the experiment (or perhaps it's better to say that I'm desperate enough to do it), I'm still not entirely comfortable. Furthermore, especially given the lack of controls, it's possible that all these reports prove for certain is the power of the placebo effect. I wish I could participate in a formal double-blind control-group study, not this ad-hoc crowd-sourced experience.*

---

*Of course, government approval and clinical supervision hardly guarantee safety, as we learned in January 2016, when one person died and five others were hospitalized during a clinical trial of a French pharmaceutical meant to treat anxiety, motor disorders, and chronic pain.

Fadiman is eager for formal medical and psychiatric research into microdosing, both with psilocybin and with LSD. He has recently been contacted by two individuals, one in Australia and one in Europe, who seek to carry out just this research. The Australian, a graduate student, wants simply to systematize the same kind of self-reporting that Fadiman is doing, with people following a common reporting system, though still sourcing their own drugs and operating independently of clinical supervision. The student cannot, he says, get governmental permission for anything else. The European researcher, however, plans a formalized clinical study of the possible benefits of microdosing, using a double-blind model with a control group. This researcher believes that the current European resurgence of interest in psychedelic research makes approval likely.

Some American scientists with whom I spoke doubt the likelihood of having such a study approved in the United States. The FDA would be troubled, they say, by any such study's "ambulatory" nature. They don't believe that an institution would be willing to seek approval for a study that dosed participants with a Schedule I substance and then sent them out into the world effectively under the influence. Other American scientists, however, disagree. They point out that researchers send people out into the world dosed with medications that we know compromise their abilities to function in all sorts of ways. We give people high doses of opioids, for example, sometimes sending them home with supplies of the drugs to self-administer. Furthermore, were that the only issue, an inpatient study could easily be crafted. These scientists believe that, given the success of the psilocybin studies at UCLA, NYU, and Johns Hopkins, it is possible, even likely, that we will see a microdosing study in the future. I hope so, and I hope my family history and my own ad-hoc experiment don't preclude my participation.

The psychedelic researchers I interviewed expressed more interest in how microdosing can increase functioning and well-being in healthy people than in its potential antidepressant benefits. Their curiosity has been piqued by reports of Silicon Valley executives and engineers who have started microdosing as a way to improve productivity and encourage creative thinking at work. Microdosing has become something of a performance-enhancing mini-trend in the tech world, enough of one to justify an inundation of articles in magazines and online extolling its virtues.* According to *Rolling Stone* magazine, the typical micro-doser is not, in fact, a middle-aged mom of four hoping to be less of a raging bitch, but an "übersmart twentysomething curious to see whether microdosing will help him or her work through technical problems and become more innovative."†

Users have begun to embrace microdosing as an alternative to the cognitive-enhancing drugs that are ubiquitous on college campuses and in Silicon Valley.‡ Stimulants such as Ritalin, Adderall, and modafinil are popular because they do in fact increase productivity and focus. However, they've been linked to decreases in neuroplasticity, likely as a result of the way they flood neural networks with dopamine, glutamate, and norepinephrine. Psychedelics enhance neuroplasticity, which makes them a compelling alternative. According to one of *Rolling Stone's* übersmart twentysomething microdosers, "Microdosing has helped me come up with some new designs to explore and new ways of thinking."

Hey, I was a techbro all along, and just didn't know it! Next time you see me, I'll be wearing a hoodie, sipping a steaming mug of "bulletproof butter coffee," and railing about the gross homeless dude pissing in the doorway of my four-and-a-half-million-dollar condo in the Mission.

All joking aside, 1960s-era research, though inconclusive and anecdotal, did seem to indicate that psychedelic drugs can

---

* See, e.g., Robert Glatter, M.D., "LSD Microdosing: The New Job Enhancer in Silicon Valley and Beyond?"; Chris Gayomali, "Forget Coffee, Silicon Valley's New Productivity Hack Is 'Microdoses' of LSD"; etc., etc., ad nauseam.
† Andrew Leonard, "How LSD Microdosing Became the Hot New Business Trip."
‡ What some people call "nootropics."

improve cognition and creativity. According to Fadiman, his study showed that, for his subjects, "in almost every case, new or unnoticed aspects of their problems opened up novel avenues toward solutions. Emotional residue from prior unsuccessful attempts no longer hindered their creative flexibility." The question certainly bears further research, though as someone who came to this experience from a place of suffering, who has sought and failed to get help using established treatment models, and who, moreover, has little interest in the recreational use of drugs or even their performance-enhancing qualities, I hope that the therapeutic value of microdosing doesn't get muffled beneath the desperate hysteria to work better, stronger, faster.

Day 17

....

Transition Day

Physical Sensations: None.

Mood: Contented.

Conflict: None.

Sleep: More than eight hours!

Work: Productive.

Pain: None!

Today, when my husband was eating his breakfast, I walked up behind him, slipped my arms around his shoulders, kissed him, and said, "I know you love me." And I left it at that. Even inside my mind.

He pressed his head into my belly, and I felt his shoulders relax beneath my arms. This poor, patient man. I love him so much. And you know what? He really does love me. Of course he does. I'm not a terrible person who doesn't deserve to be loved. I'm the woman who is crazy about him, who laughs at his jokes, even his *puns*, who delights in his company. More than that, I'm not actually unlovable. Sure, I'm volatile and mercurial, but I'm also fun. Yes, I'm occasionally bitchy, but I'm also sweet. I'm opinionated, but I'm willing to admit when I'm wrong. It is suddenly so obvious that what I need to do is just get out of my own way and enjoy my marriage and my life.

My mood was so good today that I found myself able to

approach with patience a book that I had up until now barely succeeded in paging through, let alone reading. *Be Here Now*— written, as the title page states, by "Dr. Richard Alpert, Ph.D., into Baba Ram Dass"—is printed primarily on butcher paper, with text that is not black but a pale blue that, depending on my mood, I find either insipid or soothing. One typical page is nothing more than a drawing of a mandala surrounded by the phrase "From Bindu to Ojas." There are sketches of Indian gods and instructions to the reader that "The energy is the same thing as Cosmic Consciousness" or "Energy = Love = Awareness = Light = Wisdom = Beauty = Truth = Purity." I have no idea what any of this means. When Ram Dass writes, "When I'm with the guru, there's nobody home," I can't help sympathizing. When I am with this book, there's nobody home. Until today.

With my newfound equanimity, I find myself willing to entertain the possibility that the problem is not the book's but mine. *Be Here Now* is considered one of the most influential volumes of psychedelic spiritual literature. Certainly, the first section, in which the author details his early research and experiences with LSD, is relevant to my project, if only because it describes an important moment in the history of the drug's promulgation. Moreover, I am, like Richard Alpert, "a good, Jewish, middleclass, upwardly mobile, anxiety-ridden neurotic." There are things I can learn from this book, if only I am able to stop rolling my eyes at lines about "the big ice cream cone in the sky" or how "if you are PURE SPIRIT you are *not* matter!"

In the early 1960s, Ram Dass writes, his name was Richard Alpert and he was an assistant professor of social science at Harvard who had research contracts with Yale and Stanford. The invocation of these three most illustrious of institutions is meant, I know, to reassure and impress the most anxious of readers. Despite having gone to law school at Harvard,* and thus

---

*Harvard Law School is known to alumni and others as *the* Law School, as if no others exist.

being fully cognizant of the essential similarity of the university to every other competitive institution, to my embarrassment I am in fact reassured and impressed. The mere fact that many of the early LSD pioneers in the United States attended or taught at Harvard establishes their credibility, doesn't it?* At Harvard in the mid-1960s, Alpert teamed up with Timothy Leary, a clinical-psychology lecturer and expert in the field of the quantitative assessment of personality, with a Ph.D. from Berkeley, whom Alpert describes as having recently "been bicycling around Italy, bouncing checks."† Leary, who had had a profound mystical experience while taking psilocybin in the form of what Alpert calls "Tionanactyl, the flesh of the Gods, the Magic Mushrooms of Mexico," had set up the Harvard Psilocybin Project along with (among others) Aldous Huxley, who was then a visiting professor at MIT. In addition to studying psilocybin. Leary had acquired a quantity of LSD‡ and was, Alpert writes, "busy taking it and administering it." Alpert eagerly joined in on both the self-experimentation and the research.

Among Leary and Alpert's research projects was the 1961 Concord Prison Experiment, designed to test the effects of psilocybin-assisted group therapy on rates of recidivism. They recruited a group of prisoners with three to five months remaining on their felony prison sentences, and administered the drug in three group-therapy situations, using standard personality tests before and after the therapy to assess the drug's effects. Leary and his team took the drug themselves, along with their subjects, a common practice of theirs.

Leary claimed that the therapy resulted in a marked decrease

* See, e.g., Theodore Kaczynski.

† Leary's sojourn abroad was preceded by the suicide of his wife, his marriage to and divorce from another woman, and the arrest of his thesis adviser and purported lover for solicitation of sex in a public restroom.

‡ By some accounts, a man named Michael Hollingshead, described by one of my sources as a "charming psychopath," gave Leary a mayonnaise jar full of LSD, which he had obtained from a New York City psychiatrist who had himself ordered the drug directly from Sandoz Pharmaceuticals.

in subsequent incarcerations among treated prisoners; however, a thirty-four-year follow-up study by Rick Doblin, the founder and executive director of the Multidisciplinary Association for Psychedelic Studies (MAPS), failed to find any long-term reduction in recidivism. Moreover, Doblin found Leary's original report of the study to be rife with quantitative errors and erroneous conclusions.

During the summer of 1961, Alpert and Leary spoke at an international psychiatry conference in Copenhagen. Their talk was not well received. Some critics called it little more than a muddled and incoherent tribute to psychedelic drugs. In the wake of that conference, a series of critical articles in *The Harvard Crimson* and the *Boston Herald,* a Hearst tabloid, led to an investigation by the Massachusetts Department of Health, which, though it didn't shut the Harvard experiments down, did require that all drugs be administered by a qualified physician. Leary turned his supply of psilocybin over to the student health services (the same place where, thirty years later, I was to have my first, decidedly unpsychedelic, therapy appointment), but he continued to distribute LSD widely to willing volunteers.

The year following the Copenhagen conference, Leary and Alpert supervised the Good Friday Experiment (also known as the Marsh Chapel Experiment), designed by a Harvard Ph.D. candidate in the history and philosophy of religion with a master's from the Harvard Divinity School, Walter N. Pahnke. Meant to evaluate the effects of psilocybin on spiritual experience, the study was intended to be double-blind and controlled. Twenty divinity school students were matched in pairs for religious background and training, past religious experience, and general psychological health, among other factors. Ten were dosed with psilocybin; ten others swallowed capsules of niacin. Ten research assistants were meant to be sober providers of emotional support throughout the period of the test, but, over Pahnke's objections, Leary insisted that they, too, be given psilocybin, albeit a half-dose. That was necessary, Leary claimed, to create a sense of community, but all it accomplished was a muddying of the results.

The test subjects attended a Good Friday service led by a charismatic chaplain. Though observers were not informed which students were controls and which were not, all hope of double-blind neutrality quickly evaporated. The students who were given niacin got a little nauseated, and their faces turned red. The students who were given psilocybin wandered around the chapel talking to God. Many had transcendent mystical experiences that informed the rest of their lives. A long-term follow-up study, again by Rick Doblin, determined that "the experimental subjects unanimously described their Good Friday psilocybin experience as having had elements of a genuinely mystical nature and characterized it as one of the highpoints of their spiritual life."

Leary and Alpert ended up doing battle with the Harvard administration, which was fearful that the two were encouraging the use of "mind-distorting" drugs by students. This was, of course, exactly what they were doing. Leary and Alpert responded to their bosses that there was no evidence that psychedelic drugs were dangerous, that they were in fact "safe and beneficial."* The administration was not persuaded. Leary eventually moved to California and was subsequently fired by Harvard for leaving his job without notice. Alpert was fired for distributing drugs to an undergraduate.

Leary, never overly devoted to the conventional scientific method, eventually rejected clinical inquiry entirely. He became a celebrity and a proselytizer, with a devotion to the cause of spreading the use of psychedelics that can fairly be described as religious. He believed that the drugs could change the world. Those he "turned on" included the Beats, Allen Ginsberg and Jack Kerouac, and three heirs to the Mellon fortune, who provided Leary and Alpert with a mansion in Millbrook, New York, in

*http://www.thecrimson.com/article/1962/12/13/letter-from-alpert-leary-pfollowing-is/.

which to continue spreading the gospel of LSD. Leary said, "We saw ourselves as anthropologists from the twenty-first century inhabiting a time module set somewhere in the dark ages of the 1960s. On this space module we were attempting to create a new paganism and a new dedication to life as art." Hoo boy. Is it any surprise that the local assistant district attorney, a young man named G. Gordon Liddy, became obsessed with busting Leary and his pals?

In addition to Leary and, to a lesser extent, Alpert, there were others responsible in large part for the wide dissemination of LSD beyond therapeutic, mystical, or research contexts. One, Owsley Stanley, is credited with being one of the first private individuals to synthesize the drug, with the help of a young UC Berkeley chemistry major named Melissa Cargill. Owsley produced hundreds of thousands of doses of the drug in 1965 alone. All of this production was, of course, legal: the drug had not yet been criminalized. One of Owsley's customers was a young man who had been introduced to the drug in a CIA-funded drug trial at the Palo Alto Veterans Administration Hospital. Ken Kesey was neither a psychological researcher nor particularly mystically inclined. He was a novelist, the author of *One Flew over the Cuckoo's Nest*, and the leader of a group of acolytes and hangers-on who called themselves the "Merry Pranksters." In 1964, when the publication of Kesey's second book required him to be in New York City, he and his pranksters loaded themselves up onto a Day-Glo-painted school bus and made their way cross-country, tripping all the way.* Tom Wolfe's book about the tour, *The Electric Kool-Aid Acid Test,* is another classic of psychedelic literature.†

In 1965 and 1966, Kesey organized a series of bacchanals he

---

*The survivor of many a publicity tour, I can only say that this isn't the worst solution I've encountered to the malaise of trudging from city to city, flogging one's book.

†And, more important, the inspiration for Dr. Teeth and the Electric Mayhem's bus in *The Muppet Movie.*

called "Acid Tests," featuring music (notably the Grateful Dead), strobe and black lights, and copious amounts of LSD. With these events, the use of psychedelics left the doctor's office and research laboratory and spread widely through the community. At this point, the drug was still legal. In 1967, at the Human Be-In, a "Gathering of the Tribes" in San Francisco's Golden Gate Park, Leary first exhorted the assembled crowds to "turn on, tune in, and drop out." On that day, thirty thousand people tuned in to Jefferson Airplane and the Grateful Dead, and turned on by swallowing thousands of doses of white-lightning LSD that had been prepared for the occasion by Owsley Stanley.

It was that exhortation—"Tune in, turn on, and drop out. Out of high school, junior executive, senior executive. And follow me!"*—that caused the parental panic that led to Senate hearings on campus drug use. Poorly designed and ultimately debunked studies linking LSD to birth defects were trumpeted throughout the media, as were articles with headlines like "Strip Teasing Hippie Goes Wild in Larkspur on LSD." Whereas the media had once published long interviews with, for example, Cary Grant on the personal insights and increased happiness he experienced as a result of LSD-based therapy, now *Life* magazine devoted a cover story to "The exploding threat of the mind drug that got out of control." Significant fuel was added to the prohibitionist fire because, without adequate care to monitor set and setting in order to protect users, people began turning up in emergency rooms, seeking out medical care for "bad trips." After hundreds, even thousands of panicked articles and television and radio news stories, the reputation of psychedelics was destroyed. In 1970, Nixon signed the Controlled Substances Act, putting LSD, psilocybin, and other psychedelics on Schedule I, and launching the War on Drugs with a punitive ferocity that has only just recently begun to abate.

* Robert Greenfield, *Timothy Leary: A Biography,* p. 302.

Leary was eventually arrested crossing the border into Mexico. The charge? The possession of half an ounce of marijuana, found in a locket around his daughter's neck.* While appeal of that case was pending, he was arrested again, also for marijuana possession, this time an even smaller amount. He did not, however, spend much time in prison. With the help of the Weather Underground, he escaped from the California Men's Colony at San Luis Obispo, and was smuggled to Algeria, where he came under the protection of Eldridge Cleaver. He then made his way circuitously to Kabul, but before he deplaned there he was arrested by an FBI agent. To mitigate his twenty-five-year sentence, Leary became a witness for the government in an investigation of the Weather Underground, though the information he provided was of very little value.

Meanwhile, Alpert traveled to India, where he became a follower of the Hindu guru Neem Karoli Baba, who gave him his new name. Ram Dass, unlike Leary, did not devote himself to encouraging the widespread use of psychedelics. His focus turned to spirituality, though of course his interest in the latter stemmed in part from his experiences with the former. In 1971, Ram Dass published *Be Here Now,* the book that, despite my newfound patience, I am still finding impenetrable. It is at this point that the difference between the two men becomes most striking. As my friend Ian Faloona, a climatologist and experienced meditator, put it to me, Leary and Ram Dass represent "a classic paradigm of two different paths to the ultimate reality. One gets bamboozled by the powers and tricks of the altered states, and one keeps in touch with his heart, exercising it with all his power, to go beyond the realm of smoke and phantasmagoria. As Rumi said, 'Love is the astrolabe of the mysteries of God.'"

On December 11, 1965, the day I celebrated my first birthday, one of Kesey's Acid Test parties took place in Muir Beach, the

*Or in her underwear. Reports differ.

bucolic town in which I am writing these very words. I wonder if the elderly couple from whom Ian and his wife bought the little homemade cottage they have lent me attended that Acid Test so many decades ago. If so, did they drink the spiked punch? Did they dance all night on the sand? And how did they make it up the steep stairs from the beach to their little shack clinging to the side of the hillside? I can barely manage it sober.

I am so *not* "merry," so opposed on principle to "pranksters." Nothing in this world irritates me so much as a "free spirit." I can't abide when people shirk their responsibilities, when they act without contemplation of the consequences, when they prioritize fun and freedom above all else. Don't even get me started on people who just won't stay to their right while ascending and descending perilous public staircases. For a Jewish girl, I'm quite a puritan. Though I'm enough of a libertarian to believe people have the right to ingest whatever they want, in whatever asinine way they choose, I believe that it is best to experiment with psychedelics thoughtfully and carefully. I can't think of anywhere I would have less liked to be than one of Kesey's parties. And, yes, I know that, given the extent of my antipathy, it is more than a little ironic that I ended up doing my own private electric Kool-Aid acid test.

It is also ironic—given how disparaging I am of those who use drugs in a manner I consider careless, and how uncomfortable I am being associated with them—that the scientists currently doing FDA- and DEA-sanctioned research on the benefits of psychedelic drugs by and large feel the same way about me.* Though many psychedelic researchers agreed to be interviewed for this book, few would let me quote them, even anonymously. Most feared that any association with a "personal experiment" with illegally sourced drugs would tarnish their hard-won credibility.

Their concern, by the way, is not unfounded. Drug-policy reform organizations have, in my experience, also worked very

---

*Perhaps this is not irony but, rather, poetic justice.

hard to distance themselves from the specter of psychonauts like Leary and Kesey. When I was a consultant for the Drug Policy Alliance, my colleagues were rigorously analytical attorneys, many of whom had never even tried illegal drugs. They were activists on the issue of drug policy reform because American drug policy has been a catastrophe for poor people and people of color, because they were patriotic devotees of the United States Constitution, and because they believed that the power to dictate what a person does with her consciousness should never belong to the government, even if the only thing they themselves had ever done to alter their consciousnesses was to attempt to come to grips with the rule against perpetuities. The students in my seminar on drug policy were by and large similarly motivated, as was my co-instructor. Certainly, the various organizations and individuals on whose behalf I have written amicus briefs on a wide range of drug policy issues have been models of propriety. All these people are fighting for *your* right to party, not their own.

Many of the standard-bearers of the fight for the reform of the laws pertaining to psychedelics are similarly thoughtful, reasonable, and circumspect. Jim Fadiman is, in my experience, a lion of good sense and levelheadedness. The Multidisciplinary Association for Psychedelic Studies (MAPS), which is, like the Heffter Research Institute, a prominent and well-known funder of psychedelic research, has the most reasonable of mission statements. It reads: "We envision a world where psychedelics and marijuana are safely and legally available for beneficial uses, and where research is governed by rigorous scientific evaluation of their risks and benefits." The founder of MAPS, Rick Doblin, has a Ph.D. from Harvard's Kennedy School of Government* and has done thorough and critical follow-up studies of early psychedelic research.

---

*Harvard! Again! You might be forgiven for wondering what the heck's going on there.

Though Fadiman, Doblin, and others are open about having used psychedelic drugs, this does not, to my mind, render them unreliable or discredit their work. True, their interest in the therapeutic use of psychedelic drugs stems from their own transformative personal experiences,* but I imagine the same can be said of psychotherapists, most of whom have themselves gone through therapy as part of their training. All the practitioners by whom I've been treated have made personal use of the skills they taught me. My mindfulness-based therapist meditated, my cognitive behavioral therapist cultivated her own psychological flexibility, redirected her thoughts and behaviors, and used nonviolent communication. I have no idea if my psychopharmacologist took psychiatric medications, but with all those samples lying around, how likely is it that he never tried a little something?

Still, for every sober and sensible Jim Fadiman or Rick Doblin, there's someone like Amanda Feilding, the countess of Wemyss and March, one of the most important funders of research into the therapeutic uses of psychedelics, who in 1970 cheerfully drilled a hole into her skull.

Amanda Feilding believed that trepanation, the opening of the skull to reveal the dura mater, the membrane surrounding the brain, could cure all manner of ills. Boring such a hole, she wrote, increases cranial blood volume, allowing access to a higher state of consciousness. Feilding was such a firm believer in the beneficial powers of trepanation that she made a movie of herself drilling a hole in her skull with a dentist's drill. Her guru in this madness? One Bart Hughes, a librarian by trade.

And yet the countess, wearer of floppy hats, owner of fluffy dogs, and survivor of DIY brain surgery, created and funds the Beckley Foundation, named after her estate. This charitable trust devoted to drug policy reform has done tremendously im-

---

*As did Hofmann's, as well as that of other early proponents of LSD-enhanced psychotherapy, such as Stanislav Grof.

portant work, supporting scientific research and initiatives, including studies at University College London on the potential therapeutic effects of cannabis, and at Johns Hopkins University on the usefulness of psilocybin in treating nicotine and other drug addiction. At Imperial College London, the Beckley Foundation is currently funding a study using BOLD (blood-oxygen-level dependent) fMRI to measure the effects of psilocybin on brain activity. Though horrified by the holes in Feilding's head, I'm impressed with her foundation's endeavors, and with her persistence in pursuing the scientific study of psychedelics. I believe that, without her tenacity, we would not currently be experiencing the resurgence of interest in studying the benefits of these drugs. She has, in addition to perseverance, the gift of convincing others to join her efforts. An open letter from the Beckley Foundation calling for an end to the global war on drugs was signed by dozens of people, including, among others, Nobel Prize winners and presidents from around the world.

F. Scott Fitzgerald once said, "The test of a first-rate intelligence is the ability to hold two opposed ideas in mind at the same time and still retain the ability to function." If that is the case, then surely one shouldn't condemn someone merely because one (or a dozen) of those ideas is bat-shit crazy. Still, I find it disconcerting to watch a video of a pretty young woman with whom I share an agenda, both personal and political, drilling a hole in her head and reveling in the resulting "expanded consciousness." Nothing makes me embrace my constricted consciousness more than the sight of the blood running into her smile.

Day 18

....

Normal Day
Physical Sensations: None.
Mood: Even-tempered. Pleasant.
Conflict: None.
Sleep: Adequate. Seven Hours.
Work: Remarkably productive.
Pain: Minor.

It's a relief to have another Normal Day that feels so good. I was worried that the microdose of LSD was having the effect of making Microdose Day happy but activated (raising fears of hypomania), Transition Day marvelous, and Normal Day unreliable. But today was a really good day, and I'm under the influence of nothing at all.

As someone who never took a math class after eleventh grade, and who satisfied her college natural-science distribution requirement with a class called The Origins of Human Sexual Behavior, I find it remarkable not only that I spent this really good day reading complicated articles in scientific journals, the results of the various psilocybin studies that are currently in process at UCLA, Johns Hopkins, and NYU, but that I found them so fascinating.

Though my microdosing experiment shares little with these research projects—my dose is a fraction of the ones being studied, and their goals are far more ambitious than the slight mood modification I seek—these studies are compelling and instructive. Moreover, they have relieved any residual anxieties I had about the safety of my project. It's encouraging that legitimate researchers whose approving institutions demand careful consideration of all risks are comfortable administering much higher doses of a drug that operates nearly identically to and is no more or less dangerous than LSD. I will die eventually, but it's not going to be from two drops of diluted acid every three days.

After a long hiatus, approval for human-subject research on psychedelic drugs was given by the FDA. The first such study was with the drug N,N-Dimethyltryptamine (DMT) at the University of New Mexico, conducted by Rick Strassman and published in 1994. Since then, clinical research has slowly and carefully resumed. In the first human study addressing a clinical use (a so-called Phase Two clinical protocol), the researcher Charles S. Grob, M.D., and his colleagues at Harbor-UCLA Medical Center investigated whether psilocybin could reduce anxiety, depression, and pain in patients with terminal cancer. Annie Levy, one of the participants in this twelve-subject pilot study, a middle-aged woman with short gray curls and large, luminous eyes, recalled that before the study began she was anxious and terrified. She had lost her faith, was being irritable with her husband. "I was worried about the process of dying, about suffering and being in pain."

In a room decorated with purple fabric wall hangings and fresh orchids, Annie and the other research subjects were given .2mg/kg of psilocybin, a moderate dose sufficient to make them feel the effects of the drug.* Annie lay in bed, wearing an eye mask and listening to music. Afterward, she told an interviewer, "As soon as it started working, I knew I had nothing to be afraid

---

*Charles S. Grob et al., "Pilot Study of Psilocybin Treatment for Anxiety in Patients with Advanced-Stage Cancer."

of, because it connected me with the universe." She recounted a remarkable emotional experience. "I was lying on this hospital bed and it felt like the bed had turned into this circle of hands that was holding me. I was being supported."

Her husband recalled that when they returned home "it was like someone had put on a lightbulb inside of Annie's head. She was literally glowing."

At the conclusion of the experience (approximately six hours after consuming the dose), Annie and the other subjects were evaluated and given the opportunity to discuss and process their experiences with a trained researcher. They continued to meet with the researcher periodically over the next six months—for discussion only, not for further drug treatment. None of the subjects experienced any negative physical or emotional consequences of the psilocybin. On the contrary, their despair and anxiety were substantially alleviated. The effects on Annie of this single psychedelic experience lasted until her death in 2009. Her remaining days were, more often than not, really good days.

Researchers at Johns Hopkins and NYU, also working with subjects diagnosed with terminal cancer, have used higher doses of psilocybin and seen similarly striking results. The author Michael Pollan, in an insightful and thoroughly researched article published in *The New Yorker,* interviewed researchers and subjects of both the NYU and Johns Hopkins studies. Stephen Ross, the lead scientist at NYU, told him: "I thought the first ten or twenty people were plants—that they must be faking it. They were saying things like 'I understand love is the most powerful force on the planet,' or 'I had an encounter with my cancer, this black cloud of smoke.' People who had been palpably scared of death—they lost their fear. The fact that a drug given once can have such an effect for so long is an unprecedented finding. We have never had anything like it in the psychiatric field."

The results are remarkable, as is the excitement of the researchers involved. What I find particularly interesting, however, is their focus. Their interest is specifically in the mystical experience engendered by psilocybin, which is what they believe inspires the dramatic reduction of anxiety and depression and the increase in well-being. Roland Griffiths, the psychopharmacologist in charge of the Johns Hopkins Medical School studies, came to the research, he told an interviewer, after meditation "opened up a spiritual window" for him and made him "curious about the nature of mystical experience and spiritual transformation."[*] As Pollan wrote, "Griffiths believes that the long-term effectiveness of the drug is due to its ability to occasion ... a transformative experience, but not by changing the brain's long-term chemistry, as a conventional psychiatric drug like Prozac does."

Similarly, the insights engendered by psilocybin-induced mystical experiences are theorized to be behind the remarkable recent results in studies on alcohol and tobacco addiction. The initial success of these studies should, perhaps, be no surprise, given the overtly spiritual nature of the most popular treatment for alcoholism: Alcoholics Anonymous. Most people know that the Twelve Step program instructs people to seek aid from a "higher power" in overcoming dependence. Few are aware, however, that AA was founded on a drug-induced mystical experience.

In 1934, Bill W., cofounder of AA, was treated for his alcoholism with a hallucinogenic belladonna alkaloid. The resulting mystical experience led him to become sober and inspired him to write the book and cofound the organization that have changed the lives of so many millions around the world. In the 1950s, Bill W. underwent LSD therapy, and found his experience so inspiring that he sought to have the drug made part of the AA program. His board of directors overruled him. More than half a century later, it appears that Bill W. is finally being vindicated.[†]

---

[*] David Jay Brown and Louise Reitman, "Psilocybin Studies and the Religious Experience: An Interview with Roland Griffiths, Ph.D."

[†] Perhaps if the board had been more open-minded AA might have provided a more effective treatment. Critics of AA estimate its actual success rate at somewhere between 5 and 8 percent. See, e.g., Lance M. Dodes and Zachary Dodes, *The Sober Truth.*

Though microdosing causes no mystical experiences, I am drawn to these studies, not because I am by nature a spiritual person, but because I am a skeptic. I am an atheist who believes that religion in all its forms is a delusion, occasionally benign, more often vicious, violent, and cruel. I was raised in this belief as some are raised in the belief in God. In my home, atheism was a dogma as rigid as evangelical Christianity or Wahhabist Islam. The most religious of Jewish parents sometimes tell their children that if they marry non-Jews the parents will "sit shiva" for them; they will cut off contact and mourn them as if they are dead. My father once told me that if I rejected the atheism with which I was brought up and became an Orthodox Jew, he would sit shiva for me.

When reading accounts by LSD explorers, you can't avoid the tales of their spiritual awakenings. When Ram Dass was a young man, he described himself just as I describe myself: "Inured to religion . . . I didn't have one whiff of God." Psychedelics led him to gain access to the divine, as they led Aldous Huxley and even the sober Swiss chemist Albert Hofmann. Jim Fadiman writes of "Spiritual Journeys," and the importance of the spiritual in his own life.

I keep asking the psychonauts and researchers I interview if they believe that the mystical experiences that transform the lives of people with end-stage cancer and the lives of Harvard professors like Ram Dass are *real*. When Aldous Huxley writes in *The Doors of Perception* that psychedelic drugs gave him "a glimpse of the unbearable splendour of ultimate Reality," does that ultimate reality exist outside himself, or was he just suffering from a delusion that it did? Isn't it more likely that the many people from various religious traditions who use psychedelics to gain access to the divine are merely confusing brain-centered hallucinations with God? Most of the time, the reply I get is "What difference does it make?" If the experience is transformative, why do I care so much about whether it is "real"? What do I even mean by "real"?

I was going on at perhaps tiresome length to my husband about how frustrating I find those anti-ontological, circular answers to rational questions, when I noticed a peculiar expression on his face.

"What?" I said.

"It's not like you've never had spiritual experiences," he said.

I bristled. "I have never in my life had a spiritual experience," I said. "Never."

"Uh-huh," he said blandly.

"What?"

"Esalen?"

"Oh, yeah," I said. "Esalen."

Esalen Institute, a "holistic learning and retreat center" in Big Sur, is a place where you can go on a "modern day vision quest," take a class in the "Energetics of Consciousness," or study the "Alchemy of Love and Aliveness." It is an overtly spiritual place, where meditation and yoga first gained a foothold in the West. It's also where many of the early researchers into the therapeutic uses of LSD and other psychedelics gathered to exchange information and insight. So what was I, the condescending rationalist, doing at Esalen? I could spin some yarn about how Big Sur, on the Central Coast of California, where the Santa Lucia Mountains drop abruptly into the Pacific, is one of the most beautiful places on earth. I could blame it on how much I love a good massage (Esalen hosts one of the best massage schools in the world). I could describe the stunningly beautiful hot baths, cantilevered out over the crashing surf below. I could complain about how hard it is to find a reasonably priced place to hole up and write, especially one that feeds you three delicious, wholesome meals a day made from food plucked from the garden. All that is true, but it's not the whole truth.

The truth is that part of me has for a long time been in a tentative rebellion against my parents' credo.

About a dozen years ago, when I went to Esalen, I told myself that I was depressed and stressed out, and needed time to be alone and to work. But the truth is, I was looking for something more. I spent my first two days as I would have expected to: working, eating, soaking in the hot tubs, taking ecstatic-dance (silly but fun) and yoga classes. On the third day, I woke up, danced myself into a sweat, had some breakfast, and then wandered out to the meditation yurt. I settled myself on a pillow in front of a window. Outside the window was a little canyon leading to the sea, its banks blanketed by orange flowers. I looked out at the view for a while, marveling at how pretty it was, the contrast between the flowers and the green grass, the deep-blue sky and the gray surf.

Then I closed my eyes. For about fifteen of the next twenty minutes, I alternated between cataloguing my anxieties and haranguing myself for my inability to clear my mind. Finally, exhausted by self-reproach, I just kind of zoned out. When the alarm buzzed, I opened my eyes and looked out into the canyon. The orange flowers glowed; their petals shimmered in the sunshine. And then, with a trembling rush, they took flight.

They weren't flowers but monarch butterflies, thousands upon thousands of them. They had rested still for the entire twenty minutes of my meditation, and then they rewarded me with a swirl of sudden, unexpected beauty. It felt as if someone or something had decided to show me that the world is filled with grace, and that I need only open my eyes to see it. It felt, though it pains me to say it, like a gift from the divine.

I wish I could say that I was so inspired by that experience that from that moment on I meditated every day. My depression lifted a little, but it didn't fly away. For a while, I could raise my spirits just by closing my eyes and thinking about the butterflies. But soon enough I stopped thinking of the experience as a divine gift, and instead dismissed it as a delightful coincidence. The monarchs, migrating from the Rockies to their winter home in Mexico, just happened to stop for a rest in that little hollow between the hills, and I just happened to open my eyes as they, rejuvenated, took wing. Just as it is hard for me to believe that my husband is not making a terrible mistake by loving me, it is hard for me to believe that some larger force in the universe wrangled that butterfly show just for me.

But I have always sworn that the thing I believe in more than anything else is my own fallibility. If I'm not to be a hypocrite, then I think I must at least explore the possibility that it is I who am blind, not the psychedelic researchers. Surely, it's possible that Aldous Huxley's Doors of Perception might open to admit a spiritual experience even to the likes of me? If the author of *Brave New World* believed in the "Dharma-Body of the Buddha," who is the author of *Death Gets a Timeout* to sneer?

There are so many things I believe in that are ephemeral, and I don't mean atoms and quarks. The most profoundly important thing in my life cannot be quantified or photographed. It lacks all substance, yet I not only believe in it but govern my life by it. The love I feel for my husband and my children is entirely intangible but absolutely "real." If I can love so deeply and so *specifically*—this man, not any other—if I can believe that this love is as real as the hands that type on this keyboard, if I can wrap my mind around love, why do I have such a hard time wrapping my mind around the concept of a greater spiritual meaning to life beyond our corporeal existences?

Is my mind opening? Is the microdose responsible? Or is it merely a result of being exposed to the writing and research of so many philosophers and scientists, to being immersed in this psychedelic world? I don't know the answer. All I know is that something feels like it's shifting in me. Who knows? I may end up publishing these notes scribbled in blue crayon on recycled grocery bags, replete with illustrations of mandalas and all-caps exhortations to create the CALM CENTER and BE HERE NOW.

Day 19

....

Microdose Day

*Physical Sensations: Nauseated and flushed.
    Diarrhea.*

Mood: Activated. Maybe even a little agitated.

*Conflict: Feeling a bit irritable but managed to
    tamp it down.*

*Sleep: Restless. Woke early but eventually fell
    back asleep.*

Work: A solid day's work.

Pain: None.

Microdose Day is fun and productive, but sometimes it has an edge. Senses are ever so slightly heightened, which can be pleasurable, but does incline me to a version of my infamous irritability, albeit a mellower one. My husband and I have a test we do to evaluate how irritable I am. I sit in the living room, he stands two rooms away in the kitchen, and he chomps on some almonds. I have a severe nut-noise allergy. If the sound of his chewing makes me feel like running into the kitchen to throttle him, then we know I'm a bit more activated than I should be. Today I did not run, nor did I throttle; I just stayed where I was, making a Darth Vader throttling gesture with my hands.

My conclusion? Microdosing makes me both irritable and able to tolerate irritability.

Feeling blinding rage in response to chewing is not (or not merely) a characteristic of being a jerk. It's a syndrome, though one not yet recognized by the *DSM-5*. Misophonia, or selective sound sensitivity syndrome, was first identified by two married neuroscientists, Margaret and Pawel Jastreboff. They proved that something happens in the central nervous system of those of us with misophonia when we hear certain types of sounds, especially ones like slurping, sniffing, throat clearing, gum chewing, whistling, and food chewing. We sweat; our muscles tense. We even experience unwanted sexual arousal.

The last effect is particularly bizarre. I remember once sitting in my law school final exams, being driven mad by a fellow student with a head cold. Even on a good day, I loathed this guy. He was a classic Harvard mansplainer who smirked and rolled his eyes whenever women spoke in class, even the women professors he was paying good money to smirk at. This particular morning, his thin lips were twisted into their usual sneer, but his pinched nose was red and dripping. Every few minutes, he would suck up his mucus with a cacophonous, wet snort. Each time, a wave of rage would course through my body. I felt it in my face, my gut, my arms, my legs. And then, to my horror, the feeling settled into my groin. I was overwhelmed by the urge to flip the hateful jerk over and fuck his disgusting brains out. The feeling was, to say the least, disconcerting.

When I was young, my misophonia was primarily triggered by my father, though, fortunately, without the gruesome erotic component. I would sit at the dinner table, my fingers in my ears, trying to muffle the sounds of his chewing. That he tolerated this for an instant, let alone the entire period of my adolescence, gives lie to my claims of his occasional fits of bad temper. Or perhaps his bad moods simply didn't correspond with mealtimes. At any rate, the man deserves a medal, or at least a shout-out, for forbearance.

This morning, after I found myself bickering with my husband about something pointless, I handed him a handful of almonds and walked out of the kitchen and into the living room. I heard a crunch, the smack of lips; I felt a wave of anger. Rather than do what I might once have done—hang around waiting for an excuse to pick a fight—I packed up my laptop and headed out for a café, where I could safely be enraged by the sounds of strangers chewing.

Day 20

....

Transition Day

Physical Sensations: None.

Mood: Fabulous. Truly delightful.

Conflict: None.

Sleep: Adequate.

Work: Chugging along happily.

Pain: Virtually none.

Today I've been reading accounts of "bad trips." The description of these awful, painful, grotesque, and yet life-altering trips can be terrifying. In a typical narrative, reproduced in Albert Hofmann's *LSD, My Problem Child,* Jürg Kreienbühl, a Swiss painter, writes, "'Hellish' went through my mind, and all of a sudden horror passed through my limbs." Over the next fearful hours, his beautiful young mistress's yellow-and-black shoes turned into malevolent wasps crawling over the floor. Water seemed slimy, viscous, and poisonous. He felt a pervasive sense of dread and fear. Finally, as the effects of the drug wore off, he realized that what he had been experiencing was his personality, boiled down to its essence. And that essence was selfishness. He saw himself clearly, a cynical and cold man motivated by greed and self-interest. "I loved only myself," he told Hofmann. Afterward, Kreienbühl left his mistress and returned to his wife and children, a changed man.

My fear of a "bad trip" has always prevented me from trying a typical dose of LSD. The prospect of being locked in my own, ugly mind terrifies me. What I've learned about the concept of set and setting inclines me to think that I wasn't wrong to avoid the drug in the past. The settings in which I was offered LSD were not awful, but they weren't ideal, either. Though I liked college well enough, I was never so happy that a dorm room full of other tripping students would seem like a sufficiently supportive environment. Furthermore, set is the ultimate of self-fulfilling prophecies. A mental state of fear and dread can only lead to an acid trip of fear and dread.

The day I ate those few mushrooms and swung for hours on a tire swing was pleasant enough, but not so delightful that I wanted to repeat it, or try anything stronger. And then, about five years ago, I had an experience that was so terrifying I'm surprised I'm even doing this experiment at all. Though I hadn't taken a psychedelic, I definitely had what can be described as a bad trip.

It happened while my husband was out of town, at a writers' retreat deep in the New Hampshire woods. This was a few weeks after I had weaned myself off of Ambien, using prescribed medical marijuana to fall asleep instead. I don't like to smoke, so I bought cannabis capsules from the dispensary. With the help of the marijuana, I'd drop off to sleep readily enough, though not with the effortless bliss of Ambien. That night, however, when I swallowed the capsule, the walls began to breathe.

I lay in bed watching the walls, my own breathing growing shallow. I broke out in a clammy sweat. A drink of water, I thought, might calm me. I sat up in bed and stretched one foot out to the floor. Stepping on the floor in my bedroom was like stepping onto a sponge. My toes sank into the wood planks with an audible squelch.

That's when I called my husband. He answered the phone, but the line crackled, and I missed every other word. He had almost no reception, he said. His screen showed a single indicator bar of signal.

With what I considered at the time to be admirable calm, I told him that I was about to dial 911. I was just calling to let him know.

"Please don't."

"I have to. I'm dying."

"Sweetie, I promise you, you're not dying. Do you really want our kids to end up in foster care because you are having a pot-induced delusion?"

"Here's the thing," I tried to explain. "My lungs have forgotten how to breathe. The only reason I haven't died yet is that I'm consciously inhaling and exhaling."

"That isn't true. Honey, I beg you. Just shut your eyes. You'll fall asleep and everything will be fine."

I wanted to believe him. I knew that it was at least possible that he was right. But then it occurred to me that no one actually knows what goes on in the moments immediately before someone dies. Maybe all the people who have ever overdosed actually died because they forgot to keep breathing!

My husband gently reminded me that marijuana is among the most benign substances a person can ingest. Hadn't *I* told *him* that government sources calculate a lethal dose of marijuana to be one-third a person's body weight, consumed all at once? Had I swallowed forty pounds of weed? No? Well, then, I wasn't going to die.

That was all well and good, I told him, but now I had a problem even worse than my lungs. I knew for a fact that if I didn't tell my heart to beat it would stop.

At this point, his phone cut out for the third or fourth time since we started talking. I had been frustrated when this happened before, but now I was relieved that it took him a little while to find a signal and call back. Forcing my heart to beat was requiring a tremendous amount of attention, and I had little to spare for someone who was failing to appreciate the seriousness of the circumstances. I was performing CPR on myself, *with my mind,* and I needed to focus.

He called back. We went around on the subject of voluntary and involuntary bodily functions for another two minutes, or an hour, or a week. (My sense of time was a little whacked.) Then I gasped.

"Oh my God."

"What?"

"I just died. Right there. For a split second. My heart just stopped."

My husband observed that this was not very likely, since I had been talking nonstop for the past five minutes. Even in my addled state, I could tell he was getting bored.

"Okay," I said, realizing that I'd taken up far too much of his time and attention. "This is what we're going to do. I'm going to hang up and try to sleep. But you keep your phone on for the next half-hour. If I die, I'll call you."

"If you die, you'll call me?"

"Yes. I promise."

"You've got a deal."

Sweetheart that he is, he stayed up until four in the morning, just in case I tried to call to tell him I was dead.

I didn't use marijuana again until the pain of frozen shoulder made me desperate enough to go back to the pot club. And even then, I was careful to buy only weed engineered to be nonintoxicating. I've got enough to do without having to sit around keeping my lungs working and my heart beating.

When I imagine experiencing anything like that again, but with the intensity of LSD, it makes my stomach clench in horror. Not for me, a regular LSD trip. I'm happy with my microdoses.

Day 21

....

Normal Day

Physical Sensations: None.

Mood: Fine, until the evening, when I lost my mind.

Conflict: None.

Sleep: Fine, once I fell asleep.

Work: Fine.

Pain: Moderate.

I am convinced that adolescents take up exactly the same amount of a parent's time as do toddlers. With toddlers, you spend those long hours tending to physical needs. You change diapers, spoon food into mouths, set up towers of blocks to be toppled. With adolescents, you spend those long hours fretting. Though my eldest child does an admirable job of caring for herself while she is away at college, I find I am punching the time clock with the same regularity as I did when she was thirteen months old and had just learned to walk. Back then, my day was spent chasing after her as she hurtled through space. Nowadays, I just worry.

Some research has shown that light at the blue end of the spectrum—the "short-wavelength light" emitted by e-readers, laptops, or smart phones—interferes with circadian rhythms and with the sleep-promotion hormone, melatonin. It can take as much as ninety minutes longer to fall asleep after exposure to blue light. Even a glance at a screen can reduce and delay REM sleep, and make a person less alert the following day. During this protocol, sleep feels so precarious to me that I have tried to avoid watching movies on my laptop, reading on my iPad, even on the dimmest setting, or even peeking at my phone in the hour before bed. But last night, while lying there getting ready to go to sleep, for no reason other than that I'd had a good day and was, I fear, feeling immune to trouble, I picked up my phone and opened Instagram. I was swiping through, liking photo after photo, when I came upon a photograph my eldest had posted. It was blurry, a selfie shot in a dim room. Her head was angled up and to the side, her face turned away so that her throat was in the frame. The shot was blurry, but I was able to conclude that on her neck she now sported a blue-black tattoo that looked like this:

:/

My eldest had already acquired a number of tattoos. The first was a quote from William Faulkner etched on her side beneath her arm. She got that one the summer she turned eighteen, when she spent a couple of weeks alone at home. As tattoos go, it's not bad. You might even argue that it's a reasonable choice for the child of two writers. A year later, she got a complementary inscription on the opposite side of her rib cage, a quote from a somewhat less illustrious source: a fellow college student's response to T.S. Eliot's poem "The Love Song of J. Alfred Prufrock." Those tattoos are easy enough for a mother to tolerate. They are generally hidden by clothes, and they are competently executed.

I cannot say the same for the stick-and-poke tattoos she's scrawled on her upper arm, along her wrist, on her ankle and thighs. Blue and blurry, they remind me of the marks my prisoner clients would carve into their bodies to pass the endless months and years of incarceration. I know that my daughter is not alone, that she is only one of a million artistic college students sticking and poking her body. But I really don't like those tattoos.

I was taught that Jewish law forbids tattoos. By "taught," I mean I heard it on my parents' Lenny Bruce record. When she sees his tattoo, Lenny's aunt, whom he calls the Jewish Seagull, caws, "Hah! Hah! Lenny! Vat you did! You ruined your arm! Vy'd you do that? You can't be buried in a Jewish cemetery!" The Jewish prohibition against tattoos stems from Leviticus 19:28, which states, "You shall not make gashes in your flesh for the dead nor incise any marks on yourself: I am the Lord."

"Any marks." Seems pretty clear. But of course the Bible also prohibits holding grudges against other Jews (Leviticus 19:18 "Thou shalt not avenge, nor bear any grudge against the children of thy people"), and Lord knows I hold many a grudge, especially against the children of my people (I still haven't forgiven Maxine Nudelman* for stealing my boyfriend at Camp Ramah in the summer of '76). Also forbidden? The eating of shellfish and pork. I'm typing this while stuffing my face with two tacos, one fried shrimp and the other carnitas, so obviously this has nothing to do with law, Jewish or otherwise.

I'm troubled by the tattoos because I worry that they are not an expression of artistic sensibility but of a compulsion for self-harm. Or, if I'm going to be really honest, that they are an expression of maternal failure. Surely, children who feel beloved and well taken care of don't mark their bodies with ugly things. I know this is nonsense. Whereas I see them as ugly and poorly drawn, she sees them as beautiful. They have nothing at all to do with me. They are hers and hers alone, an expression not of unhappiness or depression but of style. Her style.

This tattoo, however, was something else entirely. It was not

---

*Name changed to protect the guilty. You know who you are, "Maxine."

only ugly to me, but it was on her lovely, perfect throat, where only the highest of turtlenecks could hide it. Even though I'd spoken to my daughter as recently as yesterday afternoon, even though she'd sounded fine, cheerful if a little stressed about her finals, I flipped out. A person who thinks she might one day have a job in the "straight" world, who anticipates meeting and wanting to impress people older than herself, who imagines a range of future selves doing a range of exciting and interesting things, would never get a giant black tattoo on her neck, would she?

And then my younger daughter pointed out what I had missed. (Because, yes, by then I had gotten out of bed, with Instagram open on my phone, and my freak-out had woken her up.) The tattoo depicted an emoticon. It stood for "meh," signifying indifference.

Forget imagining a job in the straight world. A person who feels such existential apathy that she inscribes "meh" on her body does not anticipate any future at all. A person who wants one of the first things others know about her to be that she does not give a shit, is not a stable and well person. That person is depressed. That person is at risk. That person's mother needs to change out of her pajamas and get on a plane and swoop her up and bring her home and wrap her in cotton batting and protect her from everything in the world, including herself.

I am, I know, particularly anxious when it comes to my eldest child. This anxiety is based, unsurprisingly, on guilt. I have forced upon this child a Ph.D.-level expertise in her mother's mental illness. Her studies began almost as soon as she popped out of the incision in my belly, eyes wide and watching, perfect bow of a mouth ready for a kiss. A few days after we brought her home from the hospital, after the adrenaline had faded and the Vicodin worn off, I started to experience disturbing images, fantasies as vivid as dreams, though they overtook me when I was wide awake.

I would be nursing her with perfect contentment, and then, suddenly, I would see in my mind's eye an image of me smothering her. I would be walking through the house with her in my arms, humming a made-up lullaby, and as I passed the knife block on the kitchen counter, I would imagine myself grabbing a blade and slitting her throat. I would be bathing her in her little tub, and I would imagine letting go and watching her sweet face slide beneath the water.

The more I tried to suppress these horrible intrusive fantasies, the more vivid and frequent they became. I was convinced that there was something terribly wrong with me. I wondered if I was suffering from postpartum depression. I wondered if I was evil. I wondered if I was a mother or a monster.

This was in 1994, when the Web was in its infancy. Had it even occurred to me to search the Internet, there would have been nothing there to find. I didn't go to the library or consult a therapist, either. Instead, I kept mum about what I was seeing in my head, even as the images influenced how I dealt with my baby. I was fearful, worried I'd lose control and hurt her. I was anxious about being alone with her, clingy with my husband. Even after the images faded, I felt their effect on my mothering. I lacked confidence. I didn't trust myself.

The intrusive images came back again, even more intensely, when my second child was born. By that time, however, I was confident enough in my capacity to love my baby to ignore them. When they returned after the birth of my third child, in 2001, Google was finally there to help.

Surely, one of the greatest benefits of the Internet is its capacity to create community among strangers. No matter how bizarre your symptoms, you can find fellow sufferers. Convinced your skin is extruding tiny fibers? Welcome to the Morgellons community, with Joni Mitchell to sing your anthem. Find yourself imitating everything that surprises you, including the barking of a dog or a passerby's fart? You probably have Miryachit, a disease also known as Jumping Frenchman of Maine, and you can find others just like you online. None of us need ever again feel isolated in our pain.

When I turned to Google, I found out I was one of many women who suffer from the disabling, intrusive, obsessional thoughts of postpartum obsessive-compulsive disorder. Mothers with postpartum OCD do not spend their time scrubbing their houses clean (oh, how I wish that were the case). They share common ghastly, unspeakable fantasies. They imagine stabbing their babies, drowning them, throwing them out of windows. In extreme cases, these thoughts cause mothers to avoid their babies, for fear of harming them. Fortunately, those who suffer from this awful disorder don't harm their babies; tragically, they are at high risk of suicide.

The syndrome, luckily, is very responsive to treatment with SSRIs. I was on Zoloft when I had my fourth child, and I never once thought about killing him. Or least no more than any other parent does.

My firstborn bore the brunt not just of my postpartum OCD but of my inexperience and lack of confidence in dealing with it, and this pattern was repeated throughout her childhood. Besides my husband, who was an adult when we met, she has lived the longest with my untreated shifting moods, and benefited least from my efforts to stabilize them. And so I am on high alert for any sign of emotional pain in her.

I stared at the photograph of the horrible mark on her neck for a while, fighting tears. Then I sent this text:

Hey honey. Are those new tattoos on your throat?

The sub-text to this text? DON'T HURT YOURSELF. DON'T HURT YOURSELF. DON'T HURT YOURSELF.

She didn't reply.

So I sent this text:

*We love you honey. And we really want to hear from
you. Please call us.*

Subtext: I CAN BE AT THE AIRPORT IN FORTY-FIVE MIN-
UTES.

She didn't reply.

"One of us needs to get on a plane," I said to my husband. "The
last flight's in an hour."

He pointed out that it would take me nearly that long to get
to the airport.

That's when the phone rang.

My husband resisted my attempts to pry the receiver from
his fingers. He listened for a few minutes and then wordlessly
passed me the phone.

"Look at the geotag," my daughter said.

"What?" I said.

"On the photo. Read the geotag."

"Print shop 1 AM," I read.

"Print shop," she said.

"Print shop?"

"I'm in the print shop. What is in the print shop?"

"Prints?"

"Ink, Mom. There's ink in the print shop."

"You made a tattoo with print shop ink?" Stealing! Also, toxic!

She texted me another photograph. It was of her hands,
stained blue.

"I've been working for hours on my final prints. I'm covered
in ink stains."

"It's . . . an ink stain?" I whispered.

"You really need to chill."

I wonder if I would have been more "chill" if this had happened last night, between Microdose Day and Transition Day.
Would I have been better able to manage my anxiety? Would I
have hesitated before rushing to the decision to hop on a plane?

Still, a month ago, I might have been on my way to the airport by the time my daughter called. But who can know? I think perhaps the only conclusion to be drawn is that freaking out about your kids is normal, and even the most microdose-mellowed mama is still a mama. And a Jewish mama at that.

Day 22

....

Microdose Day

*Physical Sensations: A slight tingling about
    ninety minutes after dosing, a flash of
    something that feels almost like dizziness. A
    tender stomach.*

*Mood: Irritable when I woke up, but that passed
    after I took the microdose.*

Conflict: None.

Sleep: About six and a half hours.

Work: Productive, if a bit scattered.

Pain: Minor.

Though my mood is fine today, I've been wishing that I wasn't
taking LSD. Not because the protocol isn't working, but because
there's another drug I wish I could take. Remember that back
in the first chapter I told you that I'd taken MDMA six or seven
times? It wasn't in my glorious clubbing days. I didn't really
have any glorious clubbing days.* I started using MDMA about
ten years ago, with my husband. Though I know it will make
some people dismiss me as an unrepentant, drug-addled idiot,
I'm not about to stop being completely honest with you now. We

*Once, I picked up an economist at the Roxy and went back to his place. I'd use the
word "pleasant" to describe the experience, though. Not "glorious."

credit the strength of our marriage at least in part to our periodic use of the drug. Neither of us has ever taken the drug recreationally. We've never even been to a rave. We use MDMA purely as marital therapy.

We were inspired to try MDMA by a pair of guest lecturers I'd invited to speak to my seminar on the War on Drugs at UC Berkeley. Alexander Shulgin, known as Sasha, was a Bay Area pharmacologist and chemist who specialized in synthesizing and bioassaying psychoactive compounds on himself and on willing subjects. Known as the father of MDMA, Sasha Shulgin was not the first to synthesize the drug: the credit for that goes to the pharmaceutical company Merck. But Sasha was among the first to ingest the chemical. According to the story that he told my law-school class, he and some friends were on the Reno Fun Train in 1976, heading up to Tahoe for a weekend of gambling and carousing. His companions were drinking alcohol, but instead of joining them, Sasha drank a vial containing 120 milligrams of MDMA. He described the feeling like this: "I feel absolutely clean inside, and there is nothing but pure euphoria. I have never felt so great, or believed this to be possible."

Sasha, who referred to the drug as his "low-calorie martini," shared it with a friend, Leo Zeff, a former U.S. Army lieutenant colonel and psychotherapist who was so impressed with the drug's potential that he came out of retirement to proselytize about MDMA's therapeutic possibilities. Zeff trained hundreds, perhaps even thousands, of therapists around the country in how to use MDMA as a tool in their practices. Ann Shulgin, Sasha's wife, who accompanied him when he lectured to my class, told us that she herself had used MDMA, and also administered it to couples. She said that in her couples counseling practice she could accomplish more in a single six-hour session with MDMA than in six years of traditional therapy. Her patients could plumb their most vulnerable depths, safely and even joyfully, with the kind of trust that even years of therapy couldn't engender.

From about 1976 to 1981, MDMA remained a virtual secret among networks of psychotherapists who found it a profoundly important tool, especially in the treatment of couples, but who were hesitant to publicize or publish their findings for fear of hastening criminalization. Inevitably, however, word got out to recreational drug users. In 1981, a group of chemists in the Boston area—known, imaginatively, as the "Boston Group" rebranded the drug as "Ecstasy" or "XTC"—and increased the pace of production, stamping out thousands of little colorful pills decorated with characters reminiscent of SweeTarts candies. In 1983, one of their distributors, with the financial backing of investors from Texas, massively increased both production and distribution. The "Texas Group" held huge "Ecstasy parties" at bars and clubs, circulating posters and flyers, and aggressively marketing the drug. In 1985, as the psychotherapists had predicted would happen once use spread widely, the DEA placed MDMA on Schedule I, thus ending nearly a decade of successful therapeutic use.

Before the Shulgins first came to lecture to my class, the only thing I'd heard about MDMA was that it depleted spinal fluid (this turned out to be a legend of the drug war, with no basis in fact) and transformed users into sex fiends. (Another myth. Though it greatly heightens the senses, the drug actually impedes orgasm and, in men, the ability to sustain an erection.) Sasha and Ann referred to MDMA as an empathogen or entactogen, a drug that enhances feelings of emotional communion and empathy, allowing for an opening up of communication. This, they said, was what made it ideal for couples. It allowed them to discuss potentially painful or divisive issues without triggering feelings of fear and threat, but of love. A love drug!

When I first began considering following the Shulgins' advice, my husband and I had four small children, busy careers, and sleep deficits that challenged the *concept* of empathy, let alone its reliable practice. We were stressed out, and though we would never have considered our marriage anything but happy, we were definitely communicating less than before we had children. We felt a little bit, we used to say, like foremen in a factory on swing shifts. We'd pass the children off to one another with sufficient instruction to ease the transition, and then head off to our own work. When we were alone together, we were spent and exhausted, encrusted with baby cereal and just a soupçon of puke, and though we still enjoyed one another's company, at times we lost the sense of intense communion we had once had.

Still, as compelling as was the possibility of opening up the lines of communication in a circumstance that enhances feelings of empathy and love, it took years for my husband and me to work up the courage to try the drug. I was afraid of MDMA for the same reason I was afraid of LSD: I didn't want to have a bad trip, and I didn't want to die. It was only after I'd read everything I could find about the drug that I became convinced that it was not, in fact, hallucinogenic. The walls would not breathe or change color. Moreover, the drug is relatively safe so long as you're not stupid enough to source your pills from a wild-eyed stranger wearing a pacifier around his neck.

Though MDMA in its pure form is not particularly dangerous, even at high doses, there have been fatalities, including among healthy young adults.* MDMA raises body temperature and inhibits natural thermoregulation, increasing the risk of heat-stroke. For this reason, probably the worst thing to do under the influence of MDMA is dance wildly in a packed room or beneath the desert sun. MDMA can also increase heart rate and raise blood pressure, making it dangerous for those who suffer from high blood pressure or heart disease. Additionally, MDMA can cause water retention. So, for example, if one takes it at a rave, and then chugs water to counteract the possibility of dehydration, one can suffer from hyponatremia, or water toxicity.

---

*This is in stark contrast to LSD, for which, as I've stated before, there are no verifiable fatalities.

Furthermore, MDMA certainly affects the brain. We know this because tolerance develops with repeated use, and can eventually become chronic. Heavy users don't experience the positive effects of the drug, no matter how many pills they "stack," or how much they ingest. Though there is no clear answer yet as to why this is so, it seems likely that some neuroadaptive process is going on. This means, in laymen's terms, that MDMA changes your brain chemistry in some way, though we do not know whether these changes are destructive or problematic.

However, there has never been a fatality or even an injury when MDMA is used in a carefully monitored therapeutic setting. Moreover, with a single, moderate dose, there is no need to be concerned about neuroadaptive processes. My husband and I decided that if we modeled our MDMA experience on the one developed by therapists like Zeff, were careful to regulate temperature and water intake, and put in place an emergency plan, we could safely take the drug.

We prepared far in advance for our first MDMA experience. We hired a reliable, mature babysitter to take care of our kids for three days, and arranged for one of their grandmothers to be on call in case of emergency. Both to enhance the experience and to minimize side effects, we followed a protocol of supplements that we found on the Web site of the Erowid Center, a clearinghouse for information on consciousness-altering drugs. We also planned to take an SSRI after the MDMA wore off, something Erowid users recommend in order to restore our depleted serotonin. Though the medical evidence for the utility of this practice is scant, it couldn't hurt.

After first making sure emergency medical care would be readily accessible in the event of a bad reaction, we drove down the coast to a small hotel on the beach, checked into a spartan though comfortable room, and promptly collapsed on the bed in blissful unconsciousness. By the time we woke up the next morning, we were so deliriously giggly from a night of unaccustomed sleep that for a moment we considered backing out. Who needs chemicals when you can get high on a good night's rest?

Still, we'd paid for the babysitter and planned so carefully, it seemed like a waste of both time and money not to go forward.* We skipped breakfast (per the instructions on Erowid) and went for a hike out onto the cliffs above the beach. When we were precisely a thirty-minute walk from the hotel, we took the pills. My stomach clenched in panic as soon as I swallowed the drug. Forget the research! What if my spinal fluid vanished? I could feel it evaporating already. What if my brain overheated? A fried egg! That's what a brain on drugs looks like! I knew that for sure, because Nancy Reagan told me so!

"Look at me," my husband said. He held me by the shoulders and stared into my eyes. His pupils were not yet dilated.

"This is good," he said. "Nothing bad will happen."

"Promise?"

"I promise."

A few deep breaths later, as the fog lifted over the Pacific, we hiked slowly back to the room. We stripped, got into bed, and waited for the best sex of our lives. Whatever myths the Shulgins had sought to dispel, the drug must be called Ecstasy for a reason, right?

Not so much. MDMA certainly enhances the senses. It makes touch feel glorious. The drug first came on with what I can best describe as a wave of warm, sensual tingling. I even got wet. But neither of us experienced the profound sexual arousal we'd anticipated. In fact, nothing about the experience was what we had imagined it would be. We didn't rock the bed like a wrecking ball. We didn't trance-dance into a fatally overheated stupor. We didn't see fairies dancing in the sky, or any other visual hallucinations. The drug is not, as I said, hallucinogenic.

---

*And, yes, I realize this is perhaps expressive of a certainly excessive if not near-pathological frugality, but I've always been penny-wise, pound-foolish. Witness the number of shoes in my closet, all of them bought on sale, most either a half-size too small or too large.

What we did was talk. For six hours, we talked about our feelings for each other, why we love each other, how we love each other. We talked about what we felt when we first met, how our emotional connection grew and deepened, how we might deepen it still. The best way I can describe it is that we were transported emotionally back to our relationship's early and most exciting days, to the period of our most intense infatuation, but with all the compassion and depth of familiarity of a decade of companionship. We saw each other clearly, loved each other profoundly, and basked in this reciprocated love.*

The feeling lasted not for hours or for days, but for months. Actually, the truth is, it lasted forever. We've done the drug since, every couple of years, when we feel we need to recharge the batteries of our relationship. Though the experience has never again been quite so intense, it has been a reliable method of connection, of clearing away the detritus of the everyday to get to the heart of the matter. And the heart is love. We love each other so much, even when he is chewing almonds and I have to leave the house.

The empathogenic effects of MDMA have caused a revival of interest in the use of the drug in recent years to combat treatment-resistant post-traumatic stress disorder. In particular, it has been a priority of MAPS, which is funding a variety of research studies to determine, it writes, "whether MDMA-assisted psychotherapy can help heal the psychological and emotional damage caused by sexual assault, war, violent crime, and other traumas."

I spoke with Michael Mithoefer, M.D., who, along with his wife and cotherapist, Annie Mithoefer, is carrying out clinical trials to test the safety and efficacy of MDMA-assisted psychotherapy in veterans and first responders with chronic post-traumatic stress disorder that has not resolved with the use of other treatment

*I realize that for some of you the prospect of talking for six hours about your relationship seems like the very definition of a bad trip. If so, MDMA is not for you. Actually, I take that back: MDMA is *especially* for you. Hundred bucks says your spouse would agree.

methods. The protocol of their University of South Carolina studies is similar to those used in the recent wave of psilocybin research. In his earliest studies, Mithoefer and his colleagues first provided each subject with two introductory psychotherapy sessions with trained psychotherapists. Then the subjects underwent two MDMA or placebo-assisted sessions spaced three to five weeks apart, during which they talked through the incidents that had led to their trauma. After only two sessions, PTSD was resolved in 83 percent of the subjects who received MDMA. The results for talk therapy alone? A mere 25 percent. Even more remarkably, the reductions in PTSD symptoms were sustained for the long term, *without further treatment.* These results are so dramatic that not only has the Department of Defense given its blessing to further research, but there are two Veterans Administration studies now in process.

Mithoefer described to me the effect of the study on one participant, a firefighter and 9/11 first responder who was plagued by PTSD symptoms. Once, in a fit of uncontrollable anger during a session of PTSD therapy using another method, he tore the sink from the wall of the examining room. When asked what the results of the MDMA sessions were on this man, Mithoefer smiled and said, "Well, our sink is still on the wall." The reduction of the patient's PTSD symptoms was profound: he continues to report to Mithoefer that they have not returned. A recent meta-analysis by Timothy Amoroso, in the Department of Psychology at the University of New Hampshire, comparing MDMA therapy to prolonged exposure therapy in the treatment of PTSD, confirms Mithoefer's results.[*]

Word has spread amidst the network of soldiers returned from war about the efficacy of MDMA therapy. Of the more than one thousand veterans who have reached out to Mithoefer for

---

[*]T. Amoroso and M. Workman, "Treating Posttraumatic Stress Disorder with MDMA-assisted Psychotherapy."

help, his pilot study was permitted to enroll only twenty. The poignancy and tragedy of these figures cannot be overstated. The need is overwhelming, and people are desperate for help. Veterans have a suicide rate 50 percent higher than that of the general population. Rates for female vets are even worse. There is reason to believe that MDMA-assisted psychotherapy could save thousands of lives.

MAPS, which funds the Mithoefers' work, is also funding research investigating the use of MDMA to treat social anxiety in people with autism. For years, many people with autism have been using illegally obtained MDMA for this purpose, without the benefit of guidance from therapists, and have reported improvements in their social anxiety, perception, and ability to communicate. The MAPS-funded study—currently in progress at the Los Angeles Biomedical Research Institute, a joint enterprise of UCLA and Stanford University—is comparing the results of MDMA-assisted psychotherapy sessions on twelve adults with autism, none of whom have ever taken the drug before, with an inactive-placebo control group of similar subjects. The researchers have begun to see effects resembling those reported by autistic people who had used MDMA out of the research context.

Annie and Michael Mithoefer recently received formal FDA approval for MDMA conjoint therapy with couples in which one member has PTSD. Their interest in couples therapy stems from their personal use of MDMA in a therapeutic context before the drug was placed on Schedule I. They found it so useful to enhancing communication and resolving conflicts in their marriage that Mithoefer told me he believes criminalization is a real loss for the practice of couples therapy. Having a partner respond with the kind of honest, loving empathy MDMA facilitates is profoundly restorative to a marriage.

I asked Mithoefer whether he imagined that his new study, if successful, might lead beyond the confines of PTSD treatment to the treatment of the mundane communication difficulties of typical couples such as my husband and me. To my surprise and delight, he was confident that one day we might be able to undergo legally prescribed MDMA-assisted couples counseling. He said that his hope is that, by 2021, MDMA will be removed from Schedule I, and that prescriptions will be allowed. He anticipates that the FDA might confine use to licensed clinical settings, in a manner similar to methadone treatment, but he pointed out that even if the FDA approves MDMA only for use for PTSD, off-label use is likely to be allowed.*

Why, though? I asked. Won't the FDA and DEA seek to limit a drug like MDMA as much as possible?

There, he told me, is where Big Pharma might prove useful. It is in the pharmaceutical industry's financial interest to encourage widespread use of products, and so it has lobbied aggressively to prevent any limitations on off-label use for any drug. Mithoefer imagines that Big Pharma won't even allow this narrow wedge in the door—the thinking being, if the FDA limits off-label use of MDMA, it will set a precedent for other drugs to be so limited. Others in the field, however, are less optimistic. They point out that the FDA occasionally does approve drugs with off-label limitations. They believe that MDMA, even if approved, is likely to be so limited.

But if Mithoefer is right, my husband and I need only wait five years to perform our marriage-recharging ritual legally!

Still, I don't want to wait. I know from experience that taking MDMA would allow us to continue and accelerate the process of recovering and reconnecting that began after our last argument and has continued in therapy. However, it has been a long time since I've been able to obtain MDMA. My friend network

---

*Off-label drug use is when a doctor prescribes a drug that is approved for treatment of one condition, to treat a condition for which that drug is not officially indicated. For example, Zoloft is an antidepressant, but it is also sometimes prescribed off-label to help men who suffer from premature ejaculation. This, I think we can all agree, is a win/win.

has dried up, and by all accounts, what's available on the black market now is so badly compromised and toxic that even if I were willing to buy drugs from a dealer, I'd be afraid to take them. Even more important: one of the things I tell my children, perhaps the critical part of my harm-reduction message, is that drug interactions can be dangerous. Don't mix drugs, I insist. Don't mix alcohol and marijuana, don't mix antidepressants and mushrooms. Definitely don't mix LSD with MDMA. Even if the LSD is just microdoses. Even if you really miss MDMA. I feel like I am my own parent and my own child; I am straining our relationship, but still I must insist.

I've been honest with my children about MDMA. I've told them it's been helpful to their father and me, that it's a very special drug, though their peers use it foolishly. I've warned my children that the vast majority of what is called MDMA or Molly on the market is either methamphetamine or something more toxic. If they do MDMA, they must test it first. If they cannot establish through testing that a drug is pure, they must not risk taking it.

I've also counseled my children about the dangers MDMA poses to body temperature regulation and water toxicity, and explained that this is why they must not use the drug at a rave or a party, but only in a small group in a cool room. Or, better yet, one to one, with someone they love. And then I've gone beyond harm reduction to life enhancement, and explained to my children that MDMA is one of those rare experiences that are at their very best the first time you do them. About what else in life can we say that? Not sex, that's for sure! I believe that with whom you do MDMA for the first time might even be more important than with whom you have sex for the first time. Ideally, you'd have sex for the first time with someone you love, after serious contemplation and discussion, but, whatever happens, chances are it's not going to be great. And even if by some miracle it's wonderful, even if you happen to be one of the infinitesimal number of women who orgasm in their first sexual encounter, sex only gets better the more practice you have. The opposite is true about MDMA. The first time you use MDMA is the most profound, and tolerance inevitably develops.

Do it like we did, I tell my children. Don't waste that first experience. Save it for your soul mate. I anticipate that they will take this advice about as readily as they take my advice about what to wear, whom to date, and whether to get a tattoo, but I wish they'd listen to me on this one. Because your first time really should be special.

Day 23

....

Transition Day
Physical Sensations: None.
Mood: Fabulous. Truly delightful.
Conflict: None.
Sleep: Adequate.
Work: Decent.
Pain: None!

Transition Day is a joy. It's a delight. I'm nearly giddy with pleasure, though this has much to do with the fact that for the first time in over a year I am pain-free. My frozen shoulder has thawed! It doesn't hurt! I still have restricted range of motion— I can't yet buckle my bra in the back—but I don't care. I don't care if I have to spin my bra around to bring the buckle to the front for the rest of my life. The absence of pain is a marvel. A miracle.

Humans live forever on the Hedonic Treadmill; whatever our life experiences, whatever our transient miseries or joys, we eventually revert to a mood set-point that depends not on circumstance but on individual predisposition. Lose your legs in a car accident, win the lottery—it makes no difference. Within a few years, hedonic adaptation will take over, returning you to your personal set-point of contentment or misery. That is, except if you suffer from chronic pain. Research has shown that chronic pain is among the only experiences that have the capacity to shift your happiness set-point toward the unhappy end of your spectrum. This does not surprise me. If someone offered me a million dollars to go through the last eighteen months of pain again, I'd not only refuse, but I'd cram that money up the person's ass, in low-denomination bills. This shoulder has not only made me miserable; it's made me miserable to be around. But today? Today is glorious. It feels better than a million dollars.

Which is a good thing, since today I've been investigating an area of LSD research that is so outrageous, so horrible, that I have to find a tremendous equanimity to keep from spouting off like a wild-haired, lunatic conspiracy theorist. It's all I can do not to drag a soapbox out to Sproul Plaza on the UC Berkeley campus and start ranting about a CIA program, run by Nazis, that gave LSD to unsuspecting citizens.

Instead, I'll allow myself a little bit of ranting on the page.

At the end of World War II, the U.S. military set up an agency called the Joint Intelligence Objectives Agency, whose mandate was to implement Operation Paperclip, a program in which U.S. military and spies fanned out across Europe, seeking German scientists and engineers to bring home to America. Even before the war with Germany had ended, the Cold War was in full swing, and the U.S. government was desperate not just to obtain the knowledge these men held, but to keep their ideas, research, and abilities out of the hands of the Soviets. President Truman was adamant that no actual Nazis be brought back to the States, but the generals and spies ignored this edict from their ostensible commander-in-chief. When confronted with Nazi war criminals like the infamous Wernher von Braun—inventor of the German V-2 rocket and dedicated exploiter of slave labor, who was personally responsible for flogging and torturing people, and whose program resulted in the deaths of tens of thousands—the army and intelligence services whitewashed records, expunged files, and erased evidence of Nazi Party membership. They not only brought the most evil of criminals back to the United States, but gave them the highest of security clearances.

Among the scientists brought back to the States were Nazi chemists who had experimented on prisoners at Dachau, using mescaline. The newly created Central Intelligence Agency, eagerly searching for biological weapons that could both start large-scale epidemics and be used to target individuals for assassination, found out about these Dachau experiments. Their interest was piqued, even though the experiments were, by all accounts, failures. Torturer-physicians like the Nazi Colonel Hubertus Strughold* had tried to use mescaline to elicit absolute obedience in their victims, to no avail. Nonetheless, the spymasters eagerly embraced these physicians and their experiments, and arranged for them to continue their work in the United States.

When Brigadier General Charles Loucks, chief of the Operation Paperclip scientists, heard about LSD, he tasked his Nazi physicians and chemists to work with the CIA to research the potential of LSD as a mass poison and a means of controlling human behavior. The resulting project brought together the Army Chemical Corps and the CIA in an unusually cooperative endeavor. They teamed up in operations code-named Bluebird and Artichoke to develop what they called "unconventional interrogation techniques" using LSD and other drugs. For nearly twenty years, these programs and the CIA's large-scale mind-control program, code-named MK-ULTRA, tried to weaponize psychedelic drugs.† Among their methodologically suspect stud-

---

* Strughold was a longtime NASA employee who later became known as the Father of Space Medicine. One can presume that the small children victimized by his experiments with oxygen deprivation would have found this honorific ironic, had they survived.

† For a discussion of these and other experiments, see John Marks, *The Search for the "Manchurian Candidate": The CIA and Mind Control—The Secret History of the Behavioral Sciences.*

ies was one in which they set up brothels in San Francisco and New York designed to lure men whose drinks would then be spiked with LSD; their behavior was observed through one-way mirrors, as if they were some kind of twisted focus group. It's not clear what the CIA sought to learn from these "studies," beyond answering the question of what the effects of LSD are on an unsuspecting subject under peculiar conditions. The CIA also surreptitiously dosed their own officers, ostensibly to determine what might happen if an enemy agent was secretly given LSD, or if a CIA agent was so dosed by the enemy. Nothing useful was gleaned from these experiments, though many people suffered psychic and emotional discomfort, some of it long-lasting. One can hardly imagine a worse set and setting for a psychedelic experience.

Among the unwilling and unwitting victims of this "research" was a scientist named Frank Olson, a bacteriologist working for the CIA on biological and chemical weapons. In 1953, a week after being secretly dosed by his supervisor, Olson was believed to have thrown himself out of a thirteenth-story window. The CIA claimed that the LSD caused Olson to suffer a paranoid nervous breakdown. Olson's family, however, believes that he was murdered, probably because during his LSD experience he gained insight that led him not only to refuse to continue his work in germ warfare, but to threaten to expose the government program. According to Olson's family, the CIA murdered him to keep him from divulging details about the use of biological weapons by the United States in the Korean War.

Given what I've learned about how the risks of LSD have been wildly overstated, and given what we know about the CIA's role in overthrowing governments, assassinating world leaders, and setting up black sites around the world in which to torture perceived enemies, not to mention its practice of conducting unethical LSD experiments on uninformed subjects, I find the family's explanation more convincing than the Agency's.

Olson's death, whether it was suicide or murder, had little discernible effect on the CIA's continuing LSD research. According to testimony before Congress, the CIA partnered with no fewer than eighty academic and medical institutions to study LSD in order to develop it into a tool of war and assassination. This research had an unintended consequence: it introduced thousands of subjects of these various studies, among them Ken Kesey, to the drug. Unfortunately, fearful at the prospect of congressional investigation and public disclosure, the CIA destroyed the bulk of its documentation of the MK-ULTRA experiments. We know some of what they got up to, but much of their nefarious activity will forever remain a secret.

Leave it to the CIA to take a drug that is a tool of enlightenment for so many, and try to turn it into an agent of chemical warfare. We should be grateful for the one positive thing we can say about their endeavor: it failed.

Day 24

....

Normal Day

Physical Sensations: None.

Mood: Fine, though hardly joyful.

Conflict: None.

Sleep: Restless.

Work: Not great.

Pain: Minor.

Today I had a crappy day. My mood wasn't prickly; I didn't argue with my husband or yell at my kids; but my work went poorly, and I spent much of the day surfing the Web.* My sense of dissatisfaction continued until I went to therapy. Sometimes I think I pay this professional for the privilege of having a ready ear for my complaints, in order to spare my friends and family from having to listen to them. Today my topic was how my lousy workday awoke feelings of insecurity and dissatisfaction, which inevitably led to concerns about the possibility of my depression's return.

It was harder than usual to whine about these typical complaints, because I haven't yet told my therapist about my micro-

---

*How did writers procrastinate before the Internet? They probably read novels and went on long runs. If it weren't for the fucking Internet, by now I'd be skinny and have read Proust.

dose experiment. I know I'm not being fair to her. How can she treat me when she's missing such basic information? But I'm afraid she'll be shocked. Worse, that she'll judge me. Or, worst of all, simply say, "That's interesting," then nothing else, while she *silently* judges me. She might even fire me! I know it's silly to care this much about what your therapist thinks of you, but I do. Like a fourth-grade teacher's pet, I want to be her best patient, her A student, funny and successful. I don't want her to be disappointed in me. It's not lost on me how ironic it is to want to give my therapist the impression that I totally have my shit together. It's like tidying up because the housekeeper is on the way. But not telling her has felt dishonest, especially since I've been able this month to make such good use of the tools of cognitive behavioral therapy she has recommended to me. I worry that right now she's feeling I'm doing such a good job, which means she's doing such a good job. How is she going to feel when she finds out that her lessons have finally sunk in not because of her wisdom or tenacity but because I'm taking acid behind her back?

My therapist is very young, and very beautiful. (Her beauty is irrelevant to either her competence or this story, but I cannot help mentioning it, because this is the kind of beauty that makes it difficult to concentrate on one's own minor desperations.) She is also very sensible. She practices cognitive behavioral therapy—none of that wishy-washy, self-indulgent analytic crap for her. Or for me, frankly. I prefer to take my self-indulgence with a bracing dose of pragmatism.

Today I complained to her about my shitty workday. I am not blocked, I assured her, just lazy. I kept getting great ideas, starting to write, and then fizzling out, losing interest, and binge-watching episodes of *Jessica Jones*. This has happened to me before, I told her. I'm a terrible procrastinator. Or is it that I'm a great procrastinator? Possibly the actual *best* procrastinator.

My poor, long-suffering therapist listened to this for as long as she could, then stopped me and posed the following hypothetical:

Imagine you have a closet full of Ayelet robots. These robots are the idealized version of you. They are every bit as competent as you at your best. No, they are *more* competent! They are better than you. They can write better than you can. They can produce prizewinning novels, insightful and incisive essays, dazzlingly thrilling screenplays. They can wow audiences with mind-blowing lectures. They are better mothers than you. They can cook glorious meals for your children, create exciting and thrilling experiences for your family to enjoy. They are better wives than you. They are ever ready with a supportive ear. Sex with the Ayelet robot is consistently earth-shaking.

My therapist is no nerd, and so she wasn't even aware that she was presenting me with a Superman hypothetical. In a classic DC Comic, Superman had a closet full of robot surrogates about which he said, "Each is designed to use one of my super-powers when needed! I send out the robots when Clark's absence would be suspicious! Or when I suspect that criminals are waiting to use kryptonite against me!" Superman's robots were labeled "X-Ray Vision," "Flying," "Super-Strength," "Super-Breath."* Mine might be labeled "Plotter," "Empathetic Listener," "Metaphor Generator," "Trenchant Social Analyst," "Tough but Fair Disciplinarian," "Fictional World Creator," "Imaginative Game Player," "Character Creator," "Chef," "Public Speaker," "Math Whiz" (my kids always need help with their homework, and my math skills stalled out somewhere around fifth grade), "Travel Agent," etc. And those are just the G-rated robots. I'll spare you the others.

Imagine you have a closet full of robots at the ready, my therapist said. Which of your various obligations would you assign to a robot? Which tasks and activities would you reserve for yourself, because you enjoy them too much to delegate them even to a robot who's better than you?

---

*Remember how Superman was always blowing up a hurricane gale?

Her question brought me up short. I've been thinking about it ever since.

Would I let my robot make dinner? Hell, yeah, though I kind of do that anyway (if by "robot" you mean "husband"). I love family dinner, and my husband's an amazing cook, so no robots at the actual table. Homework? Definitely. Carpool? It depends. I hate driving, especially in the early morning, but the kids are their most voluble in the car. I don't want the robot to have those important and revelatory conversations with them. Would I ask my robot to write my novels for me? If she really could do it better, then I might. I wouldn't let her do my writing every single day, but I'd definitely let her take over on days like today. I wonder how many mornings a week I would consider the prospect of a day spent hunched over a keyboard, sweating myself into a self-hating misery only to produce a constipated paragraph of crappy prose, and then decide to whistle up a robot and take myself out for a walk? Too many, I fear. Would I assign a robot the task of writing screenplays? Not the first draft—those are fun to write—but definitely the rewrites. Robot Ayelet will be in charge of all Hollywood notes calls and revisions. But I wouldn't cede to her these pages. I'm having too much fun writing them.

What about leisure activities? I'd read my own books and watch my own movies and TV, but Robot Ayelet is headed for the gym. I'd be happy never to waste another minute of my life lifting a hand weight or squatting. (I'm not sure how her fitness would transfer to me, but robotics is a young science, and I'm sure we will figure it out!) I guess I'll do my own hiking, but not every day. Robot Ayelet and I can split the forest walks down the middle. I wouldn't let Robot Ayelet near my husband, especially since she's such a sex goddess.*

It's remarkable how clarifying it is to contemplate which parts of my life I'd turn over to Robot Ayelet. We all lead lives of obligation, some of which we can't avoid. Back to School Night

---

* Maybe I'd call in a sub for the occasional blow job. I'll tap in later.

and Pilates are necessary evils. But I work, after all, for myself. If I'd just as soon assign a task to a work robot, maybe I shouldn't be doing it at all.

Robot Ayelet would never need to microdose. Every one of her days would be really good. She'd be perpetually cheerful, focused, centered. Oh God—the thought suddenly occurs to me—am I microdosing in order to turn myself into Robot Ayelet? No! That can't be. I don't want to be a soulless, perpetually cheerful robot!

There is, however, a way to consider the robot question that's relevant to my experiment. If the point of microdosing is to look at things in a different way, to learn how to respond to life's mundane adversities with equanimity rather than irritability, then part of that must be to figure out what things in my life I need to approach differently. The robot dilemma poses the question of what in your life do you value, what gives you satisfaction or joy. Microdosing has given me the space in my mind to consider that question in a way I don't believe I would have otherwise. I should talk this over with my therapist. I'm going to have to tell her about the experiment. I just hope she doesn't grade me down.

Day 25

....

Microdose Day

Physical Sensations: Minor stomach upset.

Mood: Fine for most of the day, then anxious.

Conflict: None.

*Sleep: About six and a half hours. Wish it was
    more, but not feeling tired.*

Work: Productive.

Pain: Minor.

Tonight we went out to dinner with a pair of writer friends. They
asked what I was working on, and for a moment I hesitated.
I have always been forthright to, some might argue, a fault. I
believe that secrecy is toxic, that it empowers those who wish
you harm, and keeps you from eliciting the comfort of those who
care. Yet, despite the fact that I believe so strongly in the power
and virtue of honesty, until recently I've refrained from respond-
ing to the question "What's new?" with "I'm taking a small dose
of LSD every three days; what's new with you?"

Though I've kept this experiment a secret from almost everyone save the physical therapist I hypomanically blabbed to in my
earliest days, I haven't felt good about it. The easiest way to influence the way people and politicians think about an issue is to be
open about it. Gay rights flourished and gay marriage became

the law because gay people came out of the closet. Once people realized that some of their neighbors, relatives, friends, and co-workers were gay, they found it harder to discriminate against gay people as a group. I've known since I began this experiment that if I really wanted attitudes toward these drugs and the people who use them to change, I would have to come out of the psychedelic closet. But the idea of telling people made me nervous. I was worried about what people would think of me. I was afraid my credibility would be damaged, that I would be dismissed as a crazy druggie. The issue is complicated by gender. Women are far more often accused of being "crazy," even (or especially) when all we are being is assertive.

When I asked Tim Ferriss—who has been open about his use of psilocybin, even going so far as to discuss it on a Reddit AMA*—what he thought might be the reaction if I were to talk publicly or write about this experiment, he laughed. "You'll get all sorts of criticism from people who take Prozac and Xanax twice a day." I found his easygoing courage of conviction inspiring. If he can be open, I decided, so can I.

A few days ago, I began tentatively to tell people about this experiment. To my surprise, I encountered few negative reactions. Every once in a while a listener might arch an eyebrow or smile uncomfortably, as if trying to figure out whether her discomfort meant that she wasn't hip enough, or whether I really was nuts. But those have been in the decided minority. Most people have been curious, even excited. Those with histories of mood disorders were intrigued to hear that my spirits have lifted, that though I sometimes feel the familiar clutch of anxiety in my

---

*In case you're old or a Luddite (or my mom): Reddit is an online bulletin board where people have conversations about all sorts of things. There are approximately thirty-six million Reddit user accounts, though some individuals own multiple accounts. Every month Reddit receives 234 million unique views (Mom, call me and I'll explain what that means). AMA stands for "Ask Me Anything." Famous and not-so-famous people will respond on Reddit to questions from users. Obama's done a Reddit AMA. So has that dude with two penises.

chest, I am generally able to use mindfulness techniques to make it dissolve. When I told them that I have not gained weight and that my libido has not withered away, they got really excited. The side effects of SSRIs are so ubiquitous and unpleasant that the idea of a medication protocol with fewer of them is thrilling.

Friends who incline to the spiritual were disappointed when they heard that I've experienced no connection to the divine, but reassured when I mention the pleasure I've taken in the natural world, the tree outside my window, the smell of the jasmine beside the city sidewalks. Risk takers and hedonists were disappointed that I was unable to provide details of hallucinations. No kaleidoscopic colors, they asked wistfully, no feeling that the floor was shifting beneath your feet? I live in California. The last thing I want to feel is the floor shifting beneath my feet. They urged me to try a "real" dose. It'd change my life, they said, as though my problem is that my life has been too devoid of weirdness. Besides, my life is changing.

Tonight, however, was a different story. These two writer friends are about twenty years older than my husband and I, which puts them firmly in the boomer generation. They were in their twenties in the 1960s. They've traveled the world, rejected a life of secure conformity in favor of the risks and rewards of art. What better people to confide in? I thought.

"Well," I said, "I've been writing, but not working on a novel. I've been writing about microdosing with LSD."

What does that mean? the woman of the pair asked. Are you writing some kind of nonfiction article on people who use LSD?

I took a breath and then explained.

Her face froze. If she had been wearing pearls, she would have clutched them. She looked horrified, even disgusted, as if I'd told her that I'd taken up murdering baby seals. Her husband's reaction was only slightly less disturbing. He smiled uncomfortably and changed the subject. I immediately agreed, yes, the antipasto was delicious, and, no, I didn't want any more.

Their reaction launched a series of cascading anxieties. Will I be condemned for doing this? Will people reject me as a nutcase, a crank, a deluded acid freak? Will I lose whatever credibility I have in the world? Will parents not let their children come over to our house anymore, under the misapprehension that I keep drugs in my home? I have tried to remind myself about all the people who've been open about their psychedelic use and have suffered little in the way of opprobrium. There's Tim Ferriss, Steve Jobs, Jack Nicholson, Richard Feynman, *South Park*'s Trey Parker and Matt Stone, Kary Mullis. Ilana and Abbi!

As soon as dinner was over, I tried the technique for dissipating anxiety that my cognitive behavioral therapist recommends. I took a few deep breaths, exhaling for half again as long as I inhaled. I identified the physical sensation of anxiety, placing it in my upper chest and in my throat. I drew a mental line along the borders of the area of anxiety. Then I placed a soothing hand on the area and murmured, "You're freaking the fuck out, you poor thing."* I took a few more slow breaths. "You feel bad right now, but you'll be okay. You'll be okay." My chest and throat unclenched. The anxiety ebbed. I was calm again. I was okay.

Also? I had some perspective. This couple were young in the 1960s, when Timothy Leary was spreading the gospel of psychedelic recklessness. For all I know, they had complicated histories with the drug that influenced how they responded to me. In all likelihood, their discomfort had far more to do with them than with me.

---

*Her instructions were silent on the issue of profanity, but I figure it can't hurt.

Day 26

....

Transition Day

Physical Sensations: None.

Mood: Excellent.

Conflict: None.

*Sleep: Only five hours. Nowhere near enough,
    but felt fine. Uh-oh.*

Work: Productive.

Pain: Minor.

I have only one more dose of Lewis Carroll's LSD. The thirty days will be up, the bottle will be empty. So is this it? Am I finished? Is the experiment over? The answer, at least initially, was obvious. I didn't want to go back to feeling the way I did a month ago. This perspective? This equanimity? I wanted it to continue. But that meant I needed more drugs.

Resupplying should have been easy. I live in the Bay Area, a community replete with people who spend every Labor Day cavorting naked on the playa at Black Rock City. I must have been bolder in my search than when I first embarked on this experiment, because this time it was not that hard, as it turns out, to track down a Burner with access to LSD. I was given a telephone number. I sent the Burner's friend's friend (whose name I was careful not to learn) an oddly formal text, describing my microdosing experiment, using the word "Lucy" instead of LSD. After I hit "send," I started to fret. How old was this person I was trying to do a drug deal with? Do young people even listen to the Beatles anymore? My kids certainly don't. Would the person on the other end of that number have the faintest idea what I was talking about?

Within an hour, I received a reply. Either kids do listen to the Beatles or, even better, the source was someone who's been doing this a good long time. Since a single regular dose of LSD lasts for one month, I decided that I would request a few doses. It was more than I was comfortable having in my possession, but if I continued the protocol it would allow me to avoid having to engage in the stressful business of buying drugs every month. It's hard enough to buy tampons or lube. Who needs the agita?

The source, whom I decided to name Lucy after the product she sells, replied that she could supply the number of doses I requested. She said she would deliver the drugs to me at my home. That was unacceptable to me: I won't even let someone from Craigslist show up here when I'm selling a sofa; I'd never expose my kids to a drug dealer. I suggested we meet up in the hills where I like to hike. Lucy rejected this and insisted on coming to my house. Against my better judgment, I offered a time when I knew I would be home alone and prayed that she'd turn out to be one of those honest, unarmed drug dealers.

A couple of hours before Lucy was due to arrive, it occurred to me that she wasn't likely to accept credit cards. And even if she did, I'd rather not give her mine. I ran down to the corner to the ATM.

I had just pulled a few twenties out of the machine (it's amazing how cheap LSD is—fifteen dollars a regular-size dose! That's a buck-fifty per microdose!) when my phone buzzed. Lucy wanted to know if I'd consider buying sixty doses from her. I stopped in the middle of the street and glanced around, suddenly fearful I was being followed. I've seen *Goodfellas*.

"Why?" I texted back. "That's far more than I could ever use. One dose lasts a month. Why would I want enough for five years?"

She replied. "I wouldn't know how to divide it. It's liquid."

I tapped out a reply. "Just put a few drops into a dark container. Or bring your bottle when you come and drop them into my little blue bot"—

I stopped typing.

When I was a federal defender, I had a client, a Mexican woman in her forties, a mother of five, who'd been abandoned by her husband. On a rare night out, she met a man in a bar. He was from Puerto Rico, and she found his accent beguiling. They exchanged phone numbers, and he began calling her, telling her how beautiful she was, how he couldn't get her out of his mind. My client was a frumpy little woman, with feet swollen from a lifetime of menial labor and thinning strawlike hair dyed the color of raw beef. She said the last time a man had called her beautiful was on her wedding day, when she was sixteen years old.

The couple didn't meet in person again; all their conversations happened over the phone. For days he flirted with her, describing the life they'd have together, how he'd be the father her children needed. Then he asked her if she could help him. He wasn't a drug dealer, he assured her. But he had an opportunity to make a single score, one that would set them up for their life together. Did she know anyone who had access to methamphetamine?

My client laughed. She was a domestic worker, a mother. She didn't know anyone who dealt drugs. But surely she knew some who *used* drugs, he persisted. She lived in East L.A., a center of drug activity. Wasn't there someone from the neighborhood who could point her in the right direction?

Day after day the couple would speak on the phone, and he'd beg her to help him find the methamphetamine. He was curiously specific about the quantity of drugs he desired. At least fifty grams, he said. She told him she had no access to drugs, she wouldn't know whom to ask. Ask your son! he suggested. Tell him to ask around his high school. Surely, he'd be willing to do this small thing for the sake of his mother and his soon-to-be stepfather's happiness, for the sake of his own future. Tell him to think of the house the family would move into with the money his new stepfather made from the score.

My client was torn. Not about whether she'd ask her child to search for drugs—that was out of the question. She was a fond and worried mother who hovered over her children, pushing them to complete homework she couldn't understand so they would get good grades, go to college, and have the kind of life she could not have imagined for herself when she was their age. But she had fallen hard for the lover from Puerto Rico. She wanted him to love her, and she worried that if she didn't help him he'd stop calling. She would find some, she told him. She would find methamphetamine.

Weeks passed, and they spoke every day. The calls were always the same. They began with talks of her beauty and his passion, and moved quickly to the drug deal, with the quantity of methamphetamine the man sought always carefully specified. No fewer than fifty grams, my client's telephone lover would remind her. She would reassure him that she was looking for the methamphetamine. Someday soon she would find a source.

Meanwhile, she begged her boyfriend to take their relationship to the next level, to meet her in person. He would promise to meet, but not until she had the drugs. Finally, he agreed to take her to dinner, even though she'd as yet been unsuccessful in finding the methamphetamine. The truth, which he didn't know, was that she had not even bothered to look. She knew no one who had access to drugs, nor did she want to know anyone who did.

On the evening of their first real date, she opened her door not to her lover, but to a phalanx of DEA agents. The man from Puerto Rico was not her boyfriend; he was an informant. Over the course of many weeks and long conversations about how beautiful she was and how he planned to spend the rest of his life with her, he'd set her up.

She was arrested and charged with conspiracy to deliver methamphetamine, specifically fifty grams, precisely the amount that would trigger a ten-year mandatory minimum prison sentence.

In the Criminal Code, the crime of conspiracy does not have as one of its elements the actual commission of the underlying felony; the agreement itself constitutes the crime. It was irrelevant to my client's case that no actual drugs had been exchanged. By promising to find methamphetamine, she had conspired to traffic. Her sentence would be determined by the quantity of drugs she had agreed to provide.

The only question that remained for the jury was whether she was entrapped, tricked into conspiring to commit the crime. Central to that question was whether or not my client was predisposed to deal drugs. If she was, then the informant's trickery was absolutely legal—no harm done. If she wasn't, then she must be acquitted.

I had, as you can imagine, a pretty good case, made all the better by what I discovered about the informant's long and colorful personal and professional history. After being found not guilty by reason of insanity of the attempted murder of his wife, the informant had escaped from a secure psychiatric facility and made his way to Central America, where he ended up in the employ of the CIA. His job with the CIA involved transporting cocaine. The CIA referred him to the DEA, who were even more generous than the spy agency had been. Over the years, the informant, a legally insane attempted murderer, earned hundreds of thousands of taxpayer dollars. He focused on first-time offenders, setting up one after another. These people inevitably went to jail, most of them for at least ten years. Then, in one of his cases, a large quantity of cash disappeared. The informant denied knowing anything about the lost money, but when his handlers hooked him up to a lie detector, he failed unambiguously. Their response? Not to charge him with a crime, but to move him to a different jurisdiction, where the defense attorneys would have no information about his nefarious past.

I would have found out nothing about this history but for a mistake in the discovery file the U.S. attorney was required to turn over to me. Though the documents were aggressively redacted, on one page the black pen had slipped, leaving part of a case number visible. It didn't take me long to tease out the jurisdiction. Half a dozen phone calls later, I had everything I needed to eviscerate the informant on the witness stand. I knew I could convince a jury that his testimony was at best unreliable, at worst criminal perjury.

When I confronted the assistant U.S. attorney about the man, he just shrugged. Your client is guilty, he said. We have her on tape.

But the informant! I insisted. He's a murderer! A perjurer!

The assistant U.S. attorney was unmoved.

Furious, I began spreading the word to the community. There's a man on the street in East L.A. soliciting drugs, I told people. He's not a buyer or a dealer, but a DEA informant. He's also easy to recognize amidst the various Latino communities of Los Angeles; he's got a Puerto Rican accent. Tell everyone you know.

Week after week, as I prepared for trial, my client was held in the Metropolitan Detention Center, while her kids struggled to care for themselves, to make it to school on time, the older ones taking responsibility for feeding the younger, working after school to earn money to pay the bills so they wouldn't be evicted or have the power cut off. And then, one day, I got a phone call from my client's sister, who lived in San Diego.

"Your secretary called me," the sister said.

"My secretary?"

"Your secretary says that you're a government agent. That you don't really work for my sister, but for the prosecution."

"I'm a government employee, true, but I represent your sister. I'm a federal public defender. She's my client. I do what's best for her, not for the government."

"Your secretary says to fire you. He says he can help me find a better lawyer."

My secretary was busily preparing for an elaborate wedding and had no time to talk with my clients' families about their cases. Moreover, my secretary was a woman.

"The man who said he was my secretary," I asked, "did he have a Puerto Rican accent?"

"Yes."

I don't remember if I said "Fuck" out loud, but chances are good.

Then my client's sister said, "I recorded his call on my answering machine. Do you want to hear the tape?"

What I wanted was for her to get in her car and drive it to me. "Do not speed," I said. "Do not get in an accident. Do not give the tape to anyone but me. I will be waiting in the street in front of the federal building." Hoping I don't get shot by that fucking madman, I thought to myself.

Two and a half hours later, a battered minivan pulled up to the curb. A sweet-faced young woman, short like my client but not carrying the weight of five pregnancies, peered at me from behind the steering wheel. Wisely, she insisted on seeing my picture ID before she handed me the tape. I ran with it up to the U.S. attorney's office.

As he listened to the tape, the AUSA's sneer curdled.

"Well?" I said.

"How did you get this?" he asked me.

I held his gaze. "Well?" I repeated.

He threw up his hands. "We'll dismiss."

Twenty years later, as I stared at the text from Lucy, I thought of this informant and his deliberate specificity about the quantity of drugs he wanted my client to produce. I had asked for a few doses, a quantity that I felt comfortable arguing was for personal use, a quantity I felt would limit any penalty to one I was willing to risk in order to preserve my emotional well-being and the stability of my family. But sixty doses? What court would ever believe that a single person intended to use sixty doses? Sixty doses didn't add up to possession for personal use. Sixty doses added up to intent to distribute.

I was suddenly certain that Lucy was no friend of a friend of a friend. She was a confidential informant, or maybe just a cop. Remember that scene in *Pulp Fiction* where Vince (John Travolta) calls Lance the drug dealer (Eric Stoltz)? Realizing that Vince is calling about a girl who has ODed and might die, Stoltz shouts into the phone, "Prank caller! Prank caller!" and slams the phone down. That was me on the street corner.

A bead of sweat trickling down my forehead. Fingers trembling, I typed, "No thanks. I'm only interested in a small quantity for PERSONAL USE. I wouldn't know what to do with more than that."

I hit "send," then deleted the text stream from my phone. I would not be buying LSD from Lucy or from anyone else.

Shaking, I walked home and tried to prepare myself. It mattered not at all that I'd never bought the drug. The crime of conspiracy lies in the agreement, not the action. It wouldn't take them long. Meditation, it turns out, does little to calm the nerves when one is waiting to be arrested.

Spoiler alert: I'm still here.

What I won't be doing ever again, however, is buying illegal drugs. So I suppose that means the next Microdose Day will be my last.

Day 27

....

Normal Day
Physical Sensations: None.
Mood: A little irritable.
Conflict: Yup.
Sleep: Better than last night.
Work: Day off.
Pain: Minor.

Today I was doing a fund-raising event for my kid's school, a Moms' Sunday Brunch in which each attendee received a copy of my book *Bad Mother*. As the assembled moms picked at fresh strawberries and scones and drank lukewarm Peet's coffee, I talked about modern motherhood's minor calamities and occasional moments of grace. I've given this talk hundreds of times; it goes over well. People laugh, maybe they tear up a bit, every once in a rare while they disagree, but it's always friendly and supportive. That is the message of the book—that as mothers we are far too hard on both ourselves and each other, that we need to cut ourselves and each other a break.

In a portion of the talk during which I railed against the parental anxiety that has caused us to lock our children in our houses, letting them outside only for playdates and other adult-mediated activities, one of the moms interrupted me. She lived with her family in an affluent and safe part of Berkeley, she said, but she had only just begun to let her thirteen-year-old go on her own to the nearby shopping district. To get there the girl had to cross a busy street, she explained. Mom was very worried that she'd get hit by a car.

"Exactly!" I said. "That's exactly what we all do. We are so plagued by unrealistic fears that we treat our preteens like toddlers! We forget that a child of seven, even five, can learn to cross the street safely. We indulge our panic at the expense of their independence."

She smiled beatifically. No, she insisted. I misunderstood. She wasn't confessing to maternal *failing* but bragging about maternal *competence*. She was keeping her children safe. What I was advocating was irresponsibility. *I* might be a Bad Mother, but she certainly wasn't.

I wonder what would have happened if she'd learned not only that I am an irresponsible parent who advocates letting thirteen-year-olds cross streets all by themselves, but that I'm also "on drugs"? Was she the type who had Child Protective Services on speed-dial just in case she passed a bunch of kids playing alone outdoors while their lazy mom knocked back Chardonnay (or LSD) in the kitchen?

I must, however, confront the truth about why I find myself so annoyed by this woman: I am defensive. I am defensive because part of me agrees with what I imagine she would think of me. Part of me feels that what I'm doing is irresponsible. It's irresponsible for a mother to do a microdose experiment. Not because the experiment itself is risky—I am satisfied with how carefully I approached microdosing, with the research I did and the precautions I took. Moreover, after nearly a month, the only negative things I've experienced are a slight increase in insomnia and an occasional irritable mood on Microdose Day, neither of which is worse than anything I regularly suffered before. The experiment is irresponsible not because of the drug itself, but because it is a crime, just like my botched attempt to buy LSD.

It's a crime, but it really shouldn't be.

Ever since I experienced the War on Drugs firsthand as a public defender, I have been an advocate for drug policy reform. This endless war has led to terrible injustices, far worse ones than the potential prosecution of a middle-class white lady for microdosing with LSD. It has resulted in the incarceration of millions of people, primarily black and brown. It has, as the law professor Michelle Alexander illustrated so beautifully in her revolutionary book, *The New Jim Crow*, been as effective at the immiseration and oppression of communities of color as segregation ever was. And yet it has failed to achieve even its most basic goals. People still use drugs. In fact, drugs like cocaine and heroin get ever cheaper, proving economically the fruitlessness of interdiction campaigns. When one drug proves harder to make or market, a more dangerous drug takes its place.

The effects of criminalization reverberate throughout the world. The United States has compelled most countries to sign on to international treaties committing them to criminalize the same drugs we do.* With well-regulated pharmaceutical companies out of the business of producing certain drugs, the way has been cleared for the proliferation of criminal enterprises, most of which generate the bulk of their profits right here in the States. The illegal drug market is the most profitable commercial enterprise in the world—more profitable than Apple and Walmart. Drugs that cost pennies to produce in developing countries sell for vast sums on the streets of America and Europe, thus crowding out all other products those countries might otherwise have grown or produced.

Horrific violence has periodically broken out in the United States, with waves of gang- and drug-dealing-related turf wars, but the bulk of drug-trafficking misery has been experienced abroad. Drug cartels have undermined democratic institutions in Latin America, taking over local governments with cata-

---

*The Single Convention on Narcotic Drugs of 1961, the Convention on Psychotropic Substances of 1971, and the United Nations Convention Against Illicit Traffic in Narcotic Drugs and Psychotropic Substances of 1988.

strophic results. In Mexico, for example, narco-traffickers have murdered as many as 120,000 people and caused the disappearance of 25,000 in the last decade alone.

Given the myriad injustices of mass criminalization and mass incarceration, and given the astonishing financial rewards that have accrued to violent criminal syndicates by our current policy, it's time to consider a change. In May 2014, Judge Richard Posner of the U.S. Court of Appeals for the Seventh Circuit, a conservative who is the most-cited legal scholar of the last century, published a book review in the *New Republic* in which he argued for the decriminalization not only of marijuana, but of all drugs, including LSD. Posner argued that decriminalization would alleviate the deplorable conditions in prisons caused by overcrowding:

> The sale and possession of marijuana are en route to being decriminalized; and I am inclined to think that cocaine, heroin, methamphetamine, LSD, and the rest of the illegal drugs should be decriminalized as well—though not deregulated. They should be regulated by the Food and Drug Administration for safety, like other drugs, and they should be taxed heavily, like alcohol and cigarettes. Alcohol and cigarettes are "recreational" drugs, too—and quite possibly more destructive of the users than the illegal drugs are, and, in the case of alcohol, also of acquaintances, family members, drivers, and pedestrians. The revenue from a sales tax on marijuana alone would pay for a substantial chunk of the cost of our prison system.*

The fact that conservative thinkers are making these arguments is an indication that change is, if not probable, then possible.

---

*Richard A. Posner, "We Need a Strong Prison System."

Some countries around the world have begun to rethink their drug policies. In 2001, Portugal decriminalized all drugs, including heroin and cocaine. It did not *legalize* drugs. Possession and use are still prosecuted, but as administrative violations instead of crimes. Distribution is still a criminal offense. The results of this dramatic change in approach are striking. As was anticipated by advocates of harm reduction, the spread of disease, petty crime, and overdose were substantially reduced or eliminated. More interesting: the massive increase in rates of drug use and addiction that opponents of decriminalization threatened simply did not materialize. As the award-winning journalist and author Glenn Greenwald writes in a white paper published by the Cato Institute,

> By freeing its citizens from the fear of prosecution and imprisonment for drug usage, Portugal has dramatically improved its ability to encourage drug addicts to avail themselves of treatment. The resources that were previously devoted to prosecuting and imprisoning drug addicts are now available to provide treatment programs to addicts. Those developments, along with Portugal's shift to a harm-reduction approach, have dramatically improved drug-related social ills, including drug-caused mortalities and drug-related disease transmission.*

Turns out, when you stop fighting a war, fewer people die.

I asked a number of drug policy analysts, including Michelle Alexander, Dr. Carl Hart, Ethan Nadelmann (executive director of the Drug Policy Alliance), Stephen Gutwillig (its deputy executive director), and Major Neill Franklin (a thirty-four-year veteran of the Baltimore and Maryland state police departments, now the executive director of Law Enforcement Against Prohibi-

---

*Glenn Greenwald, *Drug Decriminalization in Portugal,* p. 28.

tion), to help me imagine what a world without drug prohibition might look like. They all embraced the challenge.

Ethan Nadelmann believes that to effect real change one would need to imagine the existence in our Constitution of a freedom over consciousness, in the same way that there is a right to free expression. As difficult as this is to contemplate, he points out that when the Bill of Rights was first imagined, it, too, was radical. Freedom of speech was considered something that could bring down a society. In the same way, he urges us to imagine a core freedom over our minds around which to structure any efforts to regulate drug use and abuse.

My experts all agree that there is an inherent human instinct to alter consciousness, one so powerful that there has never in human history existed a drug-free society. As Neill Franklin told me, "There have always been drugs, and there will always be drugs." At the core of our current punitive system, Stephen Gutwillig argues, is a profoundly puritanical rejection of this impulse to alter consciousness, a hatred of drugs and drug users. Ending prohibition would require letting go of this control.

I asked them to imagine a world without this puritanical impulse, or at least a world where governments recognized that drugs will always exist, and the only question is who will control their promulgation: criminal enterprises or governments. Would the ideal system be one like Portugal's, with the use of drugs decriminalized? Or would a system of full legalization be preferable, in which the production and distribution of currently illegal drugs were actually made legal? In that system, would I be able to use my sixty feet of accumulated CVS ExtraBucks to buy my next little blue bottle of diluted LSD?

Dr. Hart told me that, though he used to support a policy of decriminalization such as Portugal's, he is now in favor of the legalization of all drugs, with a regulatory system put in place like the one we currently have for the drug he views as the most dangerous—alcohol. Nadelmann and Gutwillig agree, though they don't aspire to a world where all drugs are commodified and controlled by the free market. They believe that a sensible drug policy includes a public health component, with regulators playing a role by making decisions about which drugs should be available to adults under what circumstances. They seek "to reduce the role of the criminal justice system in drug control as much as possible while still advancing health and safety." All of my experts, in fact, advocate a public health model that begins with a robust system of education for adults and children about both the benefits and the risks of drugs.

Though Dr. Hart rejects what he calls "drug-by-drug bullshit," to the Drug Policy Alliance and to Michelle Alexander, it makes sense to treat different classes of drugs in different ways. Marijuana, for example, is a drug for which they support full legalization. Unlike nearly every other medicine, marijuana has no lethal dose. Simply put, you cannot ingest enough of the drug to kill you (no matter what your freaked-out mind thinks when you've gobbled up too many edibles). This does not mean that there aren't harms associated with frequent marijuana use, especially by children and adolescents, but Gutwillig and Nadelmann believe that we can model marijuana legalization on our current approach to the far more harmful drugs nicotine and alcohol. In those situations, we leave it up to individual communities to decide how to regulate distribution.*

Recently, I took a trip to Louisiana, where you can buy alcohol not only at gas stations and supermarkets, but in drive-through liquor stores, which will sell you a Jell-O shot covered in a plas-

---

*We are actually well on our way to legalizing marijuana. In addition to Colorado, the states of Washington, Oregon, and Alaska and the District of Columbia have all recently legalized the possession and sale of small amounts of marijuana. Polls show that more than half the country favors this reform. Twenty-four states allow for the possession and distribution of medical marijuana, a policy supported by over 70 percent of the population. As people come to appreciate the tax revenues of legalized marijuana, and notice the few negative effects of these schemes, support is likely only to increase.

tic film, the way we here in California sell bubble tea.* I asked Gutwillig how he would feel about marijuana's being sold in a similar manner. He told me that he's not personally comfortable with having marijuana available outside of dedicated marijuana outlets, such as the ones currently licensed under Colorado's legalization scheme. When I posed the same question to Neill Franklin, he told me that he has no problem with seeing supermarkets sell drugs in their "natural" plant-based state—drugs like low-THC† weed or even coca leaves, which South Americans have chewed and brewed in tea for millennia as a low-grade stimulant similar to coffee. In fact, Franklin believes that under such a regulated system marijuana would end up being used as a substitute for alcohol, which he, like Dr. Hart, views as the drug associated with the most risk and negative outcomes. If marijuana use increases and alcohol use decreases, we will avoid at least some of the deaths associated with alcohol toxicity, and other harms as well. Driving under the influence of marijuana, though hardly safe, is much less dangerous than driving under the influence of alcohol. Furthermore, alcohol use is closely associated with violence, including sexual and domestic violence. Marijuana use is not.

Like marijuana, classic psychedelics such as LSD and psilocybin don't cause substantial harms if taken in appropriate doses. Gutwillig suggested online drug markets as a way to distribute psychedelics in a controlled and safe manner.

"How would that work?" I asked. "Would I be able to just go online and buy LSD?"

"Yes," he said. An adult would be able to go online and order a

---

*I'm willing to bet that the average consumer of Jell-O shots is even younger than the average consumer of bubble tea.

†Tetrahydrocannabinol, the primary psychoactive substance in marijuana. There are over a hundred cannabinoids in marijuana, including cannabidiol (CBD), which is less intoxicating and has anxiolytic, antipsychotic, antiemetic, and anti-inflammatory properties. See, e.g., M. M. Bergamaschi et al., "Safety and Side Effects of Cannabidiol, a Cannabis Sativa Constituent."

small dose of a psychedelic or of MDMA. She would be assured that what she received was in fact pure and unadulterated. In addition, she would receive warnings about potential dangers, and clear information about safe dosages relative to body mass, age, and experience. Such a system would have a substantial impact on individual and public health outcomes, because the harms associated with MDMA, and to a lesser extent psychedelics, are generally a function of dose and adulteration. As Dr. Hart says, "Focus on purity, focus on unit dose, focus on education."

If classic psychedelics and MDMA were available in a well-regulated and safety-tested manner, people would be far less likely to turn to new psychoactive substances, sometimes referred to as NPSs or alphabetamines,* synthetics with which all sorts of harms have been associated, including death.† Franklin suggested that in an ideal system there would be a role for psychedelic guides, perhaps centers where one could go to take psychedelics, offering a setting that maximized the potential for positive experiences and minimized the potential for harm. Kind of like a day spa, for tripping.

The topic of opioids is far more fraught, given the current surge in heroin use, the drug's high addiction rate (24 percent of users become addicted), and the recent dramatic spike in overdose and death. Any potential medical model for regulated heroin legalization would have to take these dangers into consideration. Fortunately, we have evidence that shows that there are far better ways to treat heroin and opioid addiction and overdose than through interdiction and imprisonment. Back in the 1990s, a psychiatrist in Liverpool, Dr. John Marks, experimented with an alternative model of treating addicts. Rather than incarcerating them or attempting to cure their addictions, he simply

---

*Drugs such as 25I-NBOMe and 5-MeO-AMT, both synthetic hallucinogens.
†The Wesleyan students who nearly died took K2 or AB-FUBINACA, a synthetic cannabinoid infinitely more dangerous than the relatively safe MDMA they thought they were getting.

focused on keeping addicts alive, healthy, and out of the criminal justice system. He did this by prescribing to each addict her drug of choice, including heroin.

The U.S. government responded with outrage, demanding that British authorities put a stop to Marks's project, but for a while at least, he was allowed to continue. His results were striking. Patients in heroin maintenance, those who actually received heroin from their physicians, did not suffer high rates of HIV and AIDS, because they were not sharing needles. There were far fewer overdoses and deaths, because the drugs they used were clean and carefully administered. Plus, the patients didn't commit crimes. All of this is to be expected: with ready access to their drugs, they didn't need to rob, cheat, or steal. The addicts in Marks's heroin maintenance program were healthy, most of them had jobs, and they had strong family ties.

What surprised everyone, however, was that addiction rates actually *decreased* in places where heroin maintenance was offered. Giving heroin to addicts didn't make them use more, or even make more people use. It actually *stopped* the spread of drug use and abuse. Why? The easiest way to think of this is like a scale. On one side of the scale is heroin. Addicts are obsessed with one thing, and one thing only: getting the next fix; doing whatever they can to get that fix takes up all of their time and energy. Marks simply removed the desperation and effort from the equation. Addicts in his program got their drugs in the morning and then spent the day with their families or at their jobs, just like Halsted, the founder of Johns Hopkins, the cocaine-and-morphine addict who invented modern surgery. Slowly but surely, the other side of the scale began to fill up with the satisfactions of work and relationships. When the scale reached the tipping point, when the pleasures of normal life outweighed the pleasure of the drug, the addicts were inspired to get clean. Every year, 5 percent of Marks's patients simply stopped using, without the help of methadone or rehab or any other intervention.

Who knows what might have happened had Marks been allowed to continue his project? But the United States wields a mighty sword when it comes to international drug policy. It put pressure on the British government, and Marks's program was eventually shut down. Within two years, twenty-five of his patients were dead, and all the rest were back on the streets or in jail—collateral damage of the unending, unwinnable worldwide war on drugs.

Inspired by Marks's results, Swiss researchers carried out a comparison study. Eight hundred volunteers were given heroin, one hundred were put on methadone, and one hundred were given morphine. They were followed for three years. The results for the eight hundred? As the author Mike Gray writes in *Drug Crazy: How We Got into This Mess and How We Can Get Out,* "Crime among the addict population dropped by 60 percent, half the unemployed found jobs, a third of those on welfare became self-supporting, nobody was homeless, and the general health of the group improved dramatically. By the end of the experiment, eighty-three patients had decided on their own to give up heroin in favor of abstinence."

In the United States, we spend more than twenty billion dollars a year on rehab, the majority of that not on evidence-based programs but on programs that have been shown again and again to be ineffective. The success rates for typical abstinence-based rehab programs are less than 25 percent. By some estimates, 90 percent of addicts who go through rehabilitation relapse within the first year.* Medication-based opioid rehabilitation programs that prescribe drug-replacement medications that alleviate the symptoms of detox, such as buprenorphine, trade name Subutex, and Suboxone, a compounded mixture of buprenorphine

---

*Interestingly, treatment with ibogaine, a psychedelic drug derived from the African iboga plant that works to alleviate withdrawal symptoms, shows much more promising (though preliminary) results in treating addiction than either drug-replacement or traditional abstinence-based programs. See Kenneth R. Alper, M.D. et al., "Treatment of Acute Opioid Withdrawal with Ibogaine."

and the opioid antagonist naloxone, are more successful, but they, too, have substantial limitations.

We can imagine a regulatory system like the one operated by Marks in Britain, which allows for the distribution of pure, unadulterated heroin and other opioids within clinical confines, and which also provides other services to addicts and other users. That system would not just maintain the health of addicts and preserve the peace, but would actually help people overcome their addictions.

It's important when talking about opioids to remember what Dr. Hart stresses. The vast majority of people who use will not become addicted, so "it's a waste of time and effort to offer them treatment." Both he and Franklin would make these drugs available to the public and provide treatment to those who need it, "making sure that the unit dose enhances safety and minimizes toxicity." They would also provide clear, honest, and thorough education about the risks and benefits of these and all drugs.

A legalization scheme for stimulants such as cocaine and methamphetamine is even more challenging to imagine than one for opioids, because stimulants are, next to alcohol, the drugs most commonly associated with antisocial behavior.* According to Dr. Hart, "Methamphetamine abuse is associated with multiple deleterious medical consequences, including paranoia mimicking full-blown psychosis."† Adopting a purely market-based approach for drugs with such potential negative consequences made Gutwillig uncomfortable, though Franklin less so. Franklin can imagine a variety of possible regulatory schemes for cocaine, amphetamine, and methamphetamine, and pointed out that we currently have a medical model for the use of stimulants that, though hardly perfect, does function tolerably well. The millions of Americans who are prescribed Adderall, a stimulant in the

*See, e.g., *Breaking Bad*.
†Carl L. Hart et al., "Is Cognitive Functioning Impaired in Methamphetamine Users? A Critical Review."

same class of drugs as methamphetamine, fill their prescriptions legally at pharmacies. A similar system for cocaine, amphetamine, and methamphetamine might allow a patient or user to go to a pharmacy, present her ID to prove she is of legal age, and receive a dose of the drug appropriate to her size and experience.

"Treat methamphetamine like Adderall?" I asked. "Does that really make sense?"

In fact, it does. According to Dr. Hart, d-amphetamine, the main ingredient in Adderall, and methamphetamine, are chemically virtually identical.* They function in the same way in the brain. Like Adderall, methamphetamine improves focus and performance. The intensity of both drugs is enhanced when they are smoked or snorted, as is commonly the case in illicit use, as opposed to swallowed in pill form. Meth is a more problematic drug than Adderall because of how it's ingested, and because it's illegally obtained and thus often adulterated—not because of anything intrinsic to the drug itself. Individuals who are prescribed pharmaceutical methamphetamine in appropriate doses suffer no more harm than those prescribed Adderall. Because of this, and despite their concerns, all my experts agree that it would make sense to treat methamphetamine like Adderall and the other stimulants in its class.

I asked my experts if they would anticipate an increase in casual drug use were we to abolish prohibition. Most agreed that rates of use are likely to rise initially, before settling down to rates comparable to what we see now. However, increased use does not, according to Franklin, "necessarily equate with problematic use. Products would be safer to use, education would be robust, and thus use would be less problematic. If we move drug use to a place of health instead of criminal justice, then there would be quicker access to treatment. What we're spend-

*M. G. Kirkpatrick et al., "Comparison of Intranasal Methamphetamine and D-Amphetamine Self-Administration by Humans."

ing now for cops, courtrooms, and prisons would go instead to public health." Less scare, more care.

Though imagining a more sane and sensible system with these experts was a fascinating exercise, I sympathize with Dr. Hart's frustration when he told me, "I'm over the rethinking of drug policy. We need to actually just do it." Fortunately, pressures to liberate us from the horrible damage caused by the War on Drugs have intensified internationally. In April 2016, the UN General Assembly held a special session on drugs, in anticipation of which former Secretary General Kofi Annan called for the decriminalization of all drugs for personal use, the increase in treatment options for drug abusers, the implementation of harm-reduction strategies such as needle exchange programs, and a focus on regulation and public education, rather than criminalization. In an op-ed in the Huffington Post, Annan wrote, "It is time to acknowledge that drugs are infinitely more dangerous if they are left solely in the hands of criminals who have no concerns about health and safety. Legal regulation protects health."*

This is remarkable, given that the slogan of the last UN General Assembly Special Session on Drugs in 1998 was "A Drug-Free World—We Can Do It!" It took nearly twenty years, but finally at least some in the international community have come to realize that we will never have a drug-free world. What we need to strive for is a world free of a drug market controlled by vicious criminal syndicates, where hundreds of thousands are murdered and hundreds of thousands more die of drug reactions and overdose, where millions are incarcerated, and where none can gain legal access to drugs that have the potential for markedly improving their lives.

I have worked on drug policy issues for over two decades. When I first began speaking about decriminalization, back in the 1990s, when politicians were inveighing against "super-

---

*Kofi Annan, "Why It's Time to Legalize Drugs."

predators" and calling for ever-more draconian penalties, people thought I was at best a naïve dreamer, and at worst a dangerous drug advocate. And yet now here we are with the United Nations practicing radical sanity. It's entirely possible that we may in fact one day see a system in which drug use is decriminalized, treatment is available to those who need it, and drugs like psilocybin and MDMA can be prescribed under certain limited conditions. I wonder what that brunch mom will say if this happens? Will we be having conversations about the age at which our children are allowed to smoke a doobie, and will that be before or after they're allowed to cross the street?

Day 28

....

Microdose Day

*Physical Sensations: Slightly dizzy about three
   hours after dose.*

Mood: Activated. Edgy.

Conflict: Disagreement with my husband.

*Sleep: A better night's sleep than on other
   Microdose Days.*

Work: Productive workday.

Pain: Minor.

It began when I lobbed a passive-aggressive salvo through the
closed bathroom door. My shoulder was hurting, I said, and it
had to be from writing while lying on the uncomfortable couch.

"Let's agree that the next time we buy a couch we will consult
one another," I said.

As if we spend our days buying couches. As if we are likely to
buy another couch in the next decade.

After a moment, my husband answered: "Your problem isn't
the couch, or my chair, or the eight-track players. Your problem
is that you want a room of your own." Here we go again. They
should write a play about us called *Who's Afraid of Admitting
Virginia Woolf Was Right?*

"I do not. I just can't work in there."

"Exactly. You can't work in there. You want your own space. But you don't feel like you deserve it."

He's said that before, and I always respond that he's the one who wants me out of his studio. We bicker over who it is that wants me out, and then we make up and resolve to share the space more cooperatively. But this time I remembered the day a few weeks ago, when, in a fit of pique, I packed away my things from his studio: the photographs of the children, my row of books, my little laptop stand. After I had put the bin in the storage shed, I had been perfectly comfortable on the uncomfortable couch. I had felt at ease, as I feel when I write in a café. In a café, the space doesn't feel like it's mine, because it's not mine. It was when I treated the studio as my husband's, and myself as the guest that I always felt I was, that I finally felt comfortable.

I remembered that feeling, and I was finally able to admit that he is right. What I want is not a corner of his space, or even a precisely delineated half of it. What I want is a room of my own. But I don't feel I deserve one.

In part, it's about money. In the words of Virginia Woolf, "Money dignifies what is frivolous if unpaid for." Though I have always been paid well enough for my writing, I earn a fraction of what my husband does. Not just the typical seventy-nine cents every woman earns to a man's dollar. Even less than that. From the very beginning, this has bothered me. There was a while, when our kids were small, when I became obsessed with the salary of the nanny we hired after our third child was born. At the end of every year, I would do an assessment. If I earned more than I paid the nanny, I was relieved. If I earned less, I was devastated. How could I justify this frivolous career when I couldn't even pay for the child care I needed because I was pursuing this frivolous career?

I was aware of how irrational I was being. We employed a nanny not so I could work, but so *we* could work. My husband was no less responsible for child care than I was. He is a feminist, born and bred, and never for a moment did he consider child care solely my expense, but both of ours. So why did I off-set the nanny's salary only against my own? Why did my mental equation not include what he was bringing in?

For the past five years, I have earned a good living. Not as much as my husband, but enough so that if I had to I could support a middle-class lifestyle for our family. Was it because I was making more money that I suddenly felt free to resent his vast collection of obsolete audio equipment and his uncomfortable couch? Could it be that simple?

Like every other young woman in a "Take Back the Night" T-shirt, I read *A Room of One's Own* in my first Women's Studies class. And my second, and my third, and I think pretty much every single Women's Studies class I ever took. Woolf's message is clear, compelling, and seductive: "A woman must have money and a room of her own if she is to write fiction."

Actually, Woolf was quite specific. If a woman is to indulge in the literary life, she must have five hundred pounds a year. According to a number of Web sites whose authority I have decided for no particular reason to trust, five hundred 1929 pounds sterling is worth $38,383.44 today. I make more than that.

So I've got the money. What I don't have is a room of my own.

My husband came out of the bathroom, dried his hands, and turned to me, loins girded for the fight he anticipated.

I cut him off at the pass. "You're right. You've been right all along. I want a room of my own."

"Finally!"

"I want my own studio."

"Exactly."

"I have been fighting with you for months—"

"Years." Okay, he was starting to get a little drunk on my capitulation, but I guess he had earned it.

"I have been fighting with you for years because I couldn't

accept that I deserved my own workspace." Finally, we could put this stupid argument to bed. We knew the answer!

My husband opened his arms and I fell into them. Then my face fell.

"We have a problem," I said. "Studio space is just too expensive. And there's nowhere here for me to work."

"What about Dr. Schaeffer's consulting room?" my husband asked. "Could you work there?"

"It's dark and gloomy," I said. "It's a vampire's lair."

"Paint it," my husband said. "Paint it white."

"But that's the original woodwork!" I reminded him of what happened with the Gamble House in Pasadena, the masterpiece of Arts and Crafts architecture designed and built by Charles and Henry Greene. The son of David and Mary Gamble, the couple for whom the house was built, put the house on the market, only to change his mind after overhearing a prospective buyer flick a derisive finger at the floor-to-ceiling teak and mahogany woodwork and say something to the effect of "First thing we'll do is paint all this dark wood white."

"Yeah, but this isn't the Gamble house," my husband said. The woodwork in our house is lovely, but it's fir, not mahogany. Moreover, we've preserved it throughout the rest of the house. "It's just the one room. And we don't ever plan on selling. Let the kids worry about the resale value."

I wasn't done arguing. "The office isn't empty," I said. "The assistant uses it. Where would she work?"

Who, he wondered, needs a room more, the assistant or the person who is ostensibly to do the work the assistant is meant to facilitate?

Well, when you put it like that, the answer was so obvious.

"She does," I said.

This feeling of being undeserving, then, and not money, was the heart of the matter. All of this rootlessness, this squatting in corners, in cafés, at the kitchen table, has been a manifestation of my insecurity—not about my failure to earn as much as my husband, but about the inherent value of my work. I don't feel I deserve a room of my own, because I feel, no matter how much I earn, that my work is worthless.

These are some of the things I've said about my work:

- "They're meant to be read with the amount of attention you can muster while breastfeeding" (about my murder mysteries).
- "It's kind of glorified Chick Lit" (about *Love and Other Impossible Pursuits*).
- "It's more of a polemic than a novel" (about *Daughter's Keeper*).
- "I'm not an artist, more of a craftsman."

I suppose much of this has to do with how I got my start, as the author of a series of commercial murder mysteries, the kind you might find on a rack in a drugstore. When I published those books, I loudly proclaimed I had no literary pretensions. I thought I was being honest, but now I realize I was just being cowardly—saying what I worried others might say about me before they had the chance to. If I dared to nurture creative ambitions, I would put myself in danger of failing to fulfill them.

Though I am proud of my books, there is a vicious voice in my head that tells me I'm worthless. Even when I hold in my hands the finished product, even as I feel my chest expand with pride, the voice says, "This book isn't any good," or "It's okay, but you'll never be able to do it again." Every single time I sit down to work, I hear that ugly whisper in my ear. How can I expect others to take me seriously as a writer when I look down on myself?

As I write this, I realize that during this past month that ugly voice has been quieter. There were even days when I didn't hear her at all. It can only be microdosing (or the mother of all placebo effects) that has allowed me to distract my inner self-loathing insecurity-monster long enough to have what has turned out to be the most productive month of my writing life.

The painter is coming on Wednesday with buckets of white paint. I know there are those who consider what I'm about to do to the paneling, wainscoting, and trim to be a sacrilege, but if Dr. Schaeffer's consulting room is to be mine, I want it to be bright and clean, antiseptic and new. My room. My own.

Day 29

....

Transition Day

Physical Sensations: None.

Mood: A little low, but as soon as I started to work, it passed.

Conflict: None.

Sleep: Decent night's sleep.

Work: Productive.

Pain: First really painful day in quite a while.

Why is my shoulder pain back? I had such a great day yesterday, with such profound realizations and resolutions. It sucks to be back in this place of pain. Although, when I sit and really consider my shoulder, I think (though I may be deluding myself) that there's a different quality to the pain. It's not merely a matter of intensity, though it is indeed less intense. It feels less . . . permanent. Or perhaps it's merely that, having experienced pain-free days, I am optimistic that this bout will soon all be over.

The experience of optimism is an unfamiliar one for me. I am by nature a pessimist, able to anticipate the possibility of doom in virtually any circumstance. Even when the glass is full, I know that it's likely to get toppled over and its contents spilled, probably right into my open laptop. I imbibed this cocktail of negativity combined with misanthropy and laced with a heady combination of arrogance and self-loathing from my father, without realizing either how unhappy it made me or that there were ten other ways to look at things and I was always choosing the worst. It wasn't until I met my husband that I realized that a belief that the fucked-up world is filled with stupid people isn't a necessary corollary of intelligence. It's actually kinda dumb.

Each morning, I find myself astonished anew at how my husband wakes up convinced that his day will contain a series of delights and pleasures, as if he's holding a golden ticket to visit Willy Wonka's factory. Unfortunately, only one of our children shares his seemingly boundless capacity for optimism. When she was younger, this child routinely woke up in the morning and announced, "This is the best day of my life!" She would probably have gotten annoyed at all the looks the rest of us exchanged over her alien sunniness, but she doesn't really get annoyed, bless her little unblackened heart. The other kids and I, on the other hand, are confident, until proven otherwise, that what we have to look forward to is a more or less typical amount of shit.

And yet here I am, feeling hopeful and optimistic. Is it micro-dosing with LSD that has allowed my newly plastic brain to wiggle its way out from beneath its typical fog of negativity?

I wonder what would have happened had my father been born ten or twenty years later. What if he had been young when psychedelics first began infiltrating the culture? He was, after all, a political revolutionary. He despised capitalism, hated "the man." If he had been a young man in the 1960s instead of in the 1940s, perhaps his ideological commitment might have been to the kind of free-range West Coast socialism that flourished right here in Berkeley, rather than to the Zionism of the Israeli kibbutz.

What if my father had taken LSD?

I'm not naïve. I don't believe that a single tab of acid would have cured his bipolar disorder, reordered his grim view of the world, made my parents' marriage happy, but it is not impossible to imagine my father's life being different. I have a friend close to my father's age, a Hungarian immigrant whom I'll call Laszlo. During the Holocaust, Laszlo, then a child, was saved by a Gentile friend of the family, who smuggled him out of the village where he had been staying with his grandparents, to his mother in Budapest. The rest of Laszlo's large extended family in the village was deported to Auschwitz and murdered. In Budapest, Laszlo, his mother, and his sister were once again saved, this time by Giorgio Perlasca, an Italian former Fascist party member who, posing as the Spanish consul general to Hungary, provided documents, protected housing, and eventually even food to over five thousand Jews. Laszlo's father, who had been conscripted earlier in the war into the Hungarian forced-labor battalions, never returned.

A college student in Budapest in 1956, Laszlo was active in the failed revolution, and was forced to flee when the Soviet military invaded. He escaped to Austria and eventually to the United States, where he, like so many of his fellows, flourished. A former engineer who came to Silicon Valley in the early days, Laszlo is a venture capitalist and a philanthropist, with a foundation that initially focused on human rights, education, and health issues, and has lately shifted its concentration to mental health in young people. Laszlo was married and divorced twice. Despite accomplishing so much, for most of his life Laszlo has also been profoundly unhappy. He told me that when his children were young they used to ask him, "Dad, how come you're never smiling? How come you never have fun?"

I first met Laszlo through a friend who knew I was researching and writing a novel set in Hungary. At the time, I seemed to be collecting Hungarian gentlemen friends of a certain age. Laszlo was an invaluable resource, and a lovely man, whose sadness was palpable. Then, when I saw him again recently, I found him profoundly changed.

Over dim sum at our mutual favorite restaurant, Laszlo told me the most remarkable story. Like my father, Laszlo missed the era of drug experimentation. During the sixties, he was focused on going to school and earning money to support his mother and sister, and eventually his wives and children. Smoking weed or taking acid was not something he had time for.

Recently, a friend who knew that Laszlo had struggled with depression suggested that he take the hallucinogenic drug aya-huasca, commonly used by native peoples of the Amazon. Laszlo initially rejected the idea. It seemed crazy. But he was in pain, and he was desperate, much as I was when I began this experiment. He agreed to accompany his friend, a physician and an expert in early-childhood trauma and its effects on mental and physical health, and fly to a place where ayahuasca could be legally consumed with the guidance of a "shaman." If Laszlo had any expectations, they were only that he might spend a night in intense intestinal discomfort while seeing wild shapes and colors. Instead, he saw his father.

Laszlo was four years old when his father vanished, and he had never understood why his father had not said goodbye. With a child's naïveté, he imagined that it was his fault that his father left, that he had been a "bad boy." That pain lingered into his adulthood. Under the influence of this brew of the *Banisteriopsis caapi* vine, Laszlo heard his father's voice.

Laszlo asked his father why he had disappeared without even a final embrace. His father told him that the answer was simple: He had never imagined that his conscription would be permanent. He believed he would be home by the end of the day, and had simply not wanted to wake his little son.

Then Laszlo asked, "Did you love me?"

Laszlo found himself staring at a pile of corpses—men in prisoners' garb who had died, frozen in formation. His father pointed to a skeleton, the only body not covered in snow. "That is my body," Laszlo's father said. "With my last breath, I blessed you and I promised to guard you all of your life."

And then, suddenly, the sadness and longing that had tormented Laszlo dissipated. He understood why he had not only survived the Nazis and the Russians, but had been so incredibly successful throughout his life. Far from being abandoned by his father, he had thrived under his protection.

The profound spiritual experience Laszlo describes is all the more remarkable given that he, like me, is not a religious person. And yet he believes that what happened to him under the influence of ayahuasca was an authentic spiritual experience. He believes that the drug wrenched open the Doors of Perception and allowed him to glimpse truth. He believes not that he fantasized those moments with his father in the snow, but that they stood side by side somewhere, someplace back in time or in another dimension. Is that true? Or did the drug help Laszlo experience what he needed to feel in order to heal?

As so many of the researchers and philosophers with whom I've spoken have asked me, what difference does it make? The experience profoundly changed Laszlo. He is happier, lighter, more content and loving. His relationship with his children is better than ever. The pain that defined his life is gone.

I don't know where my father's pain comes from, but I wish it could dissipate like Laszlo's did. However, my father isn't about to trek off to Peru and puke in a bucket in a shaman's hut. He's not even going to experiment with microdoses of LSD. That's just not who he is.

It's a truism to say we can't change anyone, not even the ones we love. You can find that sentiment on a thousand coffee mugs and inspirational Facebook photos. Just as I can't force my father to drop a tab of acid, neither can I force him to confide in me. I cannot plumb the depths of his soul by listening to his psychotherapy tapes or plying him with questions. I cannot demand that he express love in a way that's meaningful to *me*. Though the desire to do so might be understandable, it isn't fair. In my relationship with my father I am always grasping, always *needing*. But aching for the ideal gets in the way of the actual. I have resented my father because he wasn't affectionate like Shimon, empathetic like Fadiman, willing to take risks for the sake of self-knowledge like Laszlo. What's the point of all this resentment? What good has it done me? It certainly hasn't made either me or my dad any more content. There is a mutually satisfying relationship to be had with my father; just not the one I have been craving for so long. Got any pressing questions about the Gulag? Curious about the casualty rate at the Battle of Shiloh? Let me know; I'll ask my dad.

Day 30

....

Normal Day

Physical Sensations: None.

Mood: A little wistful.

Conflict: None.

Sleep: Woke in the middle of the night. Had trouble falling back to sleep.

Work: Productive.

Pain: Seems really to be resolving.

Today I completed ten cycles of observation, and the experiment is over. The protocol asks that I prepare a report of my experience, and include "insights, advice, concerns, suggestions or warnings." Um, that one's easy. Don't try to cop from a stranger who might be a cop.

I began the experiment with great nervousness and excitement. I felt almost euphoric on the first day. Within two hours of dosing, I felt like my senses were ever so slightly heightened. On a walk to get some lunch, I noticed the beauty of my neighborhood, the trees and flowers, the smell of the jasmine. After lunch, I felt slightly nauseated.

The only days on which I experienced any unusual physical or mental sensations were the Microdose Days. I never again felt the same level of heightened sensation, but I did occasionally feel I was more aware of my surroundings. One time, I felt that my hearing was sharper; I noticed the sound of my fingers tapping on my keyboard. These sensations passed quickly, gone within ninety minutes or two hours of taking the microdose. As the month progressed, I began occasionally to feel dizzy or nauseated on Microdose Day. Additionally, I felt more activated. On Day 7, I felt nearly hypomanic; my words were racing.* I never experienced those symptoms on Transition Days or Normal Days.

Since I engaged in the experiment specifically because I want more control over my mood, that is what I monitored most closely. On some Microdose Days, I experienced a sense of well-being and joy that felt nearly, though not quite, euphoric. As the month progressed, however, while I continued to experience moments of heightened joy, I also began to feel more prone to irritability on Microdose Days. Sometimes I felt edgy and anxious. On Transition Days, by contrast, I felt generally wonderful, optimistic, and easygoing. I was, by and large, my best self.

My sleep was definitely affected by the protocol. On Microdose Days, I had a much harder time falling asleep. I stayed up later, and woke up earlier the next day. My sleep sometimes remained out of whack until the Normal Day.

I had one very serious fight with my husband on a Microdose Day. This conflict was unpleasant and difficult, but I noticed a slight difference between it and the kind of argument I might have had before the experiment. Generally, when I have a conflict with my husband (or when I embarrass myself online), the end result for me is a feeling of intense shame. My guilt becomes nearly unbearable and triggers depression. I have been working on these feelings of shame and guilt with my therapist, whom I started seeing a few months before I began the experiment. Over this past month, I was successful in using the tools she taught me both to engage in more productive conflict and to be more

*That was the day when I suddenly decided to describe this experiment to a physical therapist I barely knew.

forgiving of myself after the resolution of conflict. I think I also fought in a way that was less shame-inducing.

The therapy is responsible for this change of approach, but I've been in therapy before. Many different therapists have pointed out to me how detrimental my self-blame is. It could certainly be a coincidence that the message seems to have penetrated this month in a way it never has before. But I find myself wanting to ascribe my receptivity to a change brought about by the protocol.

My diet and exercise remained more or less the same throughout the month. I was not quite as hungry on Microdose Day, but I didn't eat any less than usual. Microdosing is not, for me at least, a weight loss regimen.

The pain of my frozen shoulder substantially decreased. I have not been woken up in the middle of the night by pain for a few weeks. I don't know whether this can fairly be attributed to the microdose, however. Most people do experience an eventual easing of such symptoms, and it's been nearly eighteen months since my shoulder froze. Maybe it's just a coincidence that this is the month when it began to unfreeze.

It is in the area of work that I noticed the most dramatic change. I don't know if this is a result of the protocol itself or a result of my decision to use the structure of the protocol as a means to force myself to put words on paper each and every day. I took just a single day off during this thirty-day period, something out of the ordinary for me. Usually, I work only during the week, and even then I often find excuses not to sit down and bang out the words. I am a marvelously effective procrastinator. I get right to it. And yet, over these thirty days, I never wrote fewer than two pages a day and sometimes wrote as many as ten. I have once or twice before in my life written this much in a single month, but never with such ease and pleasure. Maybe I've turned into one of those clone robots of myself my therapist asked me to imagine!

I began the experiment because my moods have not only

made me unhappy, they have damaged the people around me. Families are hostages to the moods of their members. This was true of my family while I was growing up. When my parents were happier, when they felt optimistic, I was relaxed—at ease with the world and able to find joy. When they were angry or absent, I was fretful and sad. And, even knowing that was true, I had been unable to do things much differently. My children's experience reflects my own, as does my husband's. When my mood is low, it is hard even for someone with my husband's inherent optimism and cheerfulness not to have his good spirits chipped away.

When I asked my husband if he noticed any changes in my mood, he said, "I have noticed several changes, yes. In situations of conflict, you seem to be able to reset yourself more quickly and easily. It used to sometimes take hours, and now it can sometimes take only minutes." He wasn't sure whether this improvement could be attributed to my finally using the tools taught in cognitive behavioral therapy, or to the LSD microdosing, or to a combination of the two.

On the other hand, he did notice an increase in my anxiety on Microdose Days. "On Microdose Day, you are able to supply a narrative of catastrophe more vividly even than normal—which is already pretty vivid." I seemed altogether too able to imagine the worst. I guess that's the problem with expanding your mind: you're not entirely in control of in which direction it expands. He also noticed something about my energy and sleep. "When you slept well, you had more energy. You didn't get tired as easily. But sometimes the dosing interfered with your sleep."

My children were less equivocal. When I told them that over the last month I had been experimenting with a medication for my mood, they were not surprised. They had sensed that something was different. To them, the experiment was a resounding success. My younger daughter said, "You've been much happier. You've been controlling your emotions. Like, when you're angry, you're super-chill." My younger son agreed: "You've been nicer and happier. You've gotten angry less." My older son's response was especially sweet. "I've noticed a change, for sure. You've been kind of playing around in a way you haven't before. You're more funny and lively. There's been a lot of things we had to deal with that were stressful, but you didn't scream or yell." In all my career as a writer or a mother, those are some of the kindest reviews I've ever received.

A friend said, "Your mood is lighter, even buoyant. Even in moments of stress, you're still present. You're more flexible. Your texts and e-mails are chill and friendly, polite. You don't seem to stew. Even when you're faced with irritation, you're still quick to smile." Stewing less, smiling more. Not bad.

I have felt different and I have been different. Whether it's the microdose, or the placebo effect, over the past month I have had many days at the end of which I looked back and thought, *That was a really good day.*

When I began this experiment, I wanted to find a solution to an intractable mood problem, and in many ways I have. Microdosing with LSD worked—in the short term, at least. I have no idea if the positive effects would continue with consistent use, if in fact microdosing would be a permanent solution to the problem of my mental health. I realize now, however, that when I embarked on this month one thing I failed to consider, out of the million things I frantically considered and reconsidered again, was the ramifications of success.

Now what?

There is no doubt in my mind that if LSD were legal I would continue to take it. But it's not. There is a paradox inherent in my situation. Here I am, living in the most drug-obsessed culture in the world, where researchers estimate that somewhere between 8 and 10 percent of the population are on antidepressants,* not to mention the myriad other substances people ingest every day,

---

*Julia Calderone, "The Rise of All-Purpose Antidepressants."

prescription and otherwise, but the one drug I have found that actually helps me I am forbidden to take. I could swallow habit-forming and Alzheimer's-causing benzos by the handful, and that would be fine, but a tiny dose of a drug that seems at this point to have no discernible side effects? That's a crime. I am a basically law-abiding citizen who prides herself on her honesty; do I spend the rest of my life breaking the law?

Even if I were to decide that the positive results are worth such an ethically problematic choice, how would I ever find the drug? Whoever Lewis Carroll is, he's not been in touch with me again. For all I know, he's dead and making ghostly appearances in the hallucinations of his old friends. I've proved definitively that I am too anxious and inept to buy drugs on the illegal market. Even if I want to continue, I have no source.

And yet, if I decide that I am not willing to embark on a program that would require the continual commission of a crime, what then? Once the Doors of Perception are slammed shut, will I necessarily slip back into despondency, irritability, and familial strife? Or might the positive effects linger? After all, the individuals in the end-of-life studies who took large doses of psilocybin experienced change that lasted for months, to the ends of their lives. Though my individual doses are tiny, I've actually taken a comparable dose to theirs over the course of the month. It's not impossible to imagine that the benefits might linger, especially since one of the most important positive outcomes was my ability to take better advantage of the lessons of therapy. Perhaps the Doors of Perception, once opened to therapy, might not be so quick to slam shut.

What I long for is the kind of answer that only real research by legitimate scientists under controlled circumstances can provide. If this ad-hoc thirty-day experiment has any message, it's that more and better research is needed.

Afterword

....

I began this experiment as a search for happiness, and though microdosing with LSD elevated my mood far more effectively than SSRIs, it actually did something even more important. Over the course of the month, I came to realize that happiness, though delightful, is not really the point. I had so many really good days, but they didn't necessarily come from being happy. The microdose lessened the force of the riptide of negative emotions that so often sweeps me away, and made room in my mind not necessarily for joy, but for insight. It allowed me a little space to consider how to act in accordance with my values, not just react to external stimuli. This, not the razzle-dazzle of pleasure, was its gift.

A while after my microdose experiment ended, my husband and I took our children on a trip. After a long day driving on precarious twisting and turning roads, we pulled into the outskirts of an unlovely town. A grim drizzle started at precisely the moment when the indicator lights on the dashboard began to flicker. We stopped at a traffic light, and the engine cut out. The electrical system had failed.

We managed to pull over to the side of the road, but we were in the middle of a busy intersection and it was rush hour. All manner of vehicles trundled by us: trucks and cars, three-wheeled auto rickshaws, and scooters. We sat in the car for a while as I tried to call someone at the office of our tour operator and rental-car company. When I finally reached the emergency agent, she promised me that a replacement vehicle would be brought to us, but warned that it might take an hour. Or two. Maybe a little more.

I glanced out the window. The drizzle was flirting with turning into rain. It was dark and wet, and we'd been driving for nearly ten hours. After a few minutes, my four kids and my husband decided to get out. Better a cool rain by the side of the road than the muggy heat of the car, they announced. I stayed inside, scrolling through my phone, trying to figure out how to hustle along the tour operator. Normally, nothing makes me so irritable as this kind of snafu. I love travel, but I'm far too easily bothered by its routine challenges. Delayed flights, missed trains, lost reservations have always made me blow my stack. As much as I love the "being there" part, I dread the "getting there," because I know that if something goes wrong I'm likely to lose it.

But as I sat in that car, I realized that my searching was more pro forma than panicked. I hadn't lost it. I wasn't even really upset. What was the point, I thought, of getting all worked up? The operator had told me it would be an hour or two. What more could I do, other than drive myself crazy trying to solve a problem out of my control? At the time, I didn't even notice how out of character this sensible thought was. Desperately trying to solve problems out of my control has always been my stock in trade.

From outside, I heard a loud (and familiar) noise. I got out of the car, tromped through the dirt by the side of the road, and walked around to the rear. My kids and their father were standing in a circle in the rain. Passing headlights lit them up, and I saw that they had arranged themselves into an impromptu "cypha," and were taking turns beatboxing and rhyming freestyle. They spat rhymes about our car trouble, about the animal preserve we'd visited earlier in the week, about the beds they'd shared in different hotels, about the new food they'd tried (What rhymes with "egg hopper"? "Show stopper"! "Eye dropper"!), about each other.

The passing cars beeped at them, their drivers and passengers waving and shouting encouragement. My children waved back and kept rhyming.

My younger daughter noticed that I was standing a little outside their circle.

"Come on, Mom!" she said. "Your turn!"

I smiled and shook my head, but the others took up the chant. "Mom! Mom! Mom!"

Laughing, with the rain soaking my clothes and my hair, I stepped into the middle of the circle and began rhyming. Ineptly, foolishly. Joyfully.

I have no idea how long it took the car-rental agent to show up with the replacement vehicle. I was having too much fun to notice. Those minutes or hours remain my fondest memories of the trip. That day when I got out of my own head, stepped into the circle, and embraced the moment, in the rain—that was a really good day.

Acknowledgments

Thanks to Daniel Abrahamson, Peter Addy, Michelle Alexander, Julane Andries, Kristen Bearse, Paul Bogaards, Dr. Louann Brizendine, Sylvia Brownrigg, Sophie Chabon, Zeke Chabon, Ida-Rose Chabon, Abraham Chabon, Sean Cole, Amy Cray, Anna Dobben, Rick Doblin, Emma Dries, Clement (Clay) Dupuy, Dr. David Eagleman, Mary Evans, James Fadiman, Ian Faloona, Tim Ferriss, William Finnegan, Neill Franklin, Justine Frischmann, Madalyn Garcia, Peter Gasser, Mary Gaule, Ira Glass, August Gugelmann, Stephen Gutwillig, Daniel Handler, Zakiya Harris, Dr. Carl Hart, Jeff Holder, Dara Hyacinthe, Jennifer Jackson, Julia Kardon, Walter Kirn, Jenni Konner, Gregg Kulick, Alix Lambert, Yael Goldstein Love, Mabel, Larissa MacFarquhar, Dr. Shane MacKay, Maria Massey, Maighdlin Mau, Sonny Mehta, Dr. Michael Mithoefler, Ethan Nadelmann, Peggy Orenstein, Ann Packer, Kristi Panik, Danielle Plafsky, Michael Pollan, David Presti, Moriel Rothman-Zecher, Hans Ruge, Caissie St. Onge, George Sarlo, Nell Scovell, Ilena Silverman, Ann and Sasha Shulgin, Rebecca Skloot, Rebecca Solnit, Ed Swanson, Rebecca Traister, Gerald Valentine, Leonard Waldman, Ricki Waldman, Dr. Philip Wolfson, Amelia Zalcman, and Anne Zaroff-Evans.

And most of all, to Michael Chabon, who loves me, I know.

Bibliography

Alexander, Michelle. *The New Jim Crow: Mass Incarceration in the Age of Colorblindness*. New York: New Press, 2010.

Alper, Kenneth R., M.D., Howard S. Lotsof, Geerte M. N. Frenken, M.F.A., Daniel J. Luciano, M.D., and Jan Bastiaans, M.D. "Treatment of Acute Opioid Withdrawal with Ibogaine." *American Journal on Addictions* 8 (1999): 234–42.

American College of Neuropsychopharmacology. "Active Ingredient in Magic Mushrooms Reduces Anxiety, Depression in Cancer Patients." *ScienceDaily,* Dec. 10, 2015.

Ammerman, Seth, Sheryl Ryan, and William P. Adelman. "The Impact of Marijuana Policies on Youth: Clinical, Research, and Legal Update." *Pediatrics* 135, no. 3 (March 2015): e769–85. At doi: 10.1542/peds.2014-4147.

Amoroso, T., and M. Workman. "Treating Posttraumatic Stress Disorder with MDMA-assisted Psychotherapy: A Preliminary Meta-analysis and Comparison to Prolonged Exposure Therapy." *Journal of Psychopharmacology* 30.7 (2016): 595–600.

Anderson, Pauline. "Scant Evidence for Long-Term Opioid Therapy in Chronic Pain." *Medscape,* Jan. 13, 2015. At http://www.medscape.com/viewarticle/838056.

Annan, Kofi. "Why It's Time to Legalize Drugs." *Huffington Post,* Feb. 23, 2016. At http://www.huffingtonpost.com/kofi-annan/why-its-time-to-legalize-drugs_b_9298502.html.

Beck, Jerome, and Marsha Rosenbaum. *Pursuit of Ecstasy: The MDMA Experience*. Albany: State University of New York Press, 1994.

Bellum, Sara. "Real Teens Ask: How Many Teens Use Drugs?" *NIDA for Teens,* June 19, 2013. At https://teens.drugabuse.gov/blog/post/real-teens-ask-how-many-teens-use-drugs.

Bergamaschi, M. M., R. H. Queiroz, A. W. Zuardi, and J. A. Crippa. "Safety and Side Effects of Cannabidiol, a Cannabis Sativa Constituent." *National Center for Biotechnology Information. U.S. National Library of Medicine,* Sept. 1, 2011. At http://www.ncbi.nlm.nih.gov/pubmed/22129319.

Bertram, Eva, Morris Blachman, Kenneth Sharpe, and Peter Andrea. *Drug*

War Politics: The Price of Denial. Berkeley and Los Angeles: University of California Press, 1996.

Brown, David Jay, and Louise Reitman. "Psilocybin Studies and the Religious Experience: An Interview with Roland Griffiths, Ph.D." MAPS Bulletin 20, no. 1, Dec. 18, 2009. At https://www.maps.org/news-letters/v20n1/v20n1 -22t025.pdf.

Calderone, Julia. "The Rise of All-Purpose Antidepressants." *Scientific American,* Nov. 1, 2014. At http://www.scientificamerican.com/article/the-rise -of-all-purpose-antidepressants/.

Carhart-Harris, R. L., M. Kaelen, M. Bolstridge, T. M. Williams, L. T. Williams, R. Underwood, A. Feilding, and D. J. Nutt. "The Paradoxical Psychological Effects of Lysergic Acid Diethylamide (LSD)." *Psychological Medicine* 46, no. 7 (2016): 1379–90. At doi: 10.1017/S0033291715002901.

Carhart-Harris, Robin L., Mark Bolstridge, James Rucker, Camilla M. J. Day, David Erritzoe, Mendel Kaelen, Michael Bloomfield, James A. Rickard, Ben Forbes, Amanda Feilding, David Taylor, Steve Pilling, Valerie H. Curran, and David J. Nutt. "Psilocybin with Psychological Support for Treatment-resistant Depression: An Open-label Feasibility Study." *The Lancet* 3, no. 7 (July 2016): 619–27. At http://www.thelancet.com/journals/lanpsy /article/PIIS2215-0366(16)30065-7/abstract.

Compton, Wilson, and Nora Volkow. "Major Increases in Opioid Analgesic Abuse in the United States: Concerns and Strategies." *Drug and Alcohol Dependence* 81 (May 2005): 103–7.

Dass, Ram. *Be Here Now.* New York: Crown Publishing, 1971.

Dodes, Lance M., and Zachary Dodes. *The Sober Truth: Debunking the Bad Science Behind 12-Step Programs and the Rehab Industry.* Boston: Beacon Press, 2014.

Dyck, Erika. *Psychedelic Psychiatry: LSD from Clinic to Campus.* Baltimore: Johns Hopkins University Press, 2008.

Fadiman, James, Ph.D. *The Psychedelic Explorer's Guide: Safe, Therapeutic, and Sacred Journeys.* Rochester, Vt.: Park Street Press, 2011.

Fish, Jefferson M., ed. *How to Legalize Drugs.* North Bergen, N.J.: Book-mart Press, 1998.

Gayomali, Chris. "Forget Coffee, Silicon Valley's New Productivity Hack Is 'Microdoses' of LSD." *Gentlemen's Quarterly,* Nov. 23, 2015. At http:// www.gq.com/story/forget-coffee-silicon-valleys-new-productivity-hack-is -microdoses-of-lsd.

Glatter, Robert, M.D. "LSD Microdosing: The New Job Enhancer in Silicon Valley and Beyond?" *Forbes,* Nov. 27, 2015. At http://www.forbes.com

/sites/robertglatter/2015/11/27/lsd-microdosing-the-new-job-enhancer-in
-silicon-valley-and-beyond/#3d455c9e114d.

Goldsmith, Neal M., Ph.D. *Psychedelic Healing: The Promise of Entheogens for Psychotherapy and Spiritual Development.* Rochester, Vt.: Healing Arts Press, 2011.

Gray, Mike. *Drug Crazy: How We Got into This Mess and How We Can Get Out.* New York: Random House, 1998.

Greenfield, Robert. *Timothy Leary: A Biography.* Orlando, Fla.: Harcourt, 2006.

Greenwald, Glenn. *Drug Decriminalization in Portugal: Lessons for Creating Fair and Successful Drug Policies.* Washington, D.C.: Cato Institute, 2009.

Grob, Charles S., Alicia L. Danforth, Gurpreet S. Chopra, Marycie Hagerty, Charles R. McKay, Adam L. Halberstadt, and George R. Greer. "Pilot Study of Psilocybin Treatment for Anxiety in Patients with Advanced-Stage Cancer." *Archives of General Psychiatry* 68, no. 1 (2011): 71–78. At doi: 10.1001/archgenpsychiatry.2010.116.

Grof, Stanislav. *Realms of the Human Unconscious: Observations from LSD Research.* New York: Viking, 1975.

Gunten, Charles F. von. "The Pendulum Swings for Opioid Prescribing." *Journal of Palliative Medicine* 19.4 (2016): 348.

Hagenbach, Leiter, and Lucius Wörthmüller. *Mystic Chemist: The Life of Albert Hofmann and His Discovery of LSD.* Trans. William Geuss and Linda Sperling. Santa Fe, N.M.: Synergetic Press, 2011.

Hart, Dr. Carl. *High Price: A Neuroscientist's Journey of Self-Discovery That Challenges Everything You Know About Drugs and Society.* New York: HarperCollins, 2013.

Hart, Carl L., Joanne Csete, and Don Habibi. "Methamphetamine: Fact vs. Fiction and Lessons from the Crack Hysteria." *Open Society Institute,* Feb. 2014. At https://www.opensocietyfoundations.org/publications /methamphetamine-dangers-exaggerated.

Hart, Carl L., Caroline B. Marvin, Rae Silver, and Edward E. Smith. "Is Cognitive Functioning Impaired in Methamphetamine Users? A Critical Review." *Neuropsychopharmacology* 37, no. 3 (2011): 586–608. At http:// www.ncbi.nlm.nih.gov/pubmed/22089317.

Hendricks, Peter S., Christopher B. Thorne, C. Brendan Clarke, David W. Coombs, and Matthew W. Johnson. "Classic Psychedelic Use Is Associated with Reduced Psychological Distress and Suicidality in the United States Adult Population." *Journal of Psychopharmacology* 29, no. 3 (2015): 280–88. doi: 10.1177/0269881114565653.

Henry, Brook L., Arpi Minassian, and William Perry. "Effect of Methamphet-amine Dependence on Everyday Functional Ability." *Addictive Behaviors* 35, no. 6 (2010): 593–98. At http://www.ncbi.nlm.nih.gov/pubmed/20167435.

Hintzen, Annelie, and Torsten Passie. *The Pharmacology of LSD: A Critical Review.* New York: Oxford University Press, 2010.

Hofmann, Albert, Ph.D. *LSD, My Problem Child: Reflections on Sacred Drugs, Mysticism and Science.* Trans. Jonathan Ott. Saline, Mich.: McNaughton & Gunn, 1983.

Holland, Julie, M.D. *Moody Bitches.* New York: Penguin, 2015.

Huxley, Aldous. *The Doors of Perception and Heaven & Hell.* New York: Thinking Ink, 2011.

Jamison, Kay Redfield. *Touched with Fire.* New York: Free Press Paperbacks, 1993.

———. *An Unquiet Mind: A Memoir of Moods and Madness.* New York: Random House, 1995.

Johnson, Matthew W., Albert Garcia-Romeu, Mary P. Cosimano, and Roland R. Griffiths. "Pilot Study of the 5-HT2AR Agonist Psilocybin in the Treatment of Tobacco Addiction." *Journal of Psychopharmacology,* Sept. 11, 2014. Last modified Oct. 16, 2014. At http://jop.sagepub.com/content/early/2014/09/06/0269881114548296.short.

Kaestner, Erik J., John T. Wixted, and Sara C. Mednick. "Pharmacologically Increasing Sleep Spindles Enhances Recognition for Negative and High-Arousal Memories." *Journal of Cognitive Neuroscience* 25, no. 10 (2013): 1597–1610. At http://www.ncbi.nlm.nih.gov/pubmed/23767926.

Kirkpatrick, M. G., E. W. Gunderson, C. E. Johanson, F. R. Levin, R. W. Foltin, and C. L. Hart. "Comparison of Intranasal Methamphetamine and *D*-Amphetamine Self-Administration by Humans." *Addiction* 107 (2012): 783–91.

Leonard, Andrew. "How LSD Microdosing Became the Hot New Business Trip." *Rolling Stone,* Nov. 20, 2015.

Linnemann, T., and T. Wall. "'This Is Your Face on Meth': The Punitive Spectacle of 'White Trash' in the Rural War on Drugs." *Theoretical Criminology* 17, no. 3 (2013): 315–34.

Markoff, John. *What the Dormouse Said: How the 60s Counterculture Shaped the Personal Computer Industry.* New York: Penguin, 2005.

Marks, John. *The Search for the "Manchurian Candidate": The CIA and Mind Control—The Secret History of the Behavioral Sciences.* New York: Norton, 1991.

McKenna, Terence. *Food of the Gods: The Search for the Original Tree of*

Knowledge: A Radical History of Plants, Drugs and Human Evolution. New York: Bantam Books, 1992.

Medina, K. L., K. L. Hanson, A. D. Schweinsburg, M. Cohen-Zion, B. J. Nagel, and S. F. Tapert. "Neuropsychological Functioning in Adolescent Marijuana Users: Subtle Deficits Detectable After a Month of Abstinence." *Journal of the International Neuropsychological Society* 13, no. 5 (2007): 807–20. PMID no. 17697412.

Michaux, Henri. *Miserable Miracle.* Trans. Mary Jose Paz. New York: New York Review of Books, 2002.

Mithoefer, Michael C., Mark T. Wagner, Ann T. Mithoefer, Lisa Jerome, Scott F. Martin, Berra Yazar-Klosinski, Yvonne Michel, Timothy D. Brewerton, and Rick Doblin. "Durability of Improvement in Post-traumatic Stress Disorder Symptoms and Absence of Harmful Effects or Drug Dependency after 3,4-methylenedioxymethamphetamine-assisted Psychotherapy: A Prospective Long-term Follow-up Study." *Journal of Psychopharmacology* (Oxford, England). SAGE Publications, Jan. 2013. At http://www.ncbi.nlm.nih.gov/pubmed/23172889.

Murakawa, Naomi. "Toothless." *Du Bois Review: Social Science Research on Race* 8 (2011): 219–28. doi: 10.1017/S1742058X11000208.

Newline, Constance A. *My Self and I.* Toronto: Longman's Canada, 1962.

O'Brien, Megan S., and James C. Anthony. "Extra-Medical Stimulant Dependence Among Recent Initiates." *Drug and Alcohol Dependence.* U.S. National Library of Medicine, June 9, 2009. At http://www.sciencedirect.com/science/article/pii/S0376871609001574.

"Overdose Death Rates." At drugabuse.gov. Last modified Dec. 2015.

Passie, Torsten, John H. Halpern, Dirk O. Stichtenoth, Hinderk M. Emrich, and Annelie Hintzen, "The Pharmacology of Lysergic Acid Diethylamide: A Review." *CNS: Neuroscience & Therapeutics* 14 (2008): 295–314.

Pinchbeck, Daniel. *Breaking Open the Head: A Psychedelic Journey into the Heart of Contemporary Shamanism.* New York: Broadway Books, 2003.

Pollan, Michael. "The Trip Treatment." *New Yorker,* Feb. 9, 2015.

Posner, Richard A. "We Need a Strong Prison System." *New Republic,* July 31, 2016.

Presti, David E. *Foundational Concepts in Neuroscience: A Brain-Mind Odyssey.* New York: W.W. Norton, 2016.

Richards, William A. *Sacred Knowledge: Psychedelics and Religious Experiences.* New York: Columbia University Press, 2016.

Roberts, Thomas B., ed. *Psychoactive Sacramentals: Essays on Entheogens and Religion.* San Francisco: Council on Spiritual Practices, 2001.

Rosenbaum, Marsha. *Safety First: A Reality-based Approach to Teens, Drugs, and Drug Education.* San Francisco, Calif.: Safety First, 2004.

Rudd, Rose A., Noah Aleshire, Jon E. Ziebell, and R. Matthew Gladden. "Increases in Drug and Opioid Overdose Deaths—United States, 2000–2014." *CDC,* Jan. 1, 2016. At http://www.cdc.gov/mmwr/preview/mmwrhtml/mm6450a3.htm.

Schaler, Jeffrey A., Ph.D., ed. *Drugs: Should We Legalize, Decriminalize or Deregulate?* Amherst, N.Y.: Prometheus Books, 1998.

Sessa, Dr. Ben. *The Psychedelic Renaissance: Reassessing the Role of Psychedelic Drugs in 21st Century Psychiatry and Society.* London: Muswell Hill Press, 2012.

Sewell. R. A., J. H. Halpern, and H. G. Pope, Jr. "Response of Cluster Headache to Psilocybin and LSD." *Neurology,* June 27, 2006. At http://www.ncbi.nlm.nih.gov/pubmed/16801660.

Shannon, Michael W., Stephen W. Borron, Michael J. Burns, Lester M. Haddad, and James F. Winchester. *Haddad and Winchester's Clinical Management of Poisoning and Drug Overdose.* Philadelphia: Saunders/Elsevier, 2007.

Shroder, Tom. *Acid Test: LSD, Ecstasy, and the Power to Heal.* New York: Penguin, 2014.

Shulgin, Alexander, and Ann Shulgin. *Pikal: A Chemical Love Story.* Berkeley, Calif.: Transform Press, 1991.

———. *Tihkal: The Continuation.* Berkeley, Calif.: Transform Press, 1997.

Siff, Stephen. *Acid Hype: American News Media and the Psychedelic Experience.* Urbana: University of Illinois Press, 2015.

Simon, Jonathan. *Mass Incarceration on Trial: A Remarkable Court Decision and the Future of Prisons in America.* New York: New Press, 2014.

Slater, Lauren. "How Psychedelic Drugs Can Help Patients Fake Death." *New York Times,* April 20, 2012.

Squeglia, L. M., J. Jacobus, and S. F. Tapers, Ph.D. "The Influence of Substance Use on Adolescent Brain Development." *Clinical EEG and Neuroscience* 40, no. 1 (2009): 31–38. doi: 10.1177/155005940904000110.

Strassman, Rick J. "Adverse Reactions to Psychedelic Drugs. A Review of the Literature." *The Journal of Nervous and Mental Disease* 172.10 (1984): 577–95. At http://www.ncbi.nlm.nih.gov/pubmed/6384428.

Tagliazucchi, Enzo, Leor Roseman, Mendel Kaelen, Csaba Orban, Suresh D. Muthukumaraswamy, Kevin Murphy, Helmut Laufs, Robert Leech, John McGonigle, Nicolas Crossley, Edward Bullmore, Tim Williams, Mark Bolstridge, Amanda Feilding, David J. Nutt, and Robin Carhart-Harris.

"Increased Global Functional Connectivity Correlates with LSD-Induced Ego Dissolution." *Current Biology*, April 13, 2016. At http://dx.doi.org /10.1016/j.cub.2016.02.010.

Vollenweider, Franz X., and Michael Kometer. "The Neurobiology of Psychedelic Drugs: Implications for the Treatment of Mood Disorders." *Nature Reviews Neuroscience* 11 (Sept. 2010): 642–51.

Weil, Andrew, M.D., and Winifred Rosen. *From Chocolate to Morphine: Everything You Need to Know About Mind-Altering Drugs.* New York: Houghton Mifflin, 1993.

Wodak, Dr. Alex, and Allie Cooney. "Effectiveness of Sterile Needle and Syringe Programming in Reducing HIV/AIDS Among Injecting Drug Users." *World Health Organization,* 2004. At http://www.who.int/hiv/pub /prev_care/effectivenesssterileneedle.pdf.

Wolfe, Tom. *The Electric Kool-Aid Acid Test.* New York: Picador, 1968.

Woolf, Virginia. *A Room of One's Own.* San Diego: Harcourt, 1929.

A Note About the Author

Ayelet Waldman is the author of the novels *Love and Treasure, Red Hook Road, Love and Other Impossible Pursuits,* and *Daughter's Keeper,* as well as of the essay collection *Bad Mother: A Chronicle of Maternal Crimes, Minor Calamities, and Occasional Moments of Grace* and the Mommy Track Mystery series. She coedited the Voice of Witness book *Inside This Place, Not of It: Narratives from Women's Prisons.* Waldman was a federal public defender and taught at Loyola Law School and the UC Berkeley School of Law, where she developed a course on the legal and social implications of the war on drugs. She lives in Berkeley, California, with her husband and four children.